ISLAM: A WAY OF LIFE AND A MOVEMENT

edited by M.Tariq Quraishi

American Trust Publications
10900 W. Washington Street
Indianapolis, Indiana 46231

First Printing
Library of Congress Catalog Card No. 83-071408
ISBN No. 0-89259-055-6

American Trust Publications
10900 W. Washington Street
Indianapolis, Indiana 46231 — USA

Tel: (317) 839-8150
Telex No.: 276242 ISLAMIC BS

Title cover by Aftab Ahmad
Peshawar, Pakistan

Printed in the United States of America

Dedicated to the founding members
of the Muslim Students' Association of
the US and Canada who for the first time
in the contemporary history of Islam ventured
beyond the barriers of ethnicity and created
a transnational platform to help many
a flower bloom.

". . .it is not possible to express Islam using European terminology. The Islamic terms: *salah, zakah, khalifah, jama'a, wudu'*, and so forth are not prayer, tax, ruler, community, and washing. The definition that Islam is a synthesis between religion and materialism, that it exists in the middle between Christianity and socialism, is very rough and could be accepted only conditionally. It is more or less correct only in some aspects. Islam is neither a simple arithmetical mean between these two teachings, nor their average. *Salah, zakah, wudu'* are more indivisible, since they express an intimate and simple feeling, a certainty which is expressed with one word and one picture only, but which still represents a logically dual connotation. The parallel with man is obvious. Man is its measure and its explanation.

It is known that the Qur'an leaves an analytical reader the impression of disarrangement, and seems to be compound of diverse elements. But the Qur'an is life, not literature. Islam is a way of living rather than a way of thinking. The only authentic comment of the Qur'an can be life, and as we know, it was the life of Prophet Muhammad. Islam in the life of Muhammad, upon whom be peace, is a natural union of love and force, the sublime and the real, the divine and the human. This "explosive compound" of religion and politics produced enormous force in the life of the peoples. In a moment, Islam has coincided with the very essence of life.

Islam's middle position can be recognized by the fact that Islam has always been attacked from the two opposite directions: from the side of religion that it is too natural, actual, and tuned to the world; and from the side of science that it contains religious and mystical elements. There is only one Islam, but like man, it has both soul and body, while its contrary aspects depend on a different point of view: materialists only see Islam as a religion and mysticism / as a "right wing" tendency /, and Christians see it only as a socio-political movement / as a "left-wing" tendency /.

'Alija 'Ali Izetbegovic
from *Islam Between East and West.*

CONTENTS

THE FIRST WORD

اا » اَليَومَ أكمَلتُ لكُم دِينَكَم وَأتمَمتُ عَليكُم نِعمَتي وَرضِيتُ لكُم الإسلامَ دِيناً . «

". . .this day I have perfected your religion for you, completed my favor upon you
and have chosen for you Islam as a way of life."   (The Qur'an 5:3)

Thus says Allah in His book.

At no other time was there more need for Islamic teachings than
today. At a time when as Alexis Carrel / *Man the Unknown* / says:

> Moral sense is almost completely ignored by modern society.
> We have, in fact, suppressed its manifestations. All are imbued
> with irresponsibility. Those who discern good and evil, those who
> are industrious and provident remain poor and are looked upon
> as backward. The woman who has several children, who devotes
> herself to their education instead of her own career, is considered
> weakminded.... Robbers enjoy prosperity in peace. Gangsters
> are protected by politicians and respected by judges....
> Homosexuality flourishes. Sexual morals have been cast aside;....
> (and thus) despite the marvels of scientific civilization, human
> personality tends to dissolve.

Ironically, when in view of the sordid affairs of the world the change is
called for, it is taken for retrogression; and they who demand it are
considered as abnormal.

None of this makes sense. Something basic is missing and is badly
needed. At this time of great need, Islam as a complete way of life is not
only needed for blessings or spiritual uplifting, it is needed for survival.
There is a beautiful verse in the Qur'an which says:

» يَا أيُّها الَّذين آمَنُوا استَجِيبوا لله وللرسولِ إذا دَعاكُم لِما يُحييِكُم . «

"O you who believe, respond to God and His apostle when He calls you to that which will give you life." (The Qur'an: 8:24)

The phrase ". . .which will give you life" used to be understood as applying to life and safety from destruction in the hereafter. Now, there is evidence to prove that the violation of Islamic teachings leads to increased mortality, i.e. a higher death rate in this very world. In other words, to follow and live according to Islamic teachings leads to increased survival. Islam as a complete way of life is needed today for survival, in this world as well as in the hereafter.

Islam: A Way of Life and a Movement is a timely book presenting luminous glimpses of Islam, the needed remedy. This collective work of several contemporary scholars clearly shows that Islam in its fifteenth century is still as young, as powerful, and above all as pertinent as it was during its first century. The splendid glimpses in this book should stimulate the reader to further indulge in the acquisition of Islamic knowledge. This, however, should not be the end of it. The real joy and fulfillment will be attained when we put the beautiful teachings of Islam to work and apply them in our daily life, thanking God the Almighty for His great gift to mankind: Islam, the way of life and the way to life.

Panama City, Florida   *Ahmed Elkadi, M.D.*

ACKNOWLEDGEMENTS

Grateful acknowledgements are made to the authors whose contributions to *al-ittihad*, the quarterly journal of the Muslim Students' Association of the US and Canada, made this compilation possible. Three of them are no longer with us: Sayyid Abu Al-'Ala Maududi, without whom the contemporary Islamic scene is intellectually drab; Dr. M.A. Draz, whose intellectual probity remains peerless; and Hammudah 'Abdalati, who died young and whose best years were yet to come.

Among the living my special thanks are to Dr. M.A. Azami, who trusted me with the translation of his valuable piece on *Kuttab an-Nabi* and allowed me to include it in the present compilation; Monzer Kahf, a fine man and economist, for his *The Islamic State and the Welfare State: Similarities and Differences.* This was, in fact, his response to my questionnaire on Islamic Economy and was slated for publication in *al-ittihad*, but for some reasons could not appear.

Apart from these two works, the rest of the writings appeared in *al-ittihad* between 1969 and 1982.

My thanks are also to those who made *al-ittihad* possible in the past, such as Erdogan Gurman, Muhammad A. Sakr and their associates (1963), the year when *al-ittihad* made its debut, Ahmad H.M. Totonji (1965-66), Zafar I. 'Abdullah (1966), Mahmoud Rashdan (1969), Jamal Badawi (1970-73), M. Zahirul Hasan (1973-75), Kaukab Siddique (1976), and Anwar Beg (1977).

Thanks are also due to Linda McCullen for her diligent typing and proofreading.

Last, but not least, my sincere gratitude goes out to Drs. Anis Ahmad and Mahmoud Rashdan, who made my stay in MSA possible by their love, understanding, and support. I wish the Muslim world had more of their kind.

Introduction

ISLAMIC MOVEMENT:
DESTINY OR A
PASSING PHASE?

To many in the West, Islam is still an unknown religion. Those who are relatively informed take it as a jingoistic religion, with blood on its sleeves, at worst a pagan faith—antagonistic to human values and progress. Little do they know that Islam goes beyond religion and offers mankind an ideal system of life.

Lately, thanks to the fall of Zulfiqar 'Ali Bhutto in Pakistan, Muhammad Reza Shah in Iran, Anwar Sadat in Egypt, and the upsurge of Islamic sentiments in the Muslim world, a plethora of writings have appeared in the West. The underlying motive, however, is not one of interest in Islam as some would like to believe, but to look for ways to counteract its momentum. In such exercises the approach remains sociological—the application of a pseudo-scientific discipline to a religious experience. In other words, they presume that *Islamic fundamentalism* is tied to certain antecedents—a set of social, political, and economic conditions in whose absence there will be no upsurge of Islamic sentiments in a Muslim people. Needless to say, such a view necessarily presupposes that the Islamic movement is a child of circumstances—at best situational, a passing phase in the march of history which will die its logical death after running its course. On the contrary, the Islamic movement has an element of permanence in it which stems from its world view; it has an internal drive, a momentum which, if at all is determined, comes from the demands of its message and mission.

To be precise, when it comes to understanding the Islamic movement, how it comes into being and what makes it work, one must look at its internal dynamics. Yet the knowledge of the dynamics alone will not be enough, since a movement if it is alive as an organic whole and has lived a past life must create a history, a myth, and a lore of its own. As such, the history of the Muslim people is of as much importance as is the knowledge of Islam's internal dynamics—together they motivate *conscious* Muslims to action. We stress the internal dynamics of the Islamic movement and its lore because even if the Muslims are living under the best of a non-Islamic system, their lives will still be affected by the momentous call of Islam. They cannot close their ears, nor can they ignore its awesome presence. The tapestry of their lives is woven with its strands. To detach them from Islam, their enemies will have to cut them limb from limb.

In other words, these are not the social, political, and economic conditions which determine the Islamic movement; instead, it is the transcendental, all-embracing Islamic movement which determines the Muslim destiny.

The internal dynamics of the Islamic movement can be summarized into the following Qur'anic concepts:

First, God is One, Sovereign, and the Lawgiver. His laws govern the entire universe, and like the celestial bodies and life on this planet that run in their orbit smoothly with perfect precision, humanity should also order itself on His laws.

This is important because religion, as understood in the West and elsewhere, is dogma and worship, and as such a private affair. Part of the confusion about Islam arises from such a misunderstanding of religion. Islam is also worship, but it embraces man's total existence as an expression of his gratitude toward his God. The expression of gratitude, however, goes beyond rhetorics; it lays claim to the total personality, and calls into play every nuance of feelings. The element of gratitude distinguishes Islamic *'ibadah* (worship) from the ascetic's pursuit of spirituality. An ascetic mortifies himself with a stoic forbearance to achieve excellence over his baser self; his aim is to pave the way for personal salvation. That is why he forsakes the world and hides himself in caves. His attitude is anti-social, and his approach is esoteric. He hates worldly existence, because it tarnishes his soul. On the contrary, for a Muslim, the world is an arena of conflict, and he is thrown into it to mold it according to his vision; his spiritual elevation and his salvation lie in the process of subjugating the hostile anti-Islamic forces. He cannot attain self-fulfillment without conflict. Conflict determines his Islamicity; it validates his conviction and gives credibility to his lifestyle. He is not supposed to enjoy in solitude the blessing of life, nor is he supposed to retreat from the world. Both attitudes are marked with selfishness and cowardice. The pursuit of worship is, therefore, not an end in itself: it has social, political, and moral dimensions. With such diverse demands, it constrains extreme attitudes so that the dissipation of energies in one direction is avoided, and all elements of life can take nourishment from that great source of vitality, soul. Obviously, it calls for moderation.

That Islam by acknowledging the rights of all social components, including the right of even one's body, brought a new dimension to man's religiosity may not be far from the truth. It is because religion, as it ought to be, is to help in the growth of life as an organic whole, and not to stifle it. The Qur'an, in its own inimitable style, alludes to the prophethood of Sayyedina Muhammad, upon whom be peace, as of one who lessens the burden of mankind and releases them from shackles.

Again, sustained efforts, in the discharge of obligations, minimal as these may be, are the essence of *'ibadah* (worship). Sudden bursts of intermittent energies with long lapses are not commendable, because life itself is not a sudden leap; it is a sustained flow of energies programmed to a certain end. Its depletion leads to inactivity, a pause, or what may be called death.

Second, there is no intercession; only one's deeds will be of help before the Divine tribunal in the hereafter.
Third, mankind is one and so is the prophethood, because their origin is one.
Fourth, oppression is to be fought and not to be befriended or ignored.

These concepts are part of a Muslim conscience. They mortify them, ennoble them, and throw them into collision against the status-quo in their societies. It is an ever-present revolution which sometimes simmers, sometimes roars, and sometimes succeeds in overthrowing the oppressive regimes; but never for a moment does it cease to exist.

History—A Lash

Another aspect which equally merits attention, though often ignored, is the history of the Muslim people. This history has come into being owing to the unfolding of the Islamic message over the past 1400 years and has created its own powerful impact on the Muslim soul. For others, history may be a chronicle of the past events; but for the Muslims, it is a criterion, a promise, and a lash. It mirrors their past achievements and their present failures. To them no model of development is as alluring as the one they see in the first magnificent Islamic state of Madinah. So sharp are its contours that it still lingers in their memory, and so powerful is the nostalgia for it that even when they are hurled into the present, their faces are glued to Madinah. Without an Islamic state, a Muslim lives an agonizing life, his sense of humiliation is acute, and the chasm in his soul immense. That is why regardless of the prevailing situation in the Muslim world, each generation of Muslims, no matter how great the odds, will undertake the bold enterprise of establishing an Islamic state.

Nevertheless, if at all the Islamic movement needs a setting for launching, the world has provided one.

When an influential man like Lord Keynes suggests to the Western world, "For at least another hundred years, we must pretend to ourselves that fair is foul and foul is fair; for foul is useful and fair is not. Avarice and usury and precaution must be our gods for a little longer still;" when this lust led to 9 million dead in World War I and 35 million in World War II; when consumerism has become a cult and the world is being robbed of its primary resources to maintain the meaningless lifestyle of a population hardly one-tenth of mankind; when positive sciences have been extended to social facts and people have abused their emotions and intellect; when man's conscious has been reduced to an unfortunate cosmic accident; when anguish and despair have become the only realities; and when life itself devoid of any higher meaning has been reduced to a theater of the absurd. Could there be a more tragic setting for a change?

Yet notwithstanding the calamity that has befallen mankind, some people are still awaiting doomsday. What greater calamity could there be than the dehumanizing of people's lives; when the distinction between sin and virtue has been eliminated; when injustice and exploitation in the name of fairness are being done to the major part of humanity; when one-tenth of the world possesses seventy percent of wealth; when the poor nations are paying seventy-eight cents out of every dollar that they earn toward the payment of loans owed to the West—the time for change is due.

The Muslim world is passing through the throes of a post-colonial period. For the Muslim masses it is a period of reflection and a search for identity. They who think that the Muslims can be thwarted from reaching their destiny had better re-examine their premise.

Islamic resurgence in Muslim societies is not tied to any conditions; it is there because of its own right, and the Muslims know they cannot respond to the demand of their faith but with a total embrace. Short of it is hellfire in this world and beyond.

Islam: A Way of Life and A Movement is not just another book: it is an attempt to understand Islam as a dynamic way of life, a movement wedded to a social goal in its widest application and which demands the best from mankind.

M. Tariq Quraishi
Ramadan 4, 1403/June 26, 1983   Plainfield, Indiana

This is a variant of an editorial the writer wrote for *Islamic Horizons*, Muharram 1402/ November 1981.

Chapter I

ISLAM:
ITS MEANING
AND MESSAGE

Sayyid Abu Al-'Ala Maududi

Sayyid Abu Al-'Ala Maududi (1903-1979) is the founder of Jama'at-e Islami Pakistan, a major Islamic movement of the contemporary Muslim world. Among his important works are *Tafhim al-Qur'an* in six volumes, *Sunnat ki 'Ai'eni Hathiyat*, (The Constitutional Role of the Sunnah), *Khilafat wa-Malukiyat* (The Caliphate and the Monarchy), *Suud* (Usuary), *Ma'shiyat-e Islam* (The Islamic Economy), *Islami Riyasat* (The Islamic State), etc. A man of multidimensional personality, Maududi has left a lasting impression on this era. The present article was first published in the January 1977 issue of *al-ittihad* under the title of *What Islam Stands For?*

Let me begin by clarifying that, for us, Islam is not the name of some unique faith presented for the first time by Muhammad, upon whom be peace, who should, on that account, be called the founder of Islam. The Qur'an makes it very clear that Islam—the complete submission of man before God (Allah)—is the only faith that God has revealed to mankind from the very beginning. Noah, Abraham, Moses and Jesus, upon them be peace, propagated the same faith. They were not founders of faiths; instead, they were reiterating the faith of their predecessors.[1]

---

[1]"Say I am not an innovator of new-fangled doctrine among the Prophets" (The Qur'an 46:9).

"The religion in the view of Allah is Islam (submission to His will): The People of the Book did not dissent therefrom except through envy of each other, after knowledge had come to them" (Ibid. 3:19).

"Abraham was not a Jew nor yet a Christian, but he was true in faith, and bowed his will to Allah's (which is Islam), and he joined not gods with Allah" (Ibid. 3:67).

"Do they seek other than the religion of Allah? While all creatures in the heavens and on earth have, willing or unwilling, bowed to His will (adhered to Islam) and to Him shall they all be brought back. Say: 'We believe in Allah, and in what has been

What Distinguishes Muhammad From Other Messengers

✓ He was the last messenger of Allah.

✓ Allah revived, through him, the same genuine faith which had been conveyed by all earlier messengers.

✓ This original message was corrupted and split in various religions by peoples of different ages, who indulged in interpolations and admixture. These non-divine elements were purged by Allah, and Islam, in its pure and original form, was transmitted to mankind through Muhammad.

✓ Since there was to be no messenger after Muhammad, the Book revealed to him was preserved word-for-word[2] so that

---

revealed to us and what was revealed to Abraham, Ishmael, Isaac, Jacob, and the Tribes, and in (the books) given to Moses, Jesus, and the Prophets from their Lord: We make no distinction between one and another among them, and to Allah do we bow our will (in Islam)'. If anyone desires a religion other than Islam (submission to Allah), never will it be accepted of him; and in the hereafter he will be in the ranks of those who have lost (all spiritual good)" (Ibid. 3:83-85).

"(Noah said) ' I have been commanded to be of those who submit to Allah's will (in Islam)'" (Ibid. 10:72).

("Moses said) 'O my people! If you do (really) believe in Allah, then in Him put your trust if you are Muslims (Submit your will to His)" (Ibid. 10:84).

"(Abraham and Ismail said) 'Our Lord! make of us Muslims, bowing to Thy (will), and of our progeny a Muslim people, (bowing to Thy will)'" (Ibid. 2: 128).

"'Behold!' his Lord said to him (Abraham) 'Bow (thy will to Me)' he said: 'I bow (my will) to the Lord and Cherisher of the universe.' And this was the legacy Abraham left to his sons, and so did Jacob: 'O my sons! Allah hath chosen the faith for you; then die not except in the faith of Islam.' Were you witnesses when death appeared before Jacob? 'Behold,' he said to his sons: 'What will you worship after me? They said: 'We shall worship thy Allah and the Allah of thy fathers of Abraham, Ishmael, and Isaac, to Him we bow (in Islam')" (Ibid. 2:131-133).

"(Joseph prayed) 'Creator of the heavens and the earth, You are my protector in this world and in the hereafter, take my soul (at death) as one submitting to Your will (as a Muslim, and unite me with the righteous' " (Ibid. 12:101).

"It was We who revealed the law (to Moses); therein was guidance and light. By its standard have been judged the Jews, by the Prophets who bowed (as in Islam) to Allah's will, by the rabbis and the doctors of law" (Ibid. 5:44).

"And behold! I inspired the disciples (of Jesus) to have faith in Me and Mine Apostle: they said, 'We have faith, and be witness that we bow to Allah as Muslims' " (Ibid. 5:111).

"She (the Queen of Sheeba) said: 'O my Lord! I have indeed wronged my soul: I do (now) submit (in Islam), with Solomon, to the Lord of the Worlds'" (Ibid. 27:44).

[2]"The same religion has He established for you as that which He enjoined on Noah... that which We have sent by inspiration to you... and that which we enjoined on Abraham, Moses and Jesus: namely, that you should remain steadfast in religion, and make no division therein" (Ibid. 42:13).

"Those who reject (truth), among the People of the Book and among the

it would be a source of guidance for all times[3].

✓ The life of Muhammad, and the manner in which he conducted himself, was also recorded in a unique manner by his companions and by later compilers of the Tradition (al-Hadith). A more complete and authentic account of the life, sayings, and actions of any prophet or historic personality has never been compiled.[4]

✓ In this way, the Qur'an and the authentic *Sunnah* of the Prophet together became a reliable source for knowing Islam, its stand and its guidance.

Historicity of the Life of the Prophet

As Muslims, we believe in all the prophets who preceded Muhammad, upon whom be peace—not only those who are mentioned in the Qur'an, but also those who are not so mentioned[5] — and this is

polytheists were not going to depart (from their ways) until there should come to them clear evidence, an apostle from Allah, rehearsing scriptures kept pure and holy: herein are laws (or decrees) right and straight" (Ibid. 98: 1-3).

"We have, without doubt, sent down the message (Qur'an) and We will assuredly guard it (from corruption)" (Ibid: 15:9).

"Nay, this is a glorious Qur'an, (inscribed) in a guarded tablet" (Ibid. 85:21-22).

[3]It is an established fact that the present text of the Qur'an is exactly the same as it was presented by Prophet Mohammad, upon whom be peace, and has not undergone any change. The Prophet used to get the message transcribed soon after its revelation and this process continued till his death. These transcripts were compiled in book form and preserved by the first Caliph. The third Caliph had several copies made of this text and distributed them to different centers of the Islamic world. All copies of the Qur'an from that time onward, wherever and whenever they may have been written or printed, follow the text. The Prophet, upon whom be peace, enjoined the believers to recite the Qur'an in prayer from the first day. Scores of companions of the Prophet knew the Qur'an by heart, and every one of them memorized at least a part of the Qur'an during the life of the Prophet, upon whom be peace. Since that time, it has become customary to recite the whole of the Qur'an during the taraweeh prayers in the month of Ramadan in every Muslim country, and hundreds of thousands of people know the Qur'an by heart. No other religious book has been so well preserved, either in memory or in writing, that one should not have the slightest doubt about its authenticity.

[4]Briefly, the tradition was recorded in the following manner: anyone attributing anything to the Prophet, upon whom be peace, had to cite names of persons through whom he claimed to have received the information. The chain of narrators went back to the person with whom the tradition originated. The original narrator had to be a person who had reasonable access to the Prophet, upon whom be peace, and should have been a direct observer of an event or recipient of a saying. The lives of the narrators were carefully investigated to test their reliability. The tradition was thus compiled and the chain of narrators was recorded, along with an account of their lives. Even today we can verify every detail of the life of the Prophet, upon whom be peace, and ascertain his exact teachings.

[5]We did aforetime send apostles before you: of them there are some whose story We have related to you and some whose story We have not related to you" (The Qur'an 40:78).

such an integral part of our faith that if we were to abandon it, we would cease to be Muslims.[6] For instruction, however, we turn to Prophet Muhammad, upon whom be peace, alone. Not on account of any prejudice, but because:

✓ As the last of Allah's messengers, he brought us the latest divine dispensation.

✓ The Word of Allah, which reached us through Muhammad, is in pure divine language, free of human admixtures, and preserved in its original form. Its language is a living language, spoken, written, and understood by millions of people; and whose grammar, vocabulary, idiom, pronunciations, and script have remained unchanged from the time of revelation until today.

✓ As I have said earlier, we have a complete historical record of the life, character, conduct, sayings and actions of Prophet Muhammad, upon whom be peace, preserved with meticulous care, accuracy, and detail. Since this cannot be said of other prophets, we cannot emulate them, though we believe in them.

Universality of the Prophet's Mission

It is our belief that Muhammad's mission was for the whole world and for all times; because,

✓ Its universality has been clearly confirmed by the Qur'an.[7]

✓ It is a logical consequence of the finality of his prophet-

---

[6]"The apostle believes in what has been revealed to him from his Lord, as do the men of faith. Each one (of them) believeth in Allah, His angels, His books, and His apostles. We make no distinction (they say) between one and another of His apostles, and they say: "We hear, and we obey: (we seek) Your forgiveness, our Lord and to You is the end of all journeys" (Ibid. 2:285).

"Those who deny Allah and his apostles, and (those who) wish to separate Allah from His apostles, saying: 'We believe in some but reject others and (those who) wish to take a course midway, they are in truth (equally) unbelievers; and We have prepared for unbelievers a humiliating punishment. To those who believe in Allah and His apostles and make no distinction between any of the apostles, We shall soon give their (due) rewards: for Allah is Oft-Forgiving" (Ibid. 4: 150-152).

[7]"Say: "O men! I am sent unto you all, as the apostle of Allah, to Whom belongs the dominion of the heavens and the earth: there is no god but He: it is He who gives both life and death. So believe in Allah and His Apostle, the unlettered Prophet, who believed in Allah and His words: follow him that (so) ye may be guided" (Ibid. 7:158).

"This Qur'an hath been revealed to me by inspiration that I may warn you and all whom it reaches" (Ibid. 6:19).

"We have not sent you but as a universal (messenger) to men, giving them glad tidings, and warning them (against sin), but most men understand not" (Ibid. 34:28).

"Verily this is no less than a Message to (all) the World" (Ibid. 81:27).

hood. He had to be the guide and the leader for all men and for all ages.

✓ God has provided, through him, a complete code which is to be followed,[8] and this in itself supports the concept of finality, because without completeness, the need for other prophets would remain.

✓ It is a fact that during the last 1400 years no man has arisen whose life and work bear even the slightest resemblance to that of a prophet. Nor has anyone presented a book which could be remotely considered a divine communication. Still less has there been a man to claim legitimate authority as a law-giver for mankind.

The Place of Reason and Revelation in Islam

It must, at this point, be understood why Allah communicates with man through His prophets. This has to be examined in the context of the sources of human knowledge. At the preliminary stage we gain knowledge through empirical observation. At higher levels is deductive reasoning, accompanied by scientific investigation. Man is equipped well enough in these fields to function without divine assistance. Doubtless, there is an everpresent divine will helping man in his innovative endeavors and progressively revealing to him the mysteries of His creation. Some gifted individuals achieve, in moments of rare inspiration, new insights or discover new laws of nature. But there is another kind of knowledge which is beyond the reach of our senses or scientific study. This sphere of knowledge does not submit to scientific examination. Philosophy and science can only speculate about it. Human theories about ultimate realities, based on reason, can never achieve the level of certainty; and their formulators, conscious of their limitations, do not represent them as conclusive. As such, man is dependent on whatever knowledge is communicated to him by Allah. How is this knowledge conveyed? Undoubtedly, it is not conveyed through the operations of some publishing house, where books are printed and handed over to each man with instructions to read and discover the truth about himself, about the universe, and about the manner in which he should organize his life. To convey this knowledge to mankind, Allah chooses prophets as His messengers. He reveals truth to them, and they communicate it to the people.

---

[8]"This day I have perfected your religion for you, completed My favor upon you, and have chosen for you Islam as your religion" (Ibid. 5:3).

"Muhammad is not the father of your men, but (he is) the Apostle of Allah, and the last of the Prophets" (Ibid. 33:40).

Comprehensiveness of the Islamic Way of Life

The work of a prophet is not limited to the communication of knowledge alone. He has to explain the relationship between God and man, and man and man. He has to prescribe a moral code, enunciate the principles of culture and civilization, lay down the mode of worship, establish a framework of belief and define the moral imperatives which must govern our life. The Prophet determines the rules to serve as the basis of social and cultural relationships, economic, judicial, and political dealings, matters of war and peace, and international affairs. The Prophet does not transmit merely a code of rituals commonly regarded as "religion." He brings with him a whole system of thought and action which is called *ad-din* (the complete way of life) in Islamic terminology.

The mission of a prophet does not end with the announcement of the message. He has to guide the people by explaining to them the implications of the Islamic creed, the moral code, the divine injunctions and commandments, and the form of worship that sustains the whole system. He has to exemplify the faith so others can pattern their lives after him. He must train individuals as well as society for practical participation in the evolution of Islamic culture and civilization. The believers must grow under his guidance into an organized community so that God's word will prevail over all other words.

Not all the prophets succeeded in carrying their mission to its ultimate objective. There were many who did not succeed, not because of any personal fault or inadequacy, but because of the prejudice and intolerance of the people, or because the circumstances were not favorable. But every prophet had the same mission, and it is a fact that Muhammad, upon whom be peace, succeeded in establishing the Sovereignty of God on earth, as it is in the heavens.

Universal Application of the Message

From the very outset, the audience of the Qur'an and Prophet Muhammad, upon whom be peace, was mankind. Those who accepted the Word acquired the status of believers without any distinction. At no time did the Qur'an address itself to the people of any particular area, race, tribe, color or language. The Qur'an always calls upon the "progeny of 'Adam" or "mankind" to accept Islam. The specific instructions and injunctions are meant for those who have come to believe in Islam, and they are always addressed as "those who believe." That the message of Islam was universal in character is proved by the fact that those who accepted the message, acquired equal rights and status as believers, regardless of their origin. The Qur'an says: "The believers are all like brothers."[9] The Prophet, upon whom be peace,

---

[9]"The believers are but a single brotherhood" (Ibid. 49:10).

said: "Those who subscribe to our belief and adopt the Islamic way of life have the same rights and the same obligations as we have."[10] He also announced, "Listen! You have one God as you have one father ('Adam). There is no distinction between an Arab and a non-Arab There is no preference for black over white, or white over black. There is distinction only in submission to Allah. The most virtuous among you is the most honorable in the eyes of Allah."[11]

The Islamic Understanding of Unity

Among the fundamentals of Islam, the most important is belief in one God (Allah), not just the conviction that He exists or that He is one, but that He alone is the Creator, Master, Ruler, and Administrator of all that exists.[12] The universe exists because Allah wills it to exist; it

---

[10]*Al-Bukhari*, Salah-38, *an-Nasa'i, Tahrim,* 2.

[11]*Musnad Ahmad,* Vol. 5, p. 411; *al-Bayhaqi, Kitab al-Haj; Zad al-Ma'ad,* Ibn al-Qayyim, Vol. 4, p. 31; Egypt 1935; similar traditions are available in *al-Bukhari* and *al-Muslim.*

[12]"It is He Who created the heavens and the earth in true (proportions)" (The Qur'an 6:73).

"Say: 'Who is the Lord and Sustainer of the heavens and the earth?' Say: '(It is) Allah'. Say: 'Do you then take (for worship) protectors other than Him, such as have no power either for good or for harm to themselves?' Say: 'Are the blind equal with those who see? Or the depths of darkness equal with light?' Or do they assign to Allah partners who have created (anything) as He has created, so that the creation seemed to them similar? Say: 'Allah is the Creator of all things: He is the One, the Supreme and Irresistible'" (Ibid. 13:16).

"(This Qur'an) a revelation from Him Who created the earth and the heavens on high. (Allah) Most Gracious is firmly established on the throne (of Authority). To Him belongs what is in the heavens and on earth, and all between them, and all beneath the soil. If thou pronounce the word aloud, (it is no matter): for verily He knows what is secret and what is yet more hidden. Allah! There is no god but He; to Him belong the Most Beautiful Names" (Ibid. 20:4-8).

"Your Lord is Allah, Who created the heavens and the earth in six days, and is firmly established on the throne (of Authority): He draws the night as a veil over the day, each seeking the other in rapid succession. He created the sun, the moon and the stars, (all) governed by laws under His command. Is it not His to create and to govern? Blessed be Allah, the Cherisher and Sustainer of the Worlds!" (Ibid. 7:54).

"He rules (all) affairs from the heavens to the earth: in the end will (all affairs) go up to Him, on a Day, the space whereof will be (as) a thousand years of your reckoning" (Ibid. 32:5).

"Don't you know that to Allah belongs the dominion of the heavens and the earth? And besides Him you have neither patron nor helper" (Ibid. 2:107).

"He to Whom belongs the dominion of the heavens and the earth; no son has He begotten, nor has He a partner in His dominion. It is He Who created all things, and ordered them in due proportions" (Ibid. 25:2).

functions because Allah wills it to function.[13] All the attributes of sovereignty reside in Allah alone, and no one else has a share in them in the slightest[14] degree. He alone possesses all the attributes of divinity,

---

[13]"O men! call to mind the grace of Allah unto you! Is there a Creator, other than Allah, to give you sustenance from heaven or earth? There is no God but He: How then are you deluded away from the Truth?" (Ibid. 35:3).

"It is Allah Who sustains the heavens and the earth, lest they cease (to function): and if they should fail, there is none, not one that can sustain them thereafter: Verily He is Most Forbearing, Oft-Forgiving" (Ibid. 35:41).

[14]"If Allah touch you with affliction, none can remove it but He; if He touch you with happiness he has power over all things. He is the Irresistible, (watching) from above over His worshippers; and He is the Wise, acquainted with all things" (Ibid. 6:17-18).

"Say: 'Allah knows best how long they stayed: With Him is (the knowledge of) the secrets of the heavens and the earth: how clearly he sees, how finely He hears (everything)! They have no protector other than Him; nor does He share His Command with any person whatsoever.' And recite (and teach) what has been revealed to thee of the Book of thy Lord; none can change His words, and none wilt thou find as a refuge other than Him" (Ibid. 18: 26-27).

"To Him belongs the dominion of the heavens and the earth: And all affairs are referred back to Allah" (Ibid. 57:5).

"Allah is He, than Whom there is no other god; — The Sovereign, the Holy One, the Source of Peace (and Perfection), the Guardian of Faith, the Preserver of Safety, the Exalted in Might, the Irresistible, the Supreme: Glory to Allah! (High is He) above the partners they attribute to Him" (Ibid. 59:23).

"Blessed be He in Whose hands is Dominion: And He over all things has Power" (Ibid. 36:83).

"So glory to Him in Whose hands is the dominion of all things and to Him will you be all brought back" (Ibid. 36:83).

"Say: 'Who then has any power at all (to intervene) on your behalf with Allah, if His Will is to give you some loss or to give you some profit?' " (Ibid. 48:11).

"If Allah touch you with hurt, there is none to remove it but He: If He designs some benefit for you, there is none who can keep back His Favor: He caused it to reach whomever of His servants he pleased. And He is the Oft-Forgiving, Most Merciful" (Ibid. 10:107).

"Say: 'No one can deliver me from Allah (if I were to disobey Him), nor should I find refuge except in Him' " (Ibid. 72:22).

"Say: 'Who is it in Whose hands is the governance of all things? Who protects while against Him there is no protection? (Say) if you know' " (Ibid. 23:88).

"Doer (without let) of all that He intends" (Ibid. 85:16).

"For Allah does command according to His Will and Plan" (Ibid. 85:16).

"Allah commands, there is none who can revise His command: and He is swift in taking account" (Ibid. 13:41).

"He cannot be questioned for His acts, but they will be questioned (for theirs)" (Ibid. 21:23).

"Is not Allah the greatest of all Judges?" (Ibid. 95:8).

and none other than Allah possesses any of those attributes.[15] His vision encompasses the whole universe, and all that it contains, in a single glance. He has direct knowledge of the universe, and all that is in the universe. He knows not only its present, but its past and its future too. This omnipresence and omniscience is an attribute of Allah

---

"Say: 'O Allah! Lord of Power (and Rule), You give power to whom You please, and You strip off power from whom You please, You bestow with honor whom You please, and You bring low whom You please: In Your hand is all good, Verily, over all things You have power' " (Ibid. 3:26).

"Do they seek for other than the Religion of Allah? ... while all creatures in the heavens and on earth have, willing or unwilling, bowed to His Will (adhered to Islam), and to Him shall they all be brought back" (Ibid. 3:83).

"They say: 'Have we any share in deciding matters?' Say: 'The powers of decision are with Allah' " (Ibid. 3:154).

"In fact the earth is Allah's. He gives it as a heritage to such of His servants as He pleases" (Ibid. 7:128).

[15]"And they have taken (for worship) gods other than Allah, to give them power and glory! Instead, they (their gods) shall reject their worship, and become adversaries against them" (Ibid. 19: 81-82).

"Yet they take (for worship) gods other than Allah, (hoping) that they might be helped! They have not the power to help them: but they will be brought up (before Our Judgment-seat as a troop (to be condemned)" Ibid. 36: 74-75).

"It was not We that wronged them, they wronged their own souls. The deities, other than Allah, whom they invoked, profited them no whit when there issued the decree of your Lord, Nor did they add aught (to their lot) but perdition!" (Ibid. 11:101)

"Is then He Who creates like one that creates not? Will you not receive admonition?" (Ibid. 16:17).

"Those whom they invoke besides Allah create nothing and are themselves created" (Ibid. 16-20).

"Your God is Allah the One. As to those who believe not in the Herafter, their hearts refuse to know and they are arrogant" (Ibid. 16:22).

"Allah had said: 'Take not (for worship) two gods: for He is just One Allah: then fear Me (and Me alone)' " (Ibid. 16: 51).

"Why then was no help forthcoming to them from those whom they worshipped as gods, besides Allah, as a means of access (to Allah)? Nay, they left them in the lurch: But that was their falsehood and their invention" (Ibid. 46:28).

"(The man said) 'It would not be reasonable of me if I did not serve Him Who created me, and to Whom you shall (all) be brought back. Shall I take (other) gods besides Him? If (Allah) Most Gracious should intend some adversity for me, of no use whatever will be their intercession for me, nor can they deliver me' " (Ibid. 36: 22-23).

"They serve, besides Allah, things that hurt them not nor profit them, and they say: 'These are our intercessors with Allah.' Say: 'Do you indeed inform Allah of something He knows not in the heavens or on earth? Glory to Him! And far is He above the partners they ascribe (to Him)!' " (Ibid. 10:18).

"It is He Who is Allah in heaven and Allah on earth: and He is Full of Wisdom and Knowledge" (Ibid. 43:84).

alone and of no other.[16] There was none "before" Him and there will be none "after" Him. He has been there always and will be there always — Eternal and Abiding. All else is transient. He alone is eternally Living

---

"O men! Call to mind the grace of Allah unto you! Is there a Creator, other than Allah, to give you sustenance from heaven or earth? There is no god but He: How then are you deluded away from the Truth?" (Ibid. 35:3).

"Say: 'Think you, if Allah took away your hearing and your sight, and sealed up your hearts, who a god other than Allah could restore them to you?" (Ibid. 6:46).

"And He is Allah: there is no god but He. To Him be praise, at the first and at the last: for His is the Command, and to Him shall you (all) be brought back" (Ibid. 28:70).

"Say: 'Behold! If Allah were to make the day perpetual over you to the Day of Judgment is there other than Allah, who can give you a night in which you can rest? Will you not then see?" (Ibid. 28:72).

"Say: 'Call upon other (gods) whom you fancy, besides Allah: they have no power ... not the weight of an atom ... in the heavens or on earth; no (sort of) share have they therein, nor is any of them a helper to Allah' " (Ibid. 34:22).

"He created the heavens and the earth in true (proportions). He makes the night overlap the day, and the day overlap the night. He has subjected the sun and the moon (to His law) each one follows a course for a time appointed. Is not He the Exalted in Power... He Who forgives again and again?... Such is Allah, your Lord and Cherisher: to Him belongs (all) dominion. There is no god but He. Then how are you turned away?" (Ibid. 39:5-6).

"Or, who has created the heaven and the earth, and who sends you down rain from the sky? Yea, with it We cause to grow well-planted orchards full of beauty and delight: it is not in your power to cause the growth of the trees in them. (Can there be another) god besides Allah? Nay, they are a people who swerve from justice. Or, who has made the earth firm to live in; made rivers in its midst; set thereon mountains immovable; and made a separating bar between the two bodies of flowing water? (Can there be another) god besides Allah? Nay, most of them know not. Or, who listens to the (soul) distressed when it calls on Him, and who relieves its suffering, and makes you (Mankind) inheritors of the earth? (Can there be another) god besides Allah? Little it is that you heed! Or who guides you through the depths of darkness on land and sea, and who sends the winds as heralds of glad tidings, going before His Mercy? (Can there be another) god besides Allah? ... High is Allah above what they associate with him! Or, who orginates Creation, then repeats it, and who gives you sustenance from heaven and earth? (Can there be another) god besides Allah? Say, 'Bring forth your argument if you are telling the truth!' " (Ibid. 27:60-64).

"Yet they have taken, besides Him, gods that can create nothing but are themselves created; that have no control of hurt or good to themselves; nor can they control death nor life nor resurrection" (Ibid. 7:191-192).

"He has created the heavens and the earth for just ends: far is He above having the partners they ascribe to Him! (Ibid. 16:3).

[16]"And whether you speak secretly or loudly (it is the same for Him) He knows even what is in the minds. Shoud He not know, He that created? And He is the One that understands the finest mysteries (and) is well acquainted (with them)" (Ibid. 67:13-14).

"Do they not observe the birds above them, spreading their wings and folding them in? None can uphold them except (Allah) Most Gracious: truly it is He who watches over all things" (Ibid. 67:19).

and Present.[17] He is no one's progeny, and He has no progeny. Whatever exists, besides His Self, is His own creation, and no other can identify himself in any manner with the Lord of the universe, or claim to be his son or daughter.[18]

"With Him is (the knowledge of) the secrets of the heavens and the earth, how clearly He sees, how finely He hears (everything). They have no protector other than Him; nor does He share His command with anyone whatsoever" (Ibid. 18:26).

"It was We Who created man, and We know what suggestions his soul makes to him: for We are nearer to him than (his) jugular vein" (Ibid. 50:16).

"He knows what enters within the earth and what comes forth out of it, what comes down from heaven and what mounts up to it, and He is with you whereever you may be And Allah sees well all that you do" (Ibid. 57:4).

"Say: 'None except Allah knows what is hidden in the heavens or in earth, nor can they perceive when they shall be raised up (for Judgment)' " (Ibid. 27:65).

"He knows the unseen. From Him is not hidden the least little atom in the heavens or on earth, nor is there anything less than that or greater. Everything is in a clear Record" (Ibid. 34:3).

"With Him are the keys of the Unseen, the treasures that none knows but He. He knows whatever there is on the earth and in the sea. Not a leaf falls but with His knowledge. There is not a grain in the darkness (or depths) of the earth, nor anything fresh or dry (green or withered), but is (inscribed) in a Record clear (to those who can read)" (Ibid. 6:59).

[17]"He is the First and the Last, the Evident and the Imminent: And He has full knowledge of all things" (Ibid. 57:3).

"And call not, besides Allah, another god. There is no god but He. Everything (that exists) will perish except His own self. To Him belongs the Command, and to Him will you (all) be brought back" (Ibid. 28:88).

"All that is on earth will perish, but the personality of your Lord will abide (forever), full of Majesty, Bounty and Honor" (Ibid. 55: 26-27).

[18]"He begets not, nor is He begotten; and there is none like unto Him" (Ibid. 112:3-4).

"They say: 'Allah has begotten a son': Glory be to Him ... Nay, to Him belongs all that is in the heavens and on earth; everything renders worship to Him. To Him is due the primal origin of the heavens and the earth: When He decrees a matter he says to it: 'Be', and it is there (Ibid. 2: 116-117).

" To Him is due the primal origin of the heavens and the earth, how can He have a son when He has no consort? He created all things, and He has full knowledge of all things. That is Allah your Lord! There is no god but, He, the Creator of all things: then you worship Him" (Ibid. 6: 101-102).

"No son did Allah beget, nor is there a god along with Him" (Ibid. 23:91).

"Further, that He may warn those (also) who say, 'Allah hath begotten a son' No knowledge have they of such a thing, nor had their fathers. It is a grievous thing that issues from their mouths as a saying. What they say is nothing but falsehood' " (Ibid. 18:4-5)

"It is not befitting to (the majesty of) Allah that He should beget a son. Glory be to Him: when He determines a matter, He only says to it, 'be' and it is there" (Ibid. 19:35).

"They say: '(Allah) Most Gracious has begotten a son!' Indeed you have put forth a

He is the only Deity. To associate anyone in His worship is as great a sin as it is an act of infidelity. He responds to man's prayer, and He alone has the power to accept or reject them. Not to ask of Him is senseless arrogance, and to turn to others is sheer ignorance. To seek of Him and also of others, is to confuse the divine with the non divine.[19]

Allah's Sovereignty

The sovereignty of Allah in Islam is not just a supernatural phenomenon. It covers all aspects of political and legal sovereignty and none other than Allah can lay claim to it. In Allah alone rests the rightful authority to exercise power on this earth, and over those whom Allah has created in it. No monarch, royal family, elite class or leader of any religious group, nor democracy on the basis of the sovereignty of the people can replace Allah's sovereignty. Whoever claims such a position is a rebel, as are those who leave Allah and turn to other people in obedience. Similarly, any institution or individual attempting to assume political and legal sovereignty and restrict the jurisdiction of Allah to spheres of personal law or religious duties, is really a usurper and a rebel. The truth is that none can claim to be a law-giver on Allah's earth, and none can challenge the supreme authority of Almighty Allah in any sphere.[20]

---

thing most monstrous. At it the skies are ready to burst, the earth to split asunder, and the mountains to fall down in utter ruin, that they should invoke a son for (Allah) Most Gracious. For it is not consonant with the majesty of (Allah) Most Gracious that He should beget a son. Not one of the beings in the heavens and the earth but must come to (Allah) Most Gracious as a servant" (Ibid. 19: 88-93).

[19]"And call not, besides Allah, another god. There is no god but He" (Ibid. 28:88).

"Beware, it is only Allah to Whom sincere devotion is due" (Ibid. 39:3).

"Say (O Prophet) 'Is it someone other than Allah that you order me to worship, O you the ignorant ones?" (Ibid 39:64).

"Call upon your Lord with humility and secretly, for Allah loves not those who trespass beyond bounds. Do no mischief on the earth, after it has been set in order, but call on Him with fear and longing (in your hearts). For the Mercy of Allah is (always) near to those who do good" (Ibid. 7:55-56).

"Behold, Luqman said to his son by way of instruction: 'O my son! Join not in worship (others) with Allah. To ascribe partners to Him is a tremendous wrong' " (Ibid. 31:13).

"Say: 'Truly I am a Warner: no god is there but the One Allah, Supreme and Irresistible' " (Ibid. 38:65).

"And your Lord says: 'Call on Me; I will answer your (prayer): but those who are too arrogant to serve Me will surely find themselves in Hell — in humiliation!' " (Ibid. 40:60).

"We assuredly sent amongst every people an apostle, (with the command), 'Serve Allah and shun false gods' " (Ibid. 16:36).

[20]"Don't you see the one who takes for his god his own passion (or impulse)? Could you be guardian over him?" (Ibid. 25:43).

Tauhid and Its Implications

Certain natural consequences flow from this Islamic understanding of Allah:

✓ Allah alone is the real Deity and none other than Allah, has any right to be worshipped by man.

✓ Allah alone has authority over the forces of the universe, and He alone can fulfill or frustrate man's hopes. Man should turn to Him alone in prayer. He should never imagine that prayers can be addressed to anyone but Allah.

✓ Allah is the Master of man's destiny, and none else can interfere with the fate of others or with his own fate. Man's hopes and fears must, therefore, be directed only to Allah. None other should be the object of fear or source of favor.

✓ Allah is the Creator of the world and He alone has complete and direct knowledge of the reality of man and of the world. Only He can guide man through the complicated course of life and teach him about good and evil. Since Allah alone is the Creator and the Master, he alone has authority over the universe and man. It is an act of blasphemy for man to become independent or claim authority over other men. For man to become his own law-giver, to accept the authority of any other individual or institution as such, is equally blasphemous. The ultimate Law-giver and Master of His creation on this earth is none other than Allah, and His law has the status of the supreme law. Man can legislate subject to His supreme law. Beyond that he has no legislative authority.

"They take their priests and their anchorites to be their lords in derogation of Allah, and (they take as their Lord) Messiah the son of Mary; while they were commanded to worship but One Allah: there is no god but He. Praise and glory to Him, (far is He) from having partners they associate (with Him)" Ibid. 9:31).

"Whatever it be wherein you differ, its decision is with Allah; such is Allah my Lord, in Him I trust and to Him I turn" (Ibid. 42:10).

"What! Have they partners (in godhead)? Who have made a law of religion for them with the permission of Allah?" (Ibid. 42:21).

"Exalted be Allah, the real King, there is no god but He, the Lord of the Majestic Throne. If anyone invokes, besides Allah, any other god, he has no authority therefore" (Ibid. 23:116-117).

"Say: I seek refuge with the Lord of Mankind, the King of Mankind, the God of Mankind" (Ibid. 114: 1-3).

"(Joseph said) Leaving Allah, whoever you worship are nothing but names which you have coined, — you and your fathers, — for which Allah has sent you no authority: the Command is for none but Allah; He has commanded that you worship none but Him; that is the right religion, but most men understand not" (Ibid. 12:40).

"Follow (O men!) the revelation given unto you from your Lord, and follow not, as patrons or protectors, other than Him" (Ibid. 7:3).

Prophethood and Its Need

We now come to our second most important belief — belief in Muhammad's prophethood. Allah conveyed His message to man through Muhammad. This took two forms:

✓ Allah revealed the Qur'an to the Prophet in his own language.

✓ The *Sunnah* of the Prophet, upon whom be peace, is an unerring guide to man for all that is permissible and all that is prohibited in the eyes of Allah. Without this belief in the Prophet, belief in Allah would become a mere theoretical proposition. It is the example of practical leadership and the

---

"As to the thief, male or female, cut off his or her hands. A punishment by way of example from Allah for their crime, and Allah is Exalted in Power ... Don't you know that to Allah (alone) belongs the dominion of the heavens and the earth? He punishes whom He pleases and He forgives whom He pleases: and Allah has power over all things" (Ibid. 5: 41-43).

"We ordained in the Book for Jews: "Life for life, eye for eye, nose for nose, ear for ear, tooth for tooth, and wounds equal for equal. But if anyone remits the retaliation by way of charity, it is an act of atonement for himself. And if any fail to judge by (the light of) what Allah has revealed, they are (no better than) wrong-doers" (Ibid. 5:48).

"O you who believe! The law of retaliation is prescribed to you in cases of murder: the free for the free, the slave for the slave, the woman for the woman. But if any remission is made by the brother of the slain, then grant any reasonable demand, and compensate him with handsome gratitude; this is a concession and a mercy from your Lord. After this, whoever exceeds the limits shall be in grave penalty" (Ibid. 2:178).

"It is prescribed, when death approaches any of you if he leave any goods, that he make a bequest to parents and next of kin, according to reasonable usage; this is due from the God-fearing. If anyone changes the bequest after hearing it, the guilt shall be on those who make the change. For Allah hears and knows all things. But if anyone fears partiality or wrong doing on the part of the testator, and makes peace between (the parties concerned), there is no wrong on him: for Allah is Oft-Forgiving, Most Merciful" (Ibid. 2:180-182).

"A divorce is only permissible twice: after that, the parties should either hold together on equitable terms or separate with kindness. It is not lawful for you, (men), to take back any of your gifts (from your wives), except when both parties fear that they would be unable to keep the limits ordained by Allah. If you (judges) do indeed fear that they would be unable to keep the limits ordained by Allah, there is no blame on either of them if she gives something for her freedom. These are the limits ordained by Allah; so do not transgress them. If any do transgress the limits ordained by Allah, such persons wrong themselves as well as others" (Ibid. 2:229).

"When you divorce women, and they fulfill the term of their seculsion (iddah), do not prevent them from marrying their (former) husbands, if they mutually agree on equitable terms. This instruction is for all among you, who believe in Allah and the Last Day. That is (the course making for) most virtue and purity amongst you, and Allah knows, and you know not" (Ibid. 2:232).

"You know not whether your parents or your children are nearest to you in benefit. These are settle portions (of inheritance) ordained by Allah and Allah is All-Knowing, All-Wise" (Ibid. 4:11).

ideological guidance provided by the Prophet, upon whom be peace, that transforms belief in Allah into a culture. No one can be a Muslim unless he believes in the Prophet as he believes in Allah.[21]

Humanity of the Prophet

The position of the Prophet has been so clearly defined in Islam that we can know what he was and what he was not. The Prophet, upon whom be peace, is no more than a servant of Allah. He must make people servants of Allah and not servants of himself.[22] At least seventeen times a day Muslims recite in their prayers: "I bear witness that Muhammad is a servant of Allah and is His prophet."[23] The Qur'an leaves no doubt that the Prophet is but a human being and has no share in divinity.[24]

"Have you not turned your vision to those who declare that they believe in the revelation come to you and to those before you? Their (real) wish is to resort together for judgment (in their disputes) to the impostor, though they were ordered to reject him. But Satan's wish is to lead them astray, far away (from the Right)" (Ibid. 4:60).

"Then (after Bani Isra'el) We put you on the (right) Way of Religion; so you follow that (Way), and follow not the desires of those who know not" (Ibid. 45:18).

"Whoever does not judge according to that which has been revealed by God, they are unbelievers ... they are wrong doers ... they are rebels" (Ibid. 5: 47, 48, 50).

"Say not for any false thing that your tongues may put forth: 'This is lawful, and this is forbidden,' so as to ascribe false things to Allah. For those who ascribe false things to Allah, will never prosper" (Ibid. 16:116).

"The woman and the man guilty of adultery or fornication ... flog each of them with a hundred stripes" (Ibid. 24:2).

"And those who launch a charge against chaste women and produce not four witnesses, (to support their allegation), flog them with eighty stripes; and reject their evidence ever after, for such men are wicked transgressors" (Ibid. 24:4).

"Say: 'O People of the Book! Come to common terms as between us and you; that we worship none but Allah; that we associate no partners with Him; that we erect not from among ourselves lords and patrons other than Allah'. If then they turn back, Say: 'Bear witness that we are Muslims (bowing to Allah's Will)' " (Ibid. 3:64).

[21]"Only those are Believers who (sincerely) believe in Allah and His Apostle: when they are with him on a matter requiring collective action, they do not depart until they have asked for his leave" (Ibid. 24:62).

"Only those are Believers who have (sincerely) believed in Allah and His Apostle, and have never since doubted" (Ibid. 49:15).

[22]It is not (possible) that a man, to whom is given the Book, and Wisdom, and the prophetic office, should say to people: 'Be you my worshippers rather than Allah's (Ibid 3:79).

[23]Transmitted in *Bukhari* (BK. 10, Chs. 153-154). It is also related in *Muslim, Abu Da'ud, an-Nasa'i, Ibn Majah,* and *Musnad Ahmad.* It is an agreed-upon tradition.

[24]"I am but a human being like yourselves, (but) the inspiration has come to me, that your god is One God. Whoever expects to meet his Lord, let him work righteousness, and in the worship of his Lord admit no one as partner" (The Qur'an 18: 110).

The Prophet is neither superhuman nor is he free of human finitude. He owns no treasure of Allah, nor does he possess knowledge of the unknown,[25] like Almighty Allah. The Prophet cannot benefit or harm others, nor can he do it to himself.[26] The precise task of the Prophet is to communicate the message of Allah. He has no power to make people righteous and faithful. Nor can he call to account those who refuse to believe, and he certainly has no power to punish them for their disbelief.[27] Should the Prophet himself choose to defy Allah or fabricate things on behalf of Allah or make any change in the message revealed to him, he will incur divine displeasure and punishment.[28] Muhammad is

---

"Say you: 'I am but a man like you. It is revealed to me by inspiration that your God is One God, so stand true to Him, and ask for His forgiveness' (Ibid. 41:6).

"They say: 'We shall not believe in you, until you cause a spring to gush forth for us from the earth, or (until) you have a garden of date trees and vines, and cause rivers to gush forth in their midst, carrying abundant water; or you cause the sky to fall in pieces, as you say (will happen), against us; or you bring Allah and the angels before (us) face to face; or you have a house adorned with gold, or you mount a ladder right into the skies and we shall not even believe in your mounting until you send down to us a book that we could read.' Say: 'Glory to my Lord! Am I naught but a man who is an apostle?' (Ibid. 17: 90-93).

[25]"But I follow what is revealed to me" (Ibid 6:50).

"Say: 'I have no power over any good or harm to myself except as Allah wills. If I had knowledge of the unseen, I should have multiplied all good, and no evil should have touched me. I am but a warner, and a bringer of glad tidings to those who have faith" (Ibid. 7:188).

[26]"Say: 'I have no power over any harm or profit to myself except as Allah wills' " (Ibid. 10:49).

[27]Say: 'It is true you will not be able to guide everyone whom you love, but Allah guides those whom He wills and He knows best those who receive guidance" (Ibid. 28:56).

"Verily We have revealed the Book to you in truth for (instructing) mankind. He, then, that receives guidance benefits his own soul but he that strays injures his own soul. You are not in charge over them" (Ibid. 39:41).

"You are not overlord upon them" (Ibid. 88:22).

[28]"If you were to follow their desires after the knowledge has reached you, then you would find neither protector nor helper against Allah" (Ibid. 2:120).

"If you, after the knowledge has reached you, were to follow their (vain) desires, — then you would indeed (clearly) be in the wrong" (Ibid. 2:145).

"But when Our Clear Signs are rehearsed unto them, those who rest not their hope on their meeting with us, say: 'Bring us a Qur'an other than this, or change this.' Say: 'It is not for me, of my own accord, to change it. I follow naught but what is revealed unto me: if I were to disobey my Lord, I should myself fear the penalty of a great Day (to come)' " (Ibid. 10:15).

"And if the apostle were to invent any sayings in Our name, We should certainly seize him by his right hand, and We should certainly then cut off the artery of his heart: nor could any of you withhold him (from Our wrath)" (Ibid. 69: 44-47).

one of the Prophets of Allah, and above that, he has no status.[29] He cannot by himself prohibit or permit anything. Without a mandate from Allah, he cannot legislate[30] for the people. He has to strictly conform to divine commandments.[31] Islam ensured that the believers should not turn the Prophet into a demi-god. Some of the earlier prophets suffered this fate at the hands of their followers. They attributed all kinds of supernatural powers to their leaders and made them into God's equals or progeny or incarnations. By discouraging such exaggeration, Islam has established the true position of the Prophet as follows:

No one can claim to be a believer without believing in the Prophet.[32] He who obeys the Prophet, in fact, obeys Allah. Allah has not designated any Prophet, except to be obeyed according to His will.[33] The path of the Prophet is the path of divine guidance.[34] Whatever the Prophet, upon whom be peace, ordains must be accepted, and whatever he instructs to avoid must be avoided.[35] The Prophet, upon whom be peace, clarified this when he said: "I am a mortal like you. In matters revealed to me by God you must obey my instructions. But you know more about your own worldly affairs than I do. So my advice in

---

[29]"Muhammad is no more than an apostle: many were the apostles that passed away before him. If he died or were slain, will you then turn back on your heels?" (Ibid. 3:144).

"By the Qur'an, full of Wisdom, you are indeed one of the apostles" (Ibid. 36: 2-3).

"This is a warner, of the (series of) warners of old!" (Ibid. 53: 56).

[30]"O Prophet! Why do you forbid yourself that which Allah has made lawful to you? (Ibid. 66:1).

[31]"I but follow what is revealed to me" (Ibid. 6:50).

"It is not for me, of my own accord, to change it; I follow naught but what is revealed unto me: If I were to disobey my Lord, I should myself fear penalty of a great day (to come)" (Ibid. 10:15).

[32]"Only those are Believers who (sincerely) believe in Allah and His Apostle" (Ibid. 24:62).

[33]"(Jesus said 'I have come to you) to attest the law which was before me, and to make lawful to you part of what was (before) forbidden to you: I have come to you with a Sign from your Lord. So fear Allah and obey me' " (Ibid. 3:50), See also (43:63).

"We sent not an apostle, but to be obeyed, in accordance with the Will of Allah" (Ibid. 4:64).

"He who obeys the apostle obeys Allah, but if any turns away, We have not sent thee to watch over their (evil deeds)" Ibid. 4:80).

"(Noah said) 'So fear Allah, and obey me' " (Ibid. 26: 108, 110; 71:3).

"(All Prophets said) 'Fear Allah and obey me' " (Ibid. 26:126, 131, 144, 150, 163, 179).

[34]"Say: 'Obey Allah, and obey the Apostle'. But if you turn away, he is only responsible for the duty placed on him and you for that placed on you. If you obey him, you shall be on right guidance. The apostle's duty is only to preach clearly" (Ibid. 24:54).

[35]"Take whatever the Prophet gives you, and abstain from whatever he forbids you. Fear Allah; for Allah is strict in punishment" (Ibid. 59:7).

these matters is not binding."[36] The Sunnah of Muhammad, upon whom be peace, is, in fact, an exposition of the purpose of the Qur'an, and this exposition too was conveyed to the Prophet by Allah Himself, as the author of the Qur'an.[37] The Prophet's explanation of the Qur'an enjoys divine sanction, and none can interpret the Qur'an in conflict with or repugnant to the explanation given by the Prophet. Allah declared the life of Muhammad, upon whom be peace, as a model life.[38] None can be a true believer unless he accepts the decision of the Prophet, upon whom be peace.[39] Muslims have no independent position in a matter determined by the Prophet.[40] Before deciding any matter, Muslims must first ascertain whether any analogous matter was decided earlier by Allah and His Prophet, and if a precedent exists, they must follow it.[41]

I hope I have clarified that Allah conveyed to mankind, through the Prophet, not only a supreme law, but also a permanent scheme of values. That which is good, according to the Qur'an and the Sunnah, is good for all times, and that which is evil shall remain evil forever. That which is enjoined as duty, in the Qur'an and the Sunnah, shall always be a duty. What is declared permissible is permissible forever, and what is prohibited is prohibited for all times. In this law, no amendment, deletion, addition or abrogation is possible unless some person or a community decides to renounce Islam. As long as Muslims remain Muslims, it is impossible that in their social and legal system something which was evil yesterday will turn into good today.

Ethical Judgment: Belief in the Hereafter

The third fundamental creed of Islam is belief in the Hereafter (*al-Akhirah*). Denial of the Hereafter is denial of Islam, even though one may have belief in Allah, in the Prophet, and in the

---

[36]*Muslim*, Book 43, traditions 139-141. *Musnad Ahmad*, Vol. 1, p. 162; Vol. III, p. 152.

[37]"And We have sent down to you the Message, so that you may explain clearly to men what is sent for them, and that they may give thought" (Ibid. 16:44).

"It is for us to collect (The Qur'an) and recite it to you (afterwards) but when we recite it, follow thou its recital, then it is for us to explain it" (Ibid. 75: 17-19).

[38]"(O Muslims) you have indeed in the Apostle of Allah a beautiful pattern of (conduct) for anyone whose hope is in Allah and the Final Day, and who engages much in the praise of Allah" (Ibid. 33:21).

[39]"But no, by the Lord, they can have no (real) faith until they make you (O Prophet!) judge in all disputes between them, and find in their souls no resentment against your decisions, but accept them with the fullest conviction" (Ibid. 4:65).

[40]"It is not fitting for a Believer, man or woman, when a matter has been decided by Allah and His Apostle, to have any option about their decision. If anyone disobeys Allah and His Apostle he is indeed on a clearly wrong path" (Ibid. 33:36).

[41]"O ye who believe! put not yourselves forward before Allah and His Apostle; and fear Allah: for Allah is He Who hears and knows all things" (Ibid. 49:1).

Qur'an.[42] In its detailed form, this belief has the following essential elements:

✓ Man has not been unleashed on the earth as an irresponsible savage. He is accountable to Allah for his actions. Today's life is only a test and an examination. At the end we will all be called upon to render a complete account of our acts of commission and omission to Allah.[43]

---

[42]"If you could but see when they are confronted with their Lord (on the Day of Judgment) He will say: 'Is not this the truth?' They will say: 'Yea, by our Lord! He will say: 'Taste then the penalty, because you were denying it.' Lost indeed are they who treat it as a falsehood ... that they must meet Allah ... until suddenly the hour is on them, and they say: 'Ah! Woe unto us that we took no thought of it'. For they bear their burdens on their backs and evil indeed are the burdens that they bear!" (Ibid. 6: 30-31).

"One day He will gather them together: (they will feel) as if they did not remain (in the world) but an hour of a day having been introduced to each other. Assuredly those will be lost who denied the meeting with Allah and refused to receive true guidance" (Ibid. 10:45).

"If you do marvel (at their want of faith), strange is their saying: 'When we are (actually) dust, shall we indeed then be in a creation renewed?' They are those who deny their Lord!" (Ibid. 13:5).

"Nay, they deny the Hour (of the judgement to come) and We have prepared a blazing fire for such as deny that Hour" (Ibid. 25:11).

"The Unbelievers say (in ridicule): 'Shall we point out to you a man that will tell you, when you are all scattered to pieces in disintegration, that you shall (then be raised) in a new creation? Has he invented a falsehood against Allah, or has a spirit (seized) Him?' Nay, it is those who believe not in the Hereafter that are in (real) penalty and in farthest error" (Ibid. 34: 7-8).

"O David! We did indeed make you a vicegerent on earth, so judge between men in truth (and justice), nor follow the lusts (of thy heart), for they will mislead you from the Path of Allah: for those who wander astray from the Path of Allah is a penalty grievous for that they forget the Day of Account. Not without purpose did We create heaven and earth and all between! That was the thought of Unbelievers! But woe to the Unbelievers because of the Fire (of Hell)" (Ibid. 38: 26-27).

"But they wonder that there has come to them a warner from among themselves. So the Unbelievers say: 'This is a wonderful thing! What! when we die and become dust, (shall we live again?) That is a (sort of) return far (from our understanding).' We already know how much of them the earth takes away and with Us is a Record keeping (the full account.)" (Ibid. 50: 2-4).

"The Unbelievers think that they will not be raised up (for judgment) Say: 'Yea, by my Lord, you shall surely be raised up; then shall you be told (the truth) of all that you did: and that is easy for Allah.' " (Ibid. 64:7).

[43]"That which is on earth We have made but as a glittering show for the earth, in order that We may test them as to which of them are best in conduct." (Ibid. 18:7).

"He Who created Death and Life, that He may try which of you is best indeed." (Ibid. 67:2).

"Does man think that he will be left uncontrolled? (without being accountable)" (Ibid. 75:36).

✓ The time for accountability is fixed by Allah. The tenure allotted to mankind on this earth shall terminate on doomsday, when the present order will be annihilated and replaced by another. The whole human race will rise once again in the new world.[44]

✓ That will be the time when they will appear before Almighty Allah and everyone will face the consequences of his deeds in his individual capacity.[45]

✓ The judgment will rest not on Allah's own knowledge alone. The requirements of due process of justice will be fully observed. A complete record of the actions of every individual, without the slightest alteration, will be put in the open court, and different forms of evidence will be presented to prove man's deeds in private and in public, and the motives which inspired his conduct.[46]

"Verily We created man from a drop of mingled sperm, in order to try him, so We gave him (the gifts) of Hearing and Sight" (Ibid. 76:2).

"When the female (infant), buried alive, will be questioned: — For what crime was she killed" (Ibid. 81: 8-9).

"Woe to those who cheat. When they have to receive by measure, from men, exact full measure. But when they have to give by measure or weight to men, give less than due. Do they not think that they will be called to account on a Mighty Day? A Day when (all) mankind will stand before the Lord of the Worlds" (Ibid. 83: 1-6).

"Then, shall ye be questioned that Day about the joy (ye indulged in)" (Ibid. 102: 8).

[44]"The Trumpet will (just) be sounded, when all that are in the heavens and on earth will swoon, except such as it will please Allah (to exempt), then will a second one be sounded, when, behold, they will be standing and looking on!" (Ibid. 39:68).

"Verily the Day of Sorting Out is the time appointed for all of them" (Ibid. 44:40).

"Say: 'Yea, those of old and those of later times, all will certainly be gathered together for the meeting appointed for a Day well known' " (Ibid. 56: 49-50).

[45]"If you could but see how the wicked (do fare) in the flood of confusion at death! ... the angels stretch forth their hands, (saying), 'Yield up your soul: This day shall you receive your award ... a penalty of shame, for that you used to tell lies against Allah, and scornfully to reject of His Signs!' And behold! Ye come to Us bare and alone as We created you for the first time" (Ibid. 6: 93:94.

"To us shall return all that he talks of, and he shall appear before Us bare and alone" (Ibid. 19:80).

"And every one of them will come to Him singly on the Day of Judgment" (Ibid. 19:96).

[46]"And they will be marshalled before your Lord in ranks (with the announcement), 'Now have you come to Us (bare) as We created you first, aye, you thought We shall not fulfill the appointment made to you to meet (Us)!' And the Book (of deeds) will be placed (before you); and you will see the sinful in great terror because of what is (recorded) in it. They will say, 'Ah! Woe to us! What a book is this! It leaves out nothing small or great, but takes account of it!' They will find all that they did, placed before them, and not one will your Lord treat with injustice" (Ibid. 18: 48-49).

√ There wil be no undue intercession. Neither bribery, nor advocacy against the truth will be allowed. No one will be able to shift his burden to another. Even the closest relations, friends, leaders, religious guides, or self-styled deities will not be able to offer any help to anyone — man will stand by himself — helpless and alone to render his account and await the pronouncement of the judgment,

---

"On the Day when their tongues, their hands, and their feet will bear witness against them as to their actions" (Ibid. 24:24).

"Indeed We shall give life to the dead, and We record that which they send before and that which they leave behind, and of all things have We taken account in a clear Book (of evidence)" (Ibid. 36:12).

"That Day shall We set a seal on their mouths. But their hands will speak to Us, and their feet will bear witness to all that they did" (Ibid. 36:65).

"And the Earth will shine with the glory of its Lord: The Record (of Deeds) will be placed (open), the prophets and the witnesses will be brought forward: and a just decision pronounced between them; and they will not be wronged (in the least)" (Ibid. 39:69).

"At length, when they reach the (Fire), their hearing, their sight, and their skins will bear witness against them as to (all) their deeds. They will say to their skins: 'Why do you bear witness against us?' They will say: 'Allah has given us speech, ... (He) Who gives speech to everything: He created you for the first time, and unto Him gives speech to everything: He created you for the first time, and unto Him were you to return. You did not seek to hide yourselves, lest your hearing, your sight, and your skin should bear witness against you! But you did think that Allah knew not many of the things that you used to do!'" (Ibid. 41: 20-22).

"Or do they think that We hear not their secrets and their private counsels? Indeed (We do) and Our Messengers." (Ibid. 43:80).

"And you will see every group bowing on knee, every group will be called to its Record: 'This Day shall you be recompensed for all that you did! This Our Record speaks about you with truth: for We were wont to put on record all that you did'" (Ibid. 45: 28-29).

"Behold, two (guardian angels) appointed to take note (of his doings) one sitting on the right and one on the left. Not a word does he utter but there is a sentinel by him ready (to note it)" (Ibid. 50: 17-18).

"All that they do is noted in (their) Books (of Deeds). Every matter, small and great, is on record" (Ibid. 54: 52-53).

"Nay! but you deny the Judgement, while, verily over you (are appointed angels) to watch you, — honest and honorable, writing down (your words). They know all that you do" (Ibid. 82: 9-12).

"The Day that (all) things secret will be tested, (Man) will have no power, and no helper" Ibid. 86: 9-12).

"And the Earth will throw up her burdens (from within) and man cries (distressed) 'What is the matter with her?' On that Day will she relate her story. For that your Lord will have given her the order (to do that). On that Day will men proceed in companies sorted out to be shown the Deeds that they (had done)" (Ibid. 99: 2-6).

which shall be in the power of Allah alone.[47]

✓   The judgment will rest on one question: Did man conduct himself in accordance with the truth revealed to the Prophets? If the answer is in the affirmative, the reward will be Paradise, and if in the negative, the punishment will be Hell.

Totality of the Islamic Way of Life

Belief in the Hereafter divides people into three distinct categories. First, there are those who do not believe in the Hereafter and regard life on this earth as the ultimate. Naturally, they judge good and evil by the results that manifest themselves in this world. If an action produces beneficial results, it is good, and if it brings about harmful results, it is evil. Quite often the same action is regarded as good when the results are good, and bad when its results are bad.

---

[47]"Then (on the Day of Judgement) would those who were followed clear themselves of those who did follow (them): they would see the penalty, and all relations between them would be cut off. And those who followed would say: 'If only we had more chance, we would clear ourself of them as they have cleared themselves of us'. Thus will Allah show them (the fruits of) their deeds as (nothing but) regrets, nor will there be a way for them out of the Fire." (Ibid. 2: 166-167).

"O you who believe! Spend out of (the bounties) We have provided for you, before the Day comes when no bargaining (will avail), nor friendship, nor intercession. Those who reject Faith — they are the wrong-doers" (Ibid. 2:254).

One day shall We gather them all together, then shall We say to those who associated gods (with us): 'To your place you and those you made as our partners'. We shall separate them, and their 'partners' shall say (to them): 'It was not us that you worshipped' " (Ibid. 10: 28).

"They will all be marshalled before Allah together: then will the weak say to those who were arrogant, 'For us, we but followed you; can you avail us at all against the wrath of Allah?' They will reply, 'If we had received the guidance of Allah, we should have given it to you: to us it makes no difference (now) whether we rage, or bear (these torments) with patience: for ourselves there is no way of escape.' " (Ibid. 14: 21).

"(O Prophet) Tell My servants who have believed, that they should establish regular prayers, and spend (in charity) out of the sustenance We have given them, secretly and openly, before the coming of a Day in which there will be neither mutual bargaining, nor befriending" (Ibid. 14:31).

"When those who associated partners to Allah will see their partners, they will say: 'Our Lord! They are our partners, those whom we used to invoke besides Thee.' But they will throw back their word at them (And say): 'Indeed you are liars!' " (Ibid. 16:86).

"That Day, Allah will call to them and say: 'Where are My partners whom you imagined (to be such)?' Those against whom the charge will be proved, will say: 'Our Lord! These are the ones whom we led astray; we led them astray, as we were astray ourselves: we free ourselves (from them) in Your presence! It was not us they worshipped.' It will be said (to them): 'Call upon your partners (for help); they will call upon them, but they will not listen to them; and they will see the penalty (before them); (how they will wish) If only they

Second, there are people who do not deny the Hereafter, but who depend on the intercession or atonement of someone to absolve them of their sins. Among them, there are some who regard themselves as Allah's chosen people, who will receive only nominal punishment, however grave their sins. This deprives them of the moral advantage which they could have derived from their belief in the Hereafter. As a result, they also become very much like the people who deny the Hereafter.[48]

Third, there are those who believe in the Hereafter as Islam presents it. They do not delude themselves that they have any

---

had been open to guidance! That Day (Allah) will call to them, and say: 'What was the answer you gave to the apostles?' Then the (whole) story that day will seem obscure to them (like light to the blind) and they will not be able (even) to question each other" (Ibid. 28: 62-66).

"Nor can a bearer of burdens bear another's burden. If one heavily laden should call another to (bear) his load, not the least portion of it can be carried (by the other), even though he be nearly related" (Ibid. 35:18).

"No intercession can avail in His Presence except for those for whom He has granted permission" (Ibid. 34:23).

"Warn them of the Day that is (ever) drawing nearer, when the hearts will (come) right up to the throats to choke (them); no intimate friend nor intercessor will the wrongdoers have who could be listened to" (Ibid. 40:18).

"And who is more astray than one who invokes, besides Allah, such as will not answer him to the Day of Judgment, and who (in fact) are unconscious of their call (to them)? And when mankind is gathered together (at the Resurrection), they will be hostile to them and reject their worship (altogether)!" (Ibid. 46: 5-6).

"And no friend will ask after a friend, though they will be put in sight of each other, the sinner's desire would be that he could redeem himself from the penalty of that Day by (sacrificing) his children, his wife and his brother, his kindred who sheltered him, and all that is on earth, so it could deliver him" (Ibid. 70: 10-14).

"That Day shall a man flee from his own brother, and from his mother and his father, and from his wife and his children. Each of them that Day will have enough concern (of his own) to make him indifferent to the others" (Ibid. 80: 34-37).

"(It will be) the Day when no soul shall have power (to do) for another. The command, that Day, will be (wholly) with Allah" (Ibid. 82:19).

[48]"They are those who deny the Signs of their Lord and the fact of their having to meet Him (in the Hereafter): vain will be their works, nor shall We, on the Day of Judgment, give him any weight. That is their reward, Hell; because they rejected faith, and took My Signs and My Messengers by way of jest" (Ibid. 18:105-06).

"That Day (Allah) will call to them, and say: 'What was the answer you gave to the apostles?' " (Ibid. 28:65).

"The Unbelievers will be led to Hell in crowds; until, when they arrive there, its gates will be opened, and its keepers will say, 'Did not apostles come to you from among yourselves, rehearsing to you the Signs of your Lord, and warning you of the meeting of this Day of yours?' The answer will be: 'True, but the Decree of Punishment has been proved true against the unbelievers!' " (Ibid. 39:71).

special relationship with Allah or that anyone can intercede on their behalf.[49] They know that they alone are responsible for their actions. For them, the belief in the Hereafter becomes a great moral force. A person who believes in the accountability of his deeds finds a permanent guard stationed within himself, who cautions him and admonishes him whenever he deviates from the right path. There may be no court to summon him, no

---

"Every time a group is cast therein (in Hell), its keepers will ask, 'Did no warner come to you?' They will say: 'Yes indeed; a warner did come to us, but we rejected him and said 'Allah never sent down any (message): You are in nothing but a flagrant delusion!'" They will further say: 'Had we but listened or used our intelligence, we should not (now) be among the companions of the blazing fire!" They will then confess their sins: but far will be (forgiveness) from the companions of the blazing fire!" (Ibid. 67: 8-11).

"Then, for such as had transgressed all bounds, and had preferred the life of this world, the abode will be Hell-Fire. And for such as had entertained the fear of standing before their Lord's (tribunal) and had restrained (their) soul from lower desires, their abode will be the Garden" (Ibid. 79: 37:41).

[49]"And they (the Jews) say: 'The Fire shall not touch us but for a few numbered days.' Say: 'Have you taken a promise from Allah, for He never breaks His promise? Or is it that you say of Allah what you do not know?' Nay, those who seek gain in evil, and are girt round by their sins, — they are companions of the Fire: In it shall they abide (forever)" (Ibid. 2:80-81).

"(O Bani Isra'el) guard yourselves against a Day when one soul shall not avail another, nor shall compensation be accepted from her, nor shall intercession profit her, nor shall anyone be helped (from outside)" (Ibid. 2:123).

"Who is there that can intercede in His presence except one permitted by Him" (Ibid. 2: 255).

"They may hide (their crimes) from men, but they cannot hide (them) from Allah: He is in their midst when they plot by night a thing that He cannot approve: and Allah does compass round all that they do. Ah! These are the sort of men on whose behalf you may contend in this world; but who will contend with Allah on their behalf on the Day of Judgement, or who will carry their affairs through?" (Ibid. 4: 108-109).

"The Jews and the Christians say: 'We are sons of Allah, and His beloved.' Say: 'Why then does He punish you for your sins? Nay, you are but men, of the men He has created: He forgives whom He pleases, and He punishes whom He pleases: and to Allah belongs the dominion of the heavens and the earth, and all that is between; and unto Him is the final goal (of all)' " (Ibid. 5: 20).

"Give the warning to those in whose (hearts) is the fear that they will be brought (to judgment) before their Lord: except from Him, they will have no protector nor intercessor, that they may guard (against evil)" (Ibid. 6:51).

"No intercessor (can plead with Him) except after His leave (has been obtained)" (Ibid. 10:3).

"On that Day shall no intercession avail except for those for whom permission has been granted by (Allah) Most Gracious and whose word is acceptable to Him" (Ibid. 20:109).

"How many so-ever be the angels in the heavens, their intercession will avail nothing except after Allah has given leave for whom He pleases and that is acceptable to Him" (Ibid. 53:26).

policemen to apprehend him, no witnesses to accuse him, and no public opinion to press him; but the guard within him is ever on the alert, ready to seize him whenever he transgresses. The consciousness of this inner presence makes man fear Allah, even when he is all by himself.

He discharges his duties honestly, and refrains from doing anything prohibited. Should he succumb to temptation and violate the law of Allah, he is ever ready to offer sincere regrets; he is willing to enter into a firm contract with the future that he will not repeat the mistake. There can be no greater instrument of moral reformation nor any better method to help man develop a sound and stable character. It is the Hereafter which helps man, under all circumstances, conform to Allah's scheme of permanent values. It is for this reason that Islam attaches great importance to the belief in the Hereafter, and without it, even the belief in Allah and the Prophet is not sufficient for man's guidance.

A little earlier, I mentioned that Islam represents a whole civilization, a complete culture and a comprehensive world order. It provides moral guidance in all walks of life. That is why Islamic values are not for the ascetic who renounces the world, but for him who actively participates in different spheres of life, and works within them. The moral values which people look for in convents, monasteries and cloisters, are presented by Islam right in the current of life. Heads of government, governors of state, judges, members of the armed forces and police services, elected representatives of the people in parliaments, leaders of finance, trade and industry, college and university teachers, and students alike receive guidance to organize their lives according to the principles of Islam. There is no distinction in Islam between private and public conduct. The same moral code which one observes at home applies to one's conduct in public. Every institution of society and every department of government must conform to the laws of Islam. Politics must be based on truth and justice. Nations should deal with one another on the basis of mutual recognition of rights and due discharge of obligations. Even if there has to be war, those engaged in it should conduct themselves not as barbarians but as civilized human beings. When man decides to submit to the will of Allah and accepts His law as the supreme law, and organizes his life in accordance with the revealed moral code on the principle of accountability to Allah, the quality and character of his life cannot be limited to the precincts of prayer halls. It must extend itself to every sphere of his work as a man of God.

This is, in brief, what Islam stands for. This is no dream or utopia. For the benefit of mankind, the Prophet, upon whom be peace, and his companions developed and established it in the past, and it can be established again by its true believers.

Chapter II

COMPILATION
OF THE
QUR'AN
M.A. Draz

Dr. M. A. Draz (d. 1958) was a professor at al-Azhar (Egypt) and a scholar of high esteem. His doctoral thesis at the University of Paris ran into two volumes: *Al-Madkhal al-Qur'an al-Karim and Dastur al-Ikhlaq fi al-Qur'an*. Among his other renowned works are *Dirasat Islamiyyah and An-Naba' al-'Adhim*. His article first appeared in *al-ittihad* of Jumada al-Thani 1389/August 1969.

At the present time the Qur'an appears in the form of a single volume, its most usual make-up consisting of about 500 pages (of 15 lines each), divided into *surahs* or chapters of varying lengths. Following the introduction, composed of five short lines, the *surahs* are usually[1] arranged according to their relative lengths — the longest at the beginning,[2] followed by those of medium length, and finally the shortest (some of which consist of only one line). The text abounds in the various signs: diacritical, vocalic, orthographical and punctuation signs, all of which help the reader in his pronunciation and the observance of pauses.

But this was not the form taken by the Qur'an during the life of the Prophet, for although the text remains strictly the same as when he dictated it, its appearance has undergone considerable change. First, there was not what one might term a volume or collection. The Qur'an appeared in the form of longer or shorter fragments, which varied in length from an entire *surah* to a single verse, and sometimes only a part of a verse. The Prophet recited each passage, as he received it, to be

---

[1]Actually this order is not strictly adhered to, and there are exceptions in all the various categories, which would seem to indicate some special reason for this procedure.
[2]Thus the second *surah*, i.e., the first after the Introduction (the *Fatihah*), and which is the longest of all, takes up 40 pages.

memorized by his listeners, and then circulated among those who had not heard his actual words. Everyone waited eagerly for these passages and was keen to be given details as soon as possible after the Prophet has recited them. Even his enemies, far from being indifferent to his Qur'an, often sought to listen to the recitations. This was either to find a weak point which they could utilise to produce "rival" passages, or to attack him, or simply to gratify their passionate desire for literature. So it is not difficult to imagine the interest he must have aroused among his sympathisers and supporters. For them, the Qur'an was spiritual food and rule of conduct, the formula used in prayer and the medium for preaching. It was their liturgy, their history, their fundamental law, and the code for all the circumstances of their everyday lives.

But the sacred text was not merely a Qur'an, or *ensemble* of oral recitations, intended only to be preserved in their memories. It was also a *Kitab*, a Scripture, a Book — two aspects which mutually complement and corroborate each other. And so each passage received and recited by the Prophet was immediately set down in writing by the scribes on any suitable object within reach — the leaves of trees, pieces of wood, parchment or leather, flat stones, shoulderblades and so on. The most reliable scholars state that twenty-nine people were entrusted with this work of acting as "secretaries" to the Prophet. The best-known are the first five successors (Abu Bakr, 'Umar, 'Uthman, 'Ali, Mu'awaiyah), Zubayr Ibn al-'Awamm, Sa'd Ibn al-'Aas, 'Amr Ibn al-'Aas, Ubayy Ibn Ka'b and Zayd Ibn Thabit. But the most zealous of these were Mu'awaiyah and Zayd Ibn Thabit. Although at Makkah there were fewer persons and the work did not bear this official cachet, one thing is certain — from the beginning of the revelations, and even during the height of the persecutions, the faithful still continued to make copies of the revealed text, compiling personal manuscripts for their own private use. According to tradition, the conversion of 'Umar owed to his reading on a leaf which he found in the possession of his sister, the opening verses of *at-Taha*.

But in their written form, these documents did not originally constitute a homogeneous, classified, and numbered collection. The Prophet did not possess a single written fragment, and at this epoch, no private person possessed a complete copy. Scattered in this way, they could not even receive their definite structure in the common memory until a short time before the end of the Prophet's life. In fact, it was soon noticed that these passages did not remain completely isolated from each other, nor did they follow each other in the chronological order of their revelation. Sometimes several groups of passages were brought together to form independent units, separate from others.

Memorization by Heart

From time to time further verses were added — sometimes they were inserted into the body of the unit — following the personal direction of the Prophet, which he himself declared to be in accordance with the commands received from the celestial messenger. To leave the way clear for these progressive developments, the Muslims were obliged to wait for the completion of a certain revealed passage or series of passages, before it could be embodied into one of the units. And although at this stage there may not have been strict continuity in the sequence of the fragments in their written form, orally, at all stages of development of the revelation, each passage was given its proper place in the *surah* of which it was to become a part.

Such was the case with many of the recitations, including those dealing with prayer, education and the propagation of the Faith. Thus, during the life of the Prophet, several hundred companions (known as the "memorisers of the Qur'an") had already become adept in the reading and recitation of the Book, and knew by heart each *surah*, in the form that had been officially prescribed. For example, Ibn Mas'ud was very proud of having learned more than seventy *surahs* from the lips of the Prophet himself. And the Prophet declared that each year, during the month of Ramadan, his custom had been to make a general revision of the revealed text, reciting it in the presence of Gabriel, and that during the preceding year the divine archangel had appeared before him twice, to be present during his recitation of the Qur'an. (This would have taken place during the last year of his life — the Prophet regarded it as a sign that he was approaching his end.)

The Authorized Collection of Zayd Ibn Thabit

Barely a year had passed after the Prophet's death that it was felt necessary to bring together these scattered documents to form a properly-arranged collection, easy to consult, in which the parts of each chapter would follow each other in the order in which they had already memorized them, but to which they had so far not given any sequence or continuity. The idea was suggested by 'Umar to the first Caliph after the battle of Yamamah against the false prophet Musaylimah, during which hundreds of Muslims were killed, including seventy memorisers of the Qur'an. Fearing a possible progressive diminution in the number of these memorisers in future wars, it was hoped in this way, not only to render the whole of the written revelation immune to destruction, and easily accessible in case of need, but also to give authoritative confirmation to the form taken by this collection, which would be assembled and unified with the common consent and authority of the existing reciters and of all the companions who could each recite a more or less lengthy part.[3]

---

[3]See M.J. Rostovdoni, *Tarikh al-Qur'an wa al-Masahif*, Strassburg, 1905, pp. 26, 27.

The task was entrusted to Zayd Ibn Thabit, although at first, conscious of the heavy responsibility involved in such an undertaking, he hesitated about accepting it. But Abu Bakr insisted: "You are an intelligent man," he said. "In our eyes your integrity is above suspicion, and you used to write down the revelations at the dictation of the Prophet. You must certainly take charge of the collection of the Qur'an."[4] Yet another reason seems to have played a part in this choice. Not only was Zayd a secretary and a memoriser of the Qur'an, but in addition, he had been present during the last recitation made by the Prophet.[5] In addition to all these guarantees of authenticity, rules of procedure were established and rigorously applied. No written passage could be included unless it had been certified by two witnesses as having been drawn up, not from memory, but from the actual dictation of the Prophet, and it had to be part of the text in its most recent form. According to al-Layth Ibn Sa'd, this insistence on two witnesses definitely excluded a passage brought forward by 'Umar on the stoning of an adulterer, the reason being that 'Umar was the only witness to this passage.[6]

After all these precautions had been taken, Zayd handed the finished work to the safe keeping of Abu Bakr, who retained it during his Caliphate. Before his death the first Caliph entrusted it to the care of 'Umar, whom he had indicated as his successor. During his last moments, 'Umar, in his turn, placed it in the care of his daughter, Hafsah, one of the widows of the Prophet, because at that time the third Caliph had not yet been elected.

In addition to its completeness, this first official collection (which can be described as a dossier containing pages (*suhuf*) classified, but not yet bound) was distinguished from other copies, whether complete or partial, in the possession of private individuals, by a kind of scrupulous exactitude, excluding everything which did not form part of the actual text to be recited after its final compilation. Some persons such as Ibn Mas'ud or Ubayy Ibn Ka'b sometimes included in their versions divergent or discrepant interpretations, or took the liberty of writing in the margin short explanatory notes[7]

---

[4]Referring to this work, Leblois wrote: "How pleased everyone would have been if, after the death of Jesus, one of His closest disciples had been entrusted with the work of putting His teachings into written form!" (Leblois: *Le Qur'an et la Bible Hebraique*, p. 47, Note 5).

[5]*See* Zanjani, *Tarikh al-Qur'an*, p.17.

[6]*See* Suyuti, *Itqan*, Vol. 1, p. 58.

[7]For example, in the collection compiled by Ibn Mas'ud, we find, written beside the text, والصلاة الوسطى"the intermediary prayer", this explanation: صلاة العصر "afternoon prayer", orوهيصلاةالعصر"which is the afternoon prayer". We will not discuss whether this definition is itself the correct one — the question was a very controversial one among the Companions of the Prophet. But, even admitting, with al-Bara'ah, that this definition originally existed and was considered to be the correct one, and that it was later

(sometimes in a different color), or certain extra-textual prayer-formulas.[8] On the contrary, in the official collection, even the titles of the chapters were rigorously expurgated if found necessary. But however great the value of such a document, and however praise-worthy the one taken in its compilation, since it remained in the vigilant care of the first two Caliphs, it was still more or less a private book and did not acquire its now universal authority until the day it was published.

Caliph 'Uthman Copies of Zayd Ibn Thabit's Manuscript

It was not until the reign of the third Caliph 'Uthman, after the campaigns of Armenia and Azerbaijan, that the auspicious moment arrived for the publication of the Qur'an.

The armies of Syria and Iraq, who had assembled for the purpose, noticed a certain difference in their respective recitations. The Syrians were listening to the reading made by their compatriot Ubayy, and the Iraqis were listening to their own Ibn Mas'ud. The two groups began boasting: "Our reading is better than yours!" Alarmed at this scene, Hudhayfah Ibn al-Yaman went to Caliph 'Uthman with the urgent request to put an end to "...such disputes which might result in cleavages similar to those of the Jews and the Christians on the subject of their Books". 'Uthman at once formed a committee of four copyists. These were Zayd, of Madinah (already mentioned), and three Makkans: 'Abdullah Ibn al-Zubayr, Sa'd Ibn al-'Aas and 'Abd al-Rahman Ibn al-Harith Ibn Hisham. He entrusted them with the work of copying the original of Hafsah, making as many copies[9] as there were important towns in the Islamic State. He further specified: "If you disagree about the spelling of a word,[10] write it in the Qurayshite dialect, for it was in this dialect that the Qur'an was (originally) given." When the work was finished in complete accordance with the original text, it was given back to Hafsah, and the other copies of the Qur'an were bound and distributed as permanent and unchangeable texts,

---

abrogated and replaced by the present definition, it has never been found in juxtaposition to it in the final authoritative recited text. Witness this same controversy about the interpretations. Ibn al-Anbari relates that during the first collation Hafsah demanded the insertion of this explanatory word in the text, but since it provided no proof of authenticity, her father, 'Umar, opposed it categorically, (Cf. Suyuti, Durr Manthur, Volume 1, p. 303).

[8]Thus we find, in the collection made by Ubayy, in addition to the canonical surahs, the two famous prayers known as قنوت .

[9]Excluding 'Uthman's own personal copy, most of the "traditionalists" agree that five manuscripts were allocated to the five following towns: Makkah, Madinah, Basrah, Kufah and Damascus. But Abu Hatim al-Sijistani mentions two other copies made for the two provinces of the Yemen and Bahrain (Cf. Ibn Abu Da'ud, Kitab al-Masahif, p. 74.)

[10]Thus, the word تابوت, which at Madinah was written تابوه retained its Makkan form of spelling.

which definitely cancelled all other versions at any variance with it.

A number of Shi'ahs suspected 'Uthman of altering the Qur'anic text, or, more precisely, of having omitted certain material concerning 'Ali. If this were true the memorisers of the Qur'an (still very numerous at the time of the publication), could have verified it by comparing the passages in question with what they had learned by heart. Now, even Ibn Mas'ud, who had more than one reason for being dissatisfied with the policy, nevertheless acknowledged the accuracy of the work. He even foresaw that at some "... future date, the letter of the Qur'an would be adhered to, but the application of its precepts would be neglected."[11] In view of the zeal shown by the first Muslims, who manifested much more devotion toward the Word of God than their successors, we cannot rightly attribute to the spirit of "conformism" the fact that 'Uthman's version was unanimously accepted by everyone, without reservation or objection. The famous German Orientalist, Noeldeke, concludes that this was the best possible proof that the text "... was as complete and as accurate as could reasonably be expected".[12]

In any case, for fourteen centuries this version has been the only one in use in the Muslim world, including the Shi'ah community. Here it is interesting to read the Profession of Faith of the Imamians (the most important section of Shi'ism), which is to be found in a book written by Abu Ja'far of Qumm: "Concerning the length and contents of the Qur'an which the Most High God revealed to his Prophet Muhammad (May he and his family be blessed!), our belief is as follows: it consists of that which is today preserved between two covers for the use of men, and nothing else. The number of *surahs* recognized by the majority of Muslims is 114, but in our view, *surahs* 93 and 94 form one *surah*, numbers 105 and 106 form one *surah*, and similarly with *surahs* 8 and 9. He who says that we believe the Qur'an to be more than this is a liar."[13]

---

[11]Malik, Mu'watta.

[12]Noeldeke, *Geschichte des Korans*, Part 2, p. 93.

[13]*See* Mirza Alexandre Kazem, *Journal Asiatique*, December 1843 C.E. Thus the only difference was in the method of sub-dividing the Qur'an into *surahs*, and numbering them. Among these doctors this difference still exists only in theory. In fact, their versions differed in no way from those of the Sunnis. Though there were certain fanatical *mullahs* (Persian religious scholars) who made mention of a few words supposedly omitted by 'Uthman, they nevertheless refrained from inserting them in their text, for the simple reason that they were not authorized by the legitimate Imam. It was the same — more emphatically so — with an apocryphal chapter سورة النورين published by Garcin de Tassy under the title "An Unknown Chapter of the Qur'an", and which was criticized by Mirza Alexandre Kazem. This learned scholar in fact showed that not only is there no trace of this so-called surah in the Qur'an of the Shi'ahs, but there is no mention of it whatsoever in their traditional polemical books. Even the title نورين "Two Lights", referring to Muhammad and 'Ali, was not known among the Shi'ahs until the 7th century A.H., after Tusf. We have only to read this production, which is nothing but a

And Leblois was able to declare, with justification: "The Qur'an is today the only Sacred Book, which does not contain marked variations."[14] W. Muir, in fact, had previously declared: " 'Uthman's version has passed on to us from hand-to-hand without alteration. It has been so scrupulously preserved that there are no variations of any note — one might even say no variations whatsoever — in the innumerable copies of the Qur'an for all the warring factions, and this unanimous use of the same text, accepted by everyone right up to the present day, is one of the irrefutable proofs of the authenticity of the text which we now possess, and which dates back to the unfortunate Caliph 'Uthman[15] (who died by assassination)."

While these "verdicts" show an incontestable historical impartiality, there is, nevertheless, the need for a two-fold amendment—they are both understatements and overstatements.

The understatement lies in the fact that the source of the present-day Qur'anic text was traced back only as far as the third Caliph, whereas, as we have seen, 'Uthman's role consisted of making publicly available the manuscript compiled under the direction of Abu Bakr. We have also seen that this original was simply the integral reproduction of the text written down at the dictation of the Prophet himself, following the order in which it was *recited* (not to be confused with the order in which it was *revealed*).

On the Variations in Pronunciation

On the other hand, there is overstatement if we affirm categorically that these versions, although, graphically repetitions of each other, do not contain any variations in pronunciation. This is a well-known fact to those who have even a rudimentary knowledge of Arabic calligraphy. First, though the long vowels have almost always appeared in the body of Arabic words, this has never been the case with the short vowels, nor with certain medium vowels. Second, several groups of letters not only resemble each other, but are identical in form, and differ only through being written with signs known as diacritical points. Thus, for example, an 'l' can be read as 'n', or 't', or 'b' or 'i', depending on whether we put one or two points above it, or one or two points below it. Now these points were not in use during the life of the Prophet, or during the reign of the first three Caliphs. Although ordinary common sense was sometimes sufficient to hazard a guess at the correct pronunciation of a word, more often it could be arrived at only through some oral indication. Now according to tradition, the Prophet, when teaching,

mediocre compilation of words and expressions filched from the Qur'an, to note the shocking contrast it offers with the elegance and harmony of style of the Qur'an. (*See* also Noeldeke, Part 2, pp. 107-112.)

[14]Leblois, *op. cit.*, p. 54.

[15]W. Muir, *The Life of Mahomet*, quoted by B. St.-Hilaire, *Mahomet et le Koran*, p. 33.

did not always use the same method of pronunciation. Using the same word (or, rather the same radical), he would sometimes give several different explanations (or dissertations), all of which would be quite relevant and valid. Thus the word ملك can be read as *malik* (master, owner) and *malik* (king). Similarly, فتبينوا can be read as *fatabayyinu* [inform yourself (regarding)], and also *fatathabbitu* (act with circumspection), and these different readings are all equally traditional.

Another point of interest — the audience was not necessarily always comprised of the same people. In consequence, from the very earliest days, the companions grew to adopt different ways of reading, and these were often quite unknown to each other. Al-Bukhari relates that one day 'Umar became furious when he heard Hisham Ibn Hakim Ibn Hizam reciting *surah* 25 in a different way from that in which he had learned it from the Prophet. He had difficulty controlling his anger while Hisham was reciting his prayer. When the latter had finished, he seized him by the throat, and asked him from whom he had learned those things. "From the lips of the Prophet," replied Hisham. "You are lying," retorted 'Umar, "for the Prophet taught me otherwise," and he led him before the Messenger. The Prophet asked Hisham to recite. He approved the recitation, saying that the surah has been revealed in that way. He also invited 'Umar to recite, and then declared: "In truth, the Qur'an is revealed in seven readings or variations.[16] Recite it in whichever of these ways is easy for you." Al-Tabari related that 'Ubayy Ibn Ka'b was also shocked by a variation in the reading of surah 16, and that he also sought the decision of the Prophet who approved the two different readings.

Purpose of the Publication of the Qur'anic Text by 'Uthman

Was 'Uthman, therefore, more meticulous than his Master? Was he prohibiting something that the Prophet had authorised? We do not think so. Contrary to the general belief, it was not the abolition of all nuances in pronunciation that 'Uthman had in mind. Not only was his version of the Qur'an like all preceding ones, composed of

---

[16]Does the word سبعة really mean the number seven? Or does it signify an indefinite number, a multiplicity of numbers? The question is a controversial one. In any case these "seven readings" should not be confused with the "seven readings" selected by Ibn Mujahid. There is even no question of co-relating these two categories, as suggested by Dr. Jeffery in his Arabic preface to *Kitab al-Masahif*, p. 8. In fact, Ibn Mujahid has often been criticized for his choice of the number seven (cf. *Suyuti, Itqan*, p. 49; Noeldeke, *Geschichte des Korans*, p. 50; Tahir, *Tibyan*, p. 81), as being likely to suggest that reading attributed to these authorities could be considered as canonical and vice-versa. Whereas only methodical study and criticism would be capable *of separating* the true from the false. Contrary to the contention of Dr. Jeffery (*ibid.*), this criticism should invariably be applied to the Seven, the Ten, the Fourteen, and to all the other sources of variations.

"skeleton-words", liable to be read in different ways, but he always took the greatest care to give very explicit renderings of the different traditional recitations, whenever the calligraphy of the words indicated that there was only one way of reading them. Thus, we see the word مسيطر written with a س surmounted by a ص , or with a ص surmounted by a س . And so we find in one of the example-types: سارعوا and in the other وسارعوا ; and similarly بما تشتهي or بما تشتهيه ; سيقولون لله or سيقولون الله .

In our opinion, the publication of the Qur'anic text under the direction of 'Uthman had a two-fold purpose: (1) by authenticating and safeguarding the different readings which remained in the body of the written text, and which had a commonly recognized prophetic origin, scurrilous and impious arguments about their subject-matter were prevented. "To say that such-and-such a way of reading is better than some other way," 'Uthman explained, "is simply not conceivable."[17] (2) by excluding everything which was not absolutely identical with the original — to forestall and prevent a serious cleavage among Muslims and an eventual change in the text by the insertion, at some later date, of more or less controversial variations, or of explanatory notes which individual Muslims had, in good faith, written in their copies.

Further, we must not assume that this " 'Uthmanian" edition, and still less its prototype, contained all the variations which had probably been taught by the Prophet, under the heading of سبعة أحرف , or "seven ways of reading". For though it preserved those readings for which there was unimpeachable evidence that they had been incorporated into the authentic finished text, it excluded all versions transmitted through private channels, and which did not offer this guarantee.[18] And at quite an early date this basic principle was unanimously recognized and accepted by thousands of devout companions.[19]

We should mention that this exclusion in the case of the written document did not appear to have as its objective, or its consequence, their suppression in oral usage. Having thus enunciated a firm decision on this important point, the rule nevertheless permitted those who claimed to have heard the Prophet read the text in a certain way the liberty to follow their individual studies on their own moral responsibility, without, however, allowing them to assume any canonical authority in the matter for the community as a whole. This reasonable and impartial attitude was, in the first place, upheld by the reply of 'Uthman himself, when dealing with political insurgents: "As for the Qur'an," he explained "my only reason for prohibiting you (the inclusion of variations) was because I feared a split. But you may read

---

[17]Suyuti, *Itqan*, Vol. 1, p. 57.

[18]*Cf.* Suyuti, *Itqan*, p. 50; Baqillani, *Intisar*, quoted by Tahir, *Tibyan*, Cairo, 1934, p. 73.

[19]*See Suyuti, Ibid.*; Ibn Hajar, quoted by Zanjani, *Tarikh al-Qur'an*, p. 44.

in the manner you think convenient."[20] Second, it was upheld by the *fatwa* (edict) given by Imam Malik, in which he allowed the recitation of فامضوا according to the 'Umar reading, instead of فاسعوا (62:9).[21] "Except during the ritual prayer," declared Ibn 'Abd al-Barr, "for non-'Uthmanian readings do not constitute a Qur'an trustworthy enough for the accomplishment of this duty."[22]

Apart from this, with the exception of the ritual prayer, and the incorporation of only authorised material into the codex, all other ways of reading remained entirely free, and Islamic scholars of all ages have never lost interest in the study of these individual modes of reading. As such, on this two-fold point, the publisher of *Kitab al-Masahif*, Dr. Arthur Jeffery, is seriously in error. First, "This investigation" is not "in its infancy in the Muslim world" (Introduction, p.1). As evidence of this, one has only to consider the number of Arabic works which he has used for this particular subject. There is an abundance, not only of special treatises on orthography, phonetics and Qur'anic readings, but also of commentaries, works by philologists, "traditionalists" and legal experts. Further, far from being subjected, in this exclusive domain, to a certain "... pressure on the part of orthodoxy" (*Ibid*, p. 9, 10), these variations are always invested with a certain sacred character, and are still used in the Sunni schools, not as Qur'anic texts it is true, but as *hadith ahad*.

In spite of this evidence, the image of Christian ecclesiastical history, with which the American missionary is much more familiar, seems to have obsessed Dr. Jeffery to such a degree that he has, in his book, transposed it almost entirely to the Islamic terrain. In fact, the author has tried to show that in the Qur'anic text there is a certain evolution resembling in many ways the evolution in the text of the Gospels. He begins by making some absurd distinction between "...a few liturgical passages" in the Qur'an which were "probably" written at the moment of revelation, and other passages which were not (p. 6). And he declares — incidentally, contradicting himself — that even at the death of the Prophet, the body of revelation had not yet been collected (*cf.* p. 5 with p.7). By juggling words he then denies the "official" character of the compilation made by Abu Bakr (*cf.* pp. 6 and 212). Finally, he decides that at the time of the decision by 'Uthman, there were considerable divergences between the codices of the various metropolitan centres (p. 8), and he describes the Muslims of Kufah as being divided at that time into two factions: "Some accepting the new text sent by 'Uthman, but the great majority recognizing that of Ibn Mas'ud" (pp. 8 and 21). Thus 'Uthman's version is portrayed, not

[20]Ibn Abu Da'ud, K. al-Masahif, p. 36.
[21]Cf. Zanjani, op. cit., p. 16.
[22]Cf. Tahir, Tibyan, pp. 39-40. Ibn Abu Da'ud holds the same opinion (Masahif, p. 54).

only as one of several "rival" texts (pp. 9, 23), but also as a "new-comer", at variance with the early codices, even with the reading established at the time of the Prophet, and which ultimately gains precedence, not because of its intrinsic qualities, but thanks to the prestige of Madinah (p. 8).

This is a very erroneous method of presenting the history of the Qur'anic text, and calls for some corrective explanation. First, we must take into consideration, not only the age of the text, but also the fact that the text published by 'Uthman is completely identical with the collection assembled under the direction of Abu Bakr.[23] Modern Christian research simply confirms this conclusion. "We have already furnished proof," declares the German Orientalist Schwally, "that the two editions of Zayd are identical, and that the edition of 'Uthman is simply a copy of the Codex of Hafsah."[24] Further, we must not forget that all the material contained in this codex dates not only from the first Caliph, but can be traced back textually to the Prophet. It is true that all the variations in the recitation of the Qur'an are equally attributable, under either an oral or a written form, to the same source. It is quite possible that some divergent readings are anterior in date to those which appear in the 'Uthman collection, although both of these categories must be dated back to some period during the life of the Prophet. But we should note that this relative anteriority can hardly be regarded as a criterion of superiority. The most authentic text, as far as the recitation goes, is not necessarily the oldest, but rather the one that has been compiled with the maximum of careful study and research, and from which all divergences and discrepancies have been eliminated as far as it is humanly possible. For in the language of the companions, the expression الحرف الأول, applied to extra-textual readings, does not refer to readings which were in vogue during the time of the Prophet, generally speaking, but to the most primitive form of reading of that epoch, that is to say, the form which was later abrogated. Thus, we can demolish the very basis on which some people have tried to establish the importance of these kinds of variations.

Establishing the Authenticity of the Qur'an

Let us leave these chronological nuances. What emerges is that the most essential condition for establishing the authenticity of a text is the certitude that, in its written form, it has been adequately verified and approved by the author or his representative. It was precisely this *ensemble* of conditions which, at the time of compilation, was lacking in respect of certain variations, and thus they were excluded from the

---

[23]*Cf.* Bukhari, K, *Fada'il al-Qur'an.* B. 3; Ibn Abu Da'ud, p. 25.
[24]*Geschichte*, Part 2, p. 91.

codex-types.[25] Further, in this connection another eradicable basic weakness became apparent during their later transmission. The compiler of *Kitab al-Masahif* stated that he himself was struck by this uncertainty inherent in the extra-'Uthmanian readings (and this forms a three-fold point of view):

√   From the first point of view—their age—it was suspected that an attempt had been made to associate a later "invention" with an older authority to benefit from the prestige of its name (p. 15).

√   From the second point of view — on precision as to their sources—in a number of cases there was confusion in their attribution to one or other authority.

√   From the third point of view — the identification of the forms in which they were set out—where various lessons (readings) were attributed to the same reader, not only was it difficult to decide which of these were authentic; but in some cases, the readings seemed linguistically, to be impossible (p. 16).

Our Orientalist also acknowledges that the non-'Uthmanian readings are rarely attributed to authorities as appearing in their collections, but more often as merely forming part of their oral teaching, or recitation (p. 24). And yet, when he sets out to assemble them in order to form a collection, not only does he take the liberty of putting them all under the heading "Codex", and adding to those readings which are in no way different from the official text — as if to swell their volume and enhance their prestige — but he then adds other readings which he attributes to certain authors, but which are really the work of one of their disciples.

The Three Categories of the So-called "Readings"

But after all, what is the content of these so-called readings of the Qur'an, and what is its importance? First, we should state that not every *surah* is involved, nor is the entire length of any particular *surah*. If we examine their nature, we can distinguish different categories.

In one category, there is an insertion, or interpolation. Here the object is either to furnish a more precise explanation of some word which is implied, or "understood," such as:

(3:39); وناداه الملائكة يا زكريا   (2:127) واسمعيل يقولان   ونادته الملائكة يا زكريا

إلى قومه فقال يا قوم   (11:25); or to repeat a word which has just been explained in some detail; for example: عن قتال ؛ وعلى الصلاة ؛ وآمن المؤمنون

(2:217, 238, 285); or to develop the same meaning by means of a

---

[25]Let us consider, for example, the so-called codex of Ibn Mas'ud. On this subject Ibn Ishaq (quoted by Dr. Jeffery, p. 23, Note) declared that, of the numerous copies of this Codex, no two of them were identical. And Ibn al-Nadim, *Fihrist* declared having seen a copy in which appeared the first *Surah*. This was contrary to what was generally believed.

paraphrase, such as   فضلا من ربكم في مواسم الحج فأبتغوا حينئذ   (2:198)

والعصر ، ونوائب الدهر ، لفي خسر ، وإنه   (103:1)

لقيه الى آخر العمر   (103:2).

All these "explanations" are clearly seen to be the work of a glossarist, who has abandoned the purity of Qur'anic style and has overloaded the text with verbiage that is sometimes intolerable.

In the second category, the variation consists in replacing a word, either by a synonym, such as   يؤده يوفه   ذرة نملة   يتم يكمل الصوف   or by another word having a different meaning, but where both words should complement each other and be mutually "understood," for example:

الحج والعمرة للبيت   instead of   الحج والعمرة لله   (2:169).

In the third category there is a simple inversion, such as

في ظل من الغمام والملئكة في ظل من الغمام	(2:210)
بما تعملون بصير بصير بما تعملون	(3:156)
على قلب كل على كل قلب	(40:35)
بمثل ما أمنتم بما أمنتم	(2:137)
إلا الساعة أن تأتيهم إلا الساعة تأتيهم	(47:18).

Generally speaking, as far as these three categories are concerned — and without calling in question the respective literary values of their various readings — we may admit, *a priori*, the possibility that they are genuine variations, all of them eligible for inclusion, on the one condition that their origins have been historically established. However, in certain cases, one is tempted to suppose that some arrangement had been arrived at in the case of the tentative, or semi-official formulas, whereas the official and accepted formulas were exempt from all special kinds of criteria, whether these were of a theological nature as من المهاجرين والأنصار والذين , or of a political nature as يأتيهم الله في ظلل ، وبمثل ما   (9:100), and not   والأنصار الذين   as 'Umar believed, or of a dialectal nature as إن هذان الساحران , or of some other kind.

The One Important Consideration
In the Compilation of the Qur'an

The one important consideration which dominated the compilation of the Qur'anic text by the companions of the Prophet was the rigorous literal accordance of each passage with the document drawn up at the dictation of the Master, which was then read over again in his presence, and which finally received his definite approval. And it is this absolute objectivity which resounds eternally to their honor.

There was, however, a certain amount of quibbling and fault-finding in the case of Ibn Mas'ud (or other collectors), the object being to attack the unanimity of the companions vis-a-vis the 'Uthmanian text. The truth is that none of these disputants contested the accuracy of the published text. But, in addition to this, there were other readings which certain private individuals claimed to have been authorized by the Prophet, but who were unable to furnish any objective proof of such authorization. So they decided not to set up such readings as rival passages, replacing the version now unanimously recognized, but to conserve them side-by-side with the official text. Thus, for example, we hear that Abu Musa recommended his people not to suppress what was in his collection, but, when anything was lacking, to complete it from the Codex of 'Uthman.[26] And, when Ibn Mas'ud was dealing with some of his followers who were dissatisfied, what did he do except to remind them that all the revealed variations were valid?[27] No doubt the cause of this dissatisfaction — if ever there was any dissatisfaction[28] — was two-fold: for instance, a certain companion of the early days of Islam, after being denied the honor of becoming a member of the "censorship committee," was obliged to hand over his manuscript to be destroyed! But this spontaneous reaction must evidently have yielded not long afterwards to the influence of some calm reflection. Since Ibn Mas'ud was away in Iraq on his official functions well before the publication, he could not reasonably demand the postponement of such an urgent matter until his return on some problematic future date, when other companions were in possession, like him—and they had more than he had—of documents which had been rigorously compiled, and approved by the Prophet. As for his manuscript, in which he had no doubt inserted a number of personal renderings, or some variations which had not received unanimous approval, it probably suffered the fate as others of the same category.[29] That is to say, it ceased to have any definite authority, remained the object of diminished prestige, and was regarded as his personal responsibility.

Although the destruction of these private manuscripts seemed somehow a little too severe, at a time when so far there was no cause for any alteration, it nevertheless showed how wise and far-seeing the action of the Caliph had been.[30] It may be true that various systems of external signs were subsequently introduced into the text (invented by Abu al-Aswad Du'ali and his successors Nasr Ibn 'Asim, Yahya Ibn

---

[26]*Cf.* I.A. Da'ud, p. 35.

[27]*Ibid.*, p. 18.

[28]*Cf.* Schwally, *Geschichte*, Part 2, p. 92.

[29]*See supra* the case of 'Umar (page 18) and that of Hafsah (page 19, footnote 8).

[30]Here the caliph was not acting purely on his own initiative and without consulting the people. In a speech acknowledged by critics of the hadiths as authentic, and in which the piety of the third Caliph was stoutly defended by his successor, the latter declared that this rigorous measure was taken with the common agreement of all the Companions concerned. "If 'Uthman had not done it," declared 'Ali, "I should have done it myself." (*Cf.* I. Abu Da'ud, p. 12, 22.)

Ya'mar, Hasan al-Basri and Khalil Ibn Ahmad), but the body of the text has always remained unchanged, defying the action of time.

In all the copies now existing, whether printed or written, there can still be found a number of superfluous letters, certain supplementary (or complementary) words, and the form of spelling reserved solely for Qur'anic writing — an eloquent witness of the most pious fidelity with which this monumental Word has been transmitted from generation to generation up to the present time.

Chapter III

SOURCES OF
DYNAMISM
IN ISLAM

Fazlur Rehman

Dr. Fazlur Rehman has taught at Cambridge and McGill. He is currently a professor of Islamic thoughts, University of Chicago. Among his major works are *Methodology in History, The Philosophy of Mulla Sadra, Islam and Modernity, Major Themes of the Qur'an.* The present article was his original contribution to *al-ittihad* of Muharram 1398/January 1978.

Among those who have a fair acquaintance with Islam, let alone those who are experts in the field, it should be common knowledge that Islam's basic characteristic, which distinguishes it from most other religions and certainly other "higher" religions, is its central and direct concern with the establishment of a social order based upon certain divine imperatives through a political organization or a state. To most non-Muslims or a thorough-going secularist Muslim, it might be an accident of history that where and when Prophet Muhammad, upon whom be peace, appeared, there was no political rule already established — unlike the birth and infancy of Christianity, for example — and that, therefore, Muhammad *had to be* both a religious and a political leader; the Muslim secularist, of course, holding that these two aspects were nevertheless separate. To all non-secularist Muslims, for many of whom it has, indeed, become a slogan, this particular feature of Islam represents not only its uniqueness, but, indeed, an essential part of a divine plan for the last and most perfect of all religions. To perceptive Western scholars (like H.A.R. Gibb or Montgomery Watt, for example), even if they may not believe in any divine plan for Muhammad, it remains true that the message he brought was so centrally oriented toward social reform that its implementation necessarily required assumption of political power by the

Messenger:[1] the two aspects are, then, organically related to each other.

There is no religion worthy of the name which was not born of a higher source, and which did not uphold a vision for the betterment of man, although their formulations, approaches, and internal structures have differed widely. The Islamic vision of a global social order, first of all, necessarily entailed the establishment of the Muslim community as "the best community produced for mankind, enjoining good and forbidding evil and having faith in God." Again, "(They are) those who, if We give them power upon the earth, shall establish prayer, shall pay zakah, shall command good and forbid evil."[2] This was the task that this community was summoned to. In the following, we will try to see how this community has, at various stages of its history, conceived of itself, its task, and the method of carrying out that task. But before that, we had better dwell briefly on the essential elements of the vision itself as it emerges from the Qur'an and from the beginning of the Revelation. For although the formal establishment of the community and the declaration of its task, as well as the method of achieving it—the jihad — occurred in Madinah, the vision itself had already been born at Makkah with all its essential ingredients.

Muslims have often said that while the Madinah phase of the Prophet's life represents the socio-political or public aspect of Islam, the Makkan phase represented a stage of private or individual spiritual development, and that the former is an essential preparation for the latter. The Makkan period of general helplessness and persecution is often compared to the formative Christian experience, while the successful Madinan phase is considered political, and hence, less noble and un-Christian as is done by many Western-Christian scholars. The truth, however, would seem to be that both these facets are interdependent so far as the Qur'an and Muhammad are concerned, and that Muhammad failed in Makkah and succeeded in Madinah is a purely historical accident. For it is not true to say that in Makkah Muhammad's message was private, since the Qur'an had started out with its teaching of socio-economic reforms from the outset in Makkah. But since his social reforms required political power which he could not obtain in Makkah, he was unable to put his program of reform through and was able to execute it subsequently in Madinah. At Madinah, conversely, while he succeeded in controlling and directing public or corporate life of the community-state, the work of moral training of individuals and their spiritual education was certainly not relinquished but continued as long as he lived. One must, therefore, beware of making wrong dichotomies and

---

[1] The Qur'an. 3: 110-111.
[2] Ibid. 22:41.

drawing fallacious analogies. We must now address ourselves to the question as to what relevance all this has to our present problem viz. the sources of dynamism in Islam.

Before we come to historic Islam, we would, therefore, do well to lay a broad framework in terms of "original" or ideal Islam as is discovered in the Qur'an and the struggle of the Prophet. If we can do this, we can then see how this was fulfilled, modified, thwarted, or disrupted in historic Islam. We are aware that by setting up a criterion of judging the performance of historic Islam, we are involved with introducing values into a historical inquiry, but we submit that for the kind of subject we are dealing with, this is inevitable; and, further, that the values in question are intra-Islamic values, even though their location in the ideal Islam is admittedly a matter of interpretation.

We have said that Islam's central concern with the establishment of a social order in the world was a basic characteristic of it, that according to some modern writers, however, this was purely accidental while the essence of Islam, for them, is personal righteousness of private spirituality; and, finally, that those who reject this secularist stand have often characterized the Makkan experience of the Prophet as purely spiritual and the Madinian as socio-political. To them the former constituted an essential "preparation" for the latter. We have rejected the secularist position by saying that to build a social order through the instrumentality of a state was of the essence of Islam. We do not wish to argue the anti-secularist case any further except to say that whatever force or plausibility secularism, such as that in Turkey, has gained are only intelligible if 1) the post-prophetic Islamic developments (hallowed by the term shari'ah) are regarded as integral parts of ideal Islam, and 2) the Qur'an and the Prophet's conduct are taken piecemeal and in a superficial sense, rather than as an organic whole, which emerges only out of the context and the background of the Qur'an and the Prophet's activity. Since Muslims by and large, have not fulfilled either of the two conditions, the secularist reaction, even if false, is perfectly understandable. We have also rejected as untrue the stand that regards the Makkan career of the Prophet as purely spiritual and the Madinan as socio-political, even though such a view would find a positive echo, in varying degrees, from many Western-Christian students of Islam. The fact is that the spiritual-moral aspect of life goes hand in hand with public life, and there is a constant rhythmical, although highly delicate movement, between the two. If Muhammad's spirituality could not express itself in a public role in Makkah, it was because matters were beyond his control, and the Qur'an bears incontrovertible evidence that he was extremely impatient with that situation.

Our main point after these preliminaries is that both these terms, the spiritual side and the public-action-oriented aspect, are necessary to each other and interdependent. When, after his initial groping quest in the cave of *Hira'* for a solution to the socio-moral problems of his society, Muhammad finally got the answer, the answer came from God. This trancendental source vouchsafed to him the unshakable assurance that the answer was indubitably right: it was a *religious* answer, not the answer of an artificially and superficially confused "objective" social thought. It was creative not aggregative. Yet, so objective was this answer that it proved meaningfully accurate when tested upon the actual historical situation. It transformed that situation and was able to orient history in a definite direction. The original dynamic, then, was rooted in the values of Islam and, indeed, in the certainty of those values. It was like the certainty of mathematical truths which, when applied to the actual universe, fit the universe exactly and measure it. There are value-systems in the world that do not fit reality, and there are other systems which, if they do not fit, are forced upon reality. Islam, then, is the name of a "religious" or trancendental morality applied to a society. The transaction between morality and society required an effort, *jihad*, which was pragmatically defined. The peculiar nature of the Islamic success was thus the result of this complex of a trancendental inspiration and a society mediated by a pragmatic *jihad*. The balance between the component factors is extraordinarily delicate — you shift to pragmatic *jihad*, for example, in such a way that the transcendent goes out of focus and the result is sheer mundane-secular tyranny, or you focus on the transcendent in such a way that the *jihad* or its pragmatism goes out of focus and you get a truncated spirituality. What creatively inspired early Islam was certainly this balance of factors in the complex. Although in Islamic history, the complex as a whole was never lost sight of; nevertheless, a dialectic developed between transcendence and pragmatism characterized by tensions, with continual efforts to resolve those tensions. The character of those tensions and the proportionate strength or weakness of its terms, and to what extent the inner dynamics of their resolution contributed to Islamic vitality, is the theme of what follows.

First, a few words should be said about the nature and conduct of the Islamic community which held these tensions within itself. Ever since the days when the community of Islam (*Ummah Muslimah*) was formally launched in Madinah by the Qur'anic statements that it was "the median community" and "the best community produced for mankind, enjoining good and forbidding evil," the *mystique* of the community has steadily grown. The Qur'an explicitly recognized that the early revealed religions, in their original divine purity, were valid approaches to God outside the Muslim community and, conversely, that a person could not necessarily claim to have a valid approach to God by the mere fact that he was a member of his community. This stand obviously called for opposition to all such people, and thus gave rise to a strong community feeling at the very early stage of its infancy. Time and again the Qur'an sternly required the Muslims to sever all relationship with Islam's opponents even if they be friends or blood relations. Time and again it warns that those Muslims, who have anything to do with Islam's opponents would themselves be regarded as opponents of Islam and declares that Muslims "are but brothers among themselves." Indeed, the Muslim community took birth under conditions of active *jihad* and to gauge the demanding nature of this *jihad*, one may read only the following verse, "Say (to them, O Muhammad!) if your fathers and your sons and your brothers and your wives and clans, and the wealth that you have accumulated, and the trade whose loss you are so afraid of, and your homes with which you are so pleased — if all these are dearer to you than God and His Messenger and fighting for God's cause, then wait till God brings down His judgement (upon you); and God guides not an unrighteous people."[3]

No other large religious community was born with such ideological equipment and a sense of its right to an active exercise of virility on God's behalf. No wonder that it brought under its control, within a relatively short period of time, a large part of the then-known globe, and as it expanded, its sense of self-rectitude, by the third century of Islam, is replaced by its self-immage as self-contained, self-sufficient and taking God for granted, an accusation which the Qur'an had bluntly hurled at the Jewish and Christian communities. But when we look at the internal constitution of the community, it offers quite a different picture: a co-existence and natural tolerance of views widely differing from, indeed, sometimes diametrically opposed to each other. After the rise of its first schism, that of the Kharijites, and what it entailed by way of rebellions and civil wars, the Islamic orthodoxy (which here includes both the Sunnis and the Shi'i) learned its lesson and explicitly formulated its position, whereby no Muslim and particularly no Muslim group identifying itself with Islam may be "thrown outside" Islam, no matter how much its views differed from others. Indeed, in Islam, as has been noted often, there is no mechanism for such excommunication. This has sometimes been interpreted by some Western scholars by saying that the Islamic community defines orthodoxy by orthopraxy. Without necessarily repudiating this, it would I think, be more correct to say that the Islamic community does not Islamically disallow co-existence to a group provided it does not 1) build up an exclusivist organization excommunicating the community itself, and 2) at the same time

---

attempt to get de facto or de jure political control of the community as such. The earlier schism, the Kharijis and the latest, the Ahmadis in Pakistan, have met their respective fates exactly on the same grounds.

Short of an uncompromisingly fanatic stand against the community, then, the inner catholicity of the community would not normally make for tolerances of all kinds. This, of course, does not and cannot deny the kafir-calling game frequently indulged in by the 'ulama. But this cannot result in actual excommunication because there is no privileged person or group or corporate body in Islam vested with this power.

This does not mean, however, that Islam is an amorphous mass of religious beliefs and ideas, any combination of which may be allowed to be called "Islam" as is often said to be the case with Hinduism, for example. There is and always has been in Islam an "orthodoxy," as we shall soon see, but this orthodoxy, by constantly facing differing views around it and which it has no power to expel or exercise, has to come to terms with them sooner or later, and to a greater or lesser extent, this compromise or synthesis itself has to be constantly adjusted; when the cumulative backlog of unadjusted balances reaches a critical stage, shocks of volcanic proporations may be felt at the heart of the orthodoxy itself, shocks which eventually reshape and revitalize the orthodoxy. We must, therefore, try to define what may be called "orthodoxy" in the Islamic frame of reference.

Many Western observers have regarded Sunnism, with its theologio-legal system as the Islamic orthodoxy, and Shi'ism as the principal sectarian development. The basis of their judgement seems to be the belief that the Sunni religious-legal-political complex is nearer to the teaching of the Qur'an and Muhammad, upon whom be peace, than say Shi'ism. Others, foremost among them H.A.R. Gibb, have defined Islamic orthodoxy as simply "the majority of the Community." This definition *prima facie* looks rather funny since it seems to define orthodoxy by sheer numbers irrespective of whether or not that numerical preponderance is faithful or not so faithful or not at all faithful to the teachings of the Qur'an and the Prophet unless, of course, it is held that the teaching is so vague and indeterminate that a number of more or less plausible interpretations can be put upon it, a position which is absolutely indefensible. On close examination, however, the principle of the "majority of the Community" — a phrase espoused so warmly by early Sunni hadith—seems to rest on a deeper perception of how the majority of the Muslim community works, viz. through a broad principle of tolerance and catholicity. This is, indeed, what makes the idea of a "development orthodoxy" both possible and so fundamentally significant in Islam.

A brief account of constant action and reaction, through which Islamic orthodoxy has been forming and reforming itself, should help make this statement clear. The foremost fact to note in this connection is that before Khariji, Mu'tazili, and Shi'i politico-theological stands were formulated, there was no explicit Islamic orthodoxy of Sunnism which, indeed, came to define its stand precisely, only in relation to these schismatic developments, and after they had taken explicit stands on various issues. In one sense, therefore, one might say that Sunnism is essentially a reaction to sectarian developments which took clear shape before Sunnism did. This does not, however, mean that Sunnism is essentially negative, nor does it mean that it is a simple compromise with schisms in varying degrees. It is to be noted that the term 'Sunnah' in the expression "Ahl al-Sunnah" does not refer directly to the Sunnah of the Prophet, for neither the Khariji, nor the Mu'tazili, nor yet of course, the Shi'i repudiate the concept of the Prophetic Sunnah. The Sunnah in this context most probably means "the middle way" and its complement "al-Jama'a (the majority)" strengthens this idea since the majority, by definition, as it were, and by instinct, took the middle road, and hence, was nearer to the Prophet's teaching. It is in this sense that Abu Hanifah, for example, when accused of being a *Murji'a,* says that he only belongs to "the people of justice (moderation-'adl) and Sunnah (the middle way)."

While the law was an autonomous and positive growth, into the making of which went a multitude of factors, the orthodox theology crystallized in major part, under the impact of and in reaction to earlier sects. Its first comprehensive formulations in the 8th - 9th centuries, Ash'arism and Maturidism (although the latter is much closer to the Mu'tazilah on certain fundamental points) share the efficacy of the human will. This intolerable austerity of the orthodox theology, particularly in its Ash'arite form, was greatly softened by the adoption of Sufi spirituality insofar as the latter was amenable to orthodox discipline and could be absorbed in it. This first major dose of orthodox reform occurred at the hands of al-Ghazali whose works enjoyed increasing influence as time passed. This reform did not solve the problem of the efficacy of the human will as such, but God and man were put in much warmer and closer touch with each other than earlier official theology had ever allowed. Al-Ghazali sternly rejected the claims of philosophic reasoning to be able to produce a viable theology in favor of sufi experience and, as a result, philosophy or philosophic religion settled down as a way of life of a restricted intellectual elite far removed from the masses and their religion.

The influence of al-Ghazali on the orthodoxy adequately illustrated the way reform takes place in Islam. The extreme right wing of the orthodoxy — the *Ahl al-Hadith,* the Hanbalites, and the Zahiris — would not accept Sufism in any form and, indeed, were generally inimical to Kalam-theology as well. But one striking characteristic of Islam is, and historically has been, an intensive exchange of ideas between different schools of law, theology, and Sufism as well as among these three disciplines themselves. In the later medieval centuries, this exchange has infrequently taken place between the Sunnis and the Shi'is despite constant mutual polemic as well — indeed polemic itself has proved an important avenue of influence. Thus, the Shi'i, Nasir al-Din al-Tusi's work on theology, the *Tajrid*, upon which more Sunnis have written comme 'aries than the Shi'i, was taught in Sunni Madrasas as well as Shi'i, while works written on various sciences of Sunnis have been taught in Shi'i madrasas and have found Shi'i commentators. This constant and meaningful mutual contact has been not only through books but also through personal contacts during travels, particularly on occasions of the *hajj* (pilgrimage) to Makkah. These contacts, through different avenues, have also further heightened the community feeling among different Muslim groups — ethnic, linguistic, and ideological.

Nor does reform take place overnight and in a measured quantum since there is no machinery for this. The process is informal and slow, but its eventual result is a literal "re-formation" of the orthodoxy. Reform may even go too far when it builds up its own momentum. The recognition by the orthodoxy of a moderate sufism spoken of above, for example, produced, not long after al-Ghazali, a deluge of Sufism under which orthodox Islam was all but totally submerged. With pantheistic doctrines expounded by Sufi shaikhs and infiltrating into beautiful poetry — particularly Persian — at the level of the high-culture and with all sorts of Sufi superstitionism, miracle-mongering and tomb-worship, at the level of "low-culture", one wondered whether Islamic orthodoxy will survive at all, or whether Ibn al-'Arabi's teaching and that of his followers will spell its doom. Yet a radical reformism appeared in the fourteenth-century Middle East at the hands of Ibn Taimiyah, who to many of his contemporaries like Ibn Battutah, appeared a foolhardy idiosyncrat, if not a downright lunatic, for he attacked not only powerful Sufi shaikhs and declared Ibn al-Arabi to be an embodiment of un-Islam, but denounced Ash'aris and others — because of their insistence on the impotence of man as a consequence of the omnipotence of God — worse not only than Jews and Christians but even decisively than Magians. For the Magians committed the grave mistake of positing two Gods, but through right motives viz. the recognition of the real distinction between good and evil, without which no religion can survive, while the doctrines of Ash'arism and pantheistic Sufism annulled this most vital distinction. There were others like the Sufi Shaikh Sirhindi of [Muslim] India who aimed at a radical gnosticism of Sufism from within, and balance or even replace its drugging gnosticism with a genuine moral dynamism.

This reform was also eventually successful after a more or less lengthy period of germination. It was, in fact, so successful, that for many Modernist thinkers, this was the only real reform in Islam, being the harbinger of modernist reform through the Wahhabi-reformist impulse. It must be noted that this reform, engendered by men like Ibn Taimiyyah, while it reformed Sufism, also fairly radically changed orthodoxy by severely and effectively attacking the Ash'ari establishment, and, in so doing, brought in a definitely positive orientation toward rationalism — even though it rejected the result of Muslim philosophers. This new rationalism, in turn, affected the outlook on almost all issues — political, social and legal and by bringing law once more consciously under morality, produced a new dynamism in society. The kalam-theology itself, while rejecting certain decisively unorthodox philosophic doctrines, became heavily imbued and enmeshed with philosophical discussions, like the problem of being, a development that had started unconsciously with al-Ghazali but became conscious with Fakhr al-Din al- Razi.

We see from this brief account that orthodoxy is not something absolutely immovable and fixed in Islam, and has never been so from the very time of its conscious birth. It has simultaneously tolerated, fought against and absorbed all kinds of spiritual, intellectual, political, and social currents and ideologies. For this reason, the sharp distinction made by Marshall Hodgson[4] between what is Islamic and is Islamicate seems to be both unfortunate and untenable. Distinctions must be made — all sorts of distinctions in all sorts of perspectives, but they surely do not correspond to the fixed distinction between Islamic and Islamicate. The terms in which Hodgson himself has formulated this distinction are so self-contradictory, that instead of lending clarity to the subject, it necessarily creates confusion. The following considerations are urged by Hodgson to demonstrate the necessity of this distinction:

✓   Whereas what is Islamic proper, that is, in the religious sense belongs to the Muslims alone, to the Islamicate civilization, non-Muslims have also contributed in its different fields.

✓   Even much of what Muslims themselves have done in the name of Islam is not only Islamic but is un-Islamic.

✓   One can speak of "Islamic literature", of "Islamic art", of "Islamic philosophy," even of "Islamic despotism" but in such a sequence, one is speaking less and less of something that expressed Islam as a faith.

✓   Whereas Islamic law proper is the Shari'i law, there should be some term like "Islamicate" which should cover the non-Shari'i law practiced by Muslims themselves.

✓   On the analogy of "Christendom," we should use the term "Islamdom" to denote Islamic society, but we should necessarily then invent the term "Islamicate" to denote the civilization or the culture of which the society was the bearer.

✓   When one speaks of "Islamic literature" or "Islamic art," one

---

[4]Hodgson, Marshall, *The Venture of Islam,* Volume III, University of Chicago Press, p. 166.

means religious literature and mosque architecture, not winesongs and miniature paintings.

✓   Finally, illustrative of this relationship between "Islamic" and "Islamicate" is the analogy, with some mild difference, in the relationship between things Italian and things "Italianate," the latter term not referring to Italy itself, but meaning *a'la Italie*, in the Italian style and manner, for one speaks of Italian architecture even in England or Turkey.

These points are given above in the order in which Hodgson has stated them. I do not think we need to tarry here to point out the contradictions in the preceding points. It seems to me that there are certain sources from which Hodgson's trouble arises and it would be more profitable to talk about these. Hodgson notes in point 3 that there is a gradation of Islamicness in certain things, while he tells us in points 2 and 6 that there are things un-Islamic like wine-songs and the like. This should have warned him that all these things cannot be covered by the term "Islamicate," especially in view of the analogy he draws with Italianate in point 7, since it is absurd to speak of wine-songs or thievery or prostitution in Muslim society as Islamicate, i.e. *a la Islam* or in the style or manner of Islam. There seem to be at least three sources of confusion. First, there is a confusion between Islam in the vertical valuational sense, that Islam as an ideal and Islam as an historical, existential reality. It is not clear whether Hodgson would explicitly admit that it is open to a non-Muslim to know Islam in the first sense, but is clear from his distinctions that it is possible. Indeed, it would be a pertinent question to ask whether *The Venture of Islam*, written apparently by a non-Muslim is Islamic or Islamicate. But he is thinking not of ideal Islam, but of historic Islam, when he says that certain things are more Islamic than others, for in ideal Islam, all things must be fully or equally Islamic—as values, that is to say. The second major source of confusion, it seems, is the ideal, lurking all the time in the background, as many Muslims also believe, that an earlier period of Islam, say, the second century, was more Islamic than, say, the fifteenth. This idea is so deeply ingrained both in most Muslims' and equally in Western minds that it will require some heroically ascetic effort to overcome it and to cease thinking of Harun al-Rashid, for example, as more Islamic than, say, Mehmed I. It is primarily for this reason that Hodgson almost completely misunderstands Modernist Islam, its purpose, its depth and its Islamic value, and it is for this reason that the shari'ah law is, for him, a fixed entity, an entity possessing something uniquely sacred which nothing later can possess. Finally, and perhaps even more importantly, his use of the term Islamdom as a parallel to Christendom, excluding its civilizational expressions, and his regarding some of those expressions as peculiarly religious, clearly shows the unconscious modelling of Islam on Christianity, which a person with a Christian upbringing cannot help committing and which a person with a Muslim upbringing cannot help protesting.

We can now return to the story of the inner dynamism of Islam in terms of restatement and/or renovation of Islamic perception on the part of the community at any juncture or critical point of its life, and in doing so we hope to have become wiser by our criticism of Marshall Hodgson. The valid distinction does not consist of what is Islamic and what is Islamicate, but consists in 1) different perceptions of Islam at different times by different groups or individuals of the community, and 2) in the ability of these perceptions to harness the "orthodoxy," that is, the active life-spring of the community and to thus influence and mold different fields of life — moral, political, social, economic, and so on — to varying extents and with varying results. Since all these fields are at once and equally proper loci for the manifestation and activity of ideal Islam, it is improper to say that any one of them, for example, a mosque, school, market, parliament, or, indeed, the battlefield, is, ideally speaking, any more or less Islamic than the others. To be sure, what is actually "orthodoxy" at any given historical juncture is understandably resistant to change. The Ash'arite formulation of theology was and continued to be repugnant to large sements of the community; the Kalam-fiqh complex was extremely unwilling to have anything to do either with Sufism or with philosophic rationalism; in relationship to the Ash'ari-Sufi axis of the fourteenth century, the strongly activist-shari'atist elan of Ibn Taimiyah seemed so odd that a worldly-wise traveller like Ibn Battuta, after seeing him, had to say of him that although he was a highly learned man "there was, nevertheless, something in his head!" But equally sure, in one and all of these cases, orthodoxy had to yield and allow itself to be "re-formed" and often enough "reformed" as well. For its very life consists in this dynamic process which almost by definition is unending.

Yet, something characterized the later "medieval" centuries of Islam — the actual identity of these centuries as also of the meaning of the term "medieval" would differ in respect to different regions of the Muslim world, if, indeed, the term "medieval" is applicable at all — something which is often expressed by terms like "stagnation," "decline," "weakness," "gap," and so on by Western scholars. Politically and culturally these centuries, say from the 15th to 18th, were among the most creative and brilliant in the life of the community under the aegis of the three great Muslim empires. It must, therefore, be determined more precisely as to what happened. Muslims themselves have generally thought that, as the centuries have passed by, Muslims have been less and less good Muslims, a somber thought widely shared also by Westerners: Hence, Harun al-Rashid appears so much more Islamic than, say, Mehmed I. Schacht, however, has taught us — and this, I believe, is a very pertinent insight — that the Ottomans in their sincerity and commitment to the implementation of the shari'ah, actually outstripped the 'Abbasids. So if by "good Muslim" is meant a committed Muslim, the general, indeed, universal expression that the later centuries were less Islamic than the earlier ones (barring the very first generations of Islam) seems no more than a fiction, a pious fiction with Muslims and a historical fiction with Westerners. What is true, however, is — and this is the crucial point in the comparative Islamicity of earlier and later generations — that the interpretation of Islam in legal and institutional terms done by the first two or three centuries was generally relevant to that milieu, whereas once this earlier output was hallowed by the concept of the shari'ah and made immobile by the shari'atists, later generations more or less blindly accepted and followed it and, where they could not follow it fully, they used other devices to sanction their practice by it, but they did not rethink the shari'ah for their own situations, problems and needs. As a result, the continued imposition of this tradition was no more than dead weight around the neck of a live organism.

It was for these reasons and dissatisfaction with the status quo, that several sensitive Muslims began to be alarmed as far back as the 17th and 18th centuries in different regions of the Muslim world, their perceptions of the causes of decline and its remedy differing both with their milieus and their needs, as well as with their individual mental or spiritual make-ups. Once again, this phenomenon of pre-Modernism Islamic reform demonstrates, like earlier reformist phenomena, that where possible and necesary, relevant foreign influences are absorbed, but that essentially the reformist impulse is endemic to Islam. Indeed, in their zeal for reform, Muslims have waged *jihad* against Muslims. While the chief cry of these pre-Modernist reform movements was *ijtihad*, that is, a personal endeavor of a thinking Muslim to think out solutions for problems from Islamic sources, it was the Modernist who actually built his thought on the basis of ijtihad, incorporating systematically and on a large scale certain crucial modern Western elements in the socio-economic field.

That Modernist Islam is a genuinely Islamic response to the contemporary situation, should be clear enough in the light of the developments sketched out in the preceding lines. It has all the characteristics of an Islamic reform: the ferment of ideas, dissatisfaction with status quo, the agitation at the practical level, a new interpretation of Islam and, above all, the unfailing test of any Islamic reform which we have spoken of the above viz. the slow but effective absorption by the "orthodoxy" of the ferment going on around it. Things that were almost inconceivable seven or eight decades ago — for example, emancipation of women — are a matter of fact today; but that this reform is occurring in an Islamic background is clear from the fact that the Muslim woman, for all that we can see, is not going to be a replica of what the Western woman is trying to become and is, in fact, in the process of becoming, with drastic consequences for the family institution. Yet so many Westerners are deluded by appearances (and in social change situations, appearances are sometimes excessive) and assert that the Muslim society is becoming no more than an imitation of the West, and that it is bound to lose its distinctive character. The result is that the Modernist reform looks to them identical with "Westernization."

This kind of judgment is partly the result of a deep-seated assumption that whatever currency is culturally valid today, anywhere in the world, is the Western technology to which, of course, all societies in the world are positively responding in various degrees. But partly also the problem is that the student is observing a contemporary scene and cannot look at it with the necessary time-distance required for a full and objective observation just as, in Aristotle's words, we require a medium to perceive objects which we cannot perceive if we put them directly on our eyes. It is for these reasons that, for example a brilliant scholar like Marshall Hodgson is so woefully inadequate in his entire attitude toward modern Islam. In fact, his statements on one and the same page seem to me contradictory: "The presently 'awakened' Muslim lands were not asleep but, as most briefly stunned by the effects of the Modern transformation itself; and their latter-day activity is only secondarily a product of corresponding movements within the West. Fundamentally, it grows out of two centuries of the developing modern experience in Islamdom itself..." But "...it could be maintained that, in most historically significant senses, in this sixth (Modern) period the Islamicate society is ceasing to exist. From this point of view, what we are going to read about is not the evolution, as before, of a single civilization but rather a number of situations and events that have resulted from the *former* existence of such civilization: chiefly the separate responses of several Muslim people to a new modern world society of which they are all coming to form a part, and in which religion does not make a decisive difference."

The modern influx of ideas from the West in the Muslim society and the problems this has posed have, of course, been on an unprecedented scale. But just as challenges have been of unprecedented dimensions, so are the opportunities to meet them. In this essay, we hope to have provided the reader with some clues as the direction new developments may be going: whether Islam might solve modernity or modernity might dissolve Islam. One significant development characteristic of the modern period has been that the more Muslims have awakened to modernity, they have awakened to the possibilities of Islam proportionately. In fact, Muslim modernists are not the traditional 'ulema but are the authors of what is at the same time the rediscovery of the original Islam and an Islamic vision for the future, where Islam is not just a "religion" but a total and comprehensive way of life, covering equally both what for Hodgson are Islam and Islamicate, a distinction most Modernists sternly reject. On this view, Muslim-state secularism is a version of Islamic Modernism. Which version will win out in the end depends basically on the extent to which and the direction in which, orthodoxy is "re-formed."

Chapter IV

MUHAMMAD'S PROPHETHOOD: AN ANALYTICAL VIEW

Jamal A. Badawi

Dr. Jamal A. Badawi is a well-known speaker and writer on Islam. He teaches industrial management at Saint Mary's University, Halifax N.S., Canada. His article was first published by *al-ittihad* in its spring 1973 issue.

A great deal has been said about the prophet of Islam by Muslims and non-Muslims alike. What has been said, however, has been largely colored by the writer's preconditioning; whether he is a believer or a critic of Islam.

For Muslims, Muhammad's prophethood is indisputable. They firmly believe that he is a true Prophet and Messenger of God, through whom divine revelations throughout history were culminated and perfected. thus forming the universal divine message to mankind. For critics of Islam, generally, it is Muhammad, upon whom be peace, rather than God, who is the founder of Islam, the author of its teachings, and the composer of its holy book, the Qur'an. How could a sincere and "neutral" researcher examine both claims and arrive at his own conclusions?

The search for an answer to this question may be facilitated if one simple rule of objective research is observed. The researcher should try to rid himself of the predominance of emotions, prejudices and preconceptions. This is a demanding requirement of a believer, a critic, and an objective researcher. It is demanding because no man can free himself completely of emotions, prejudices, and preconceptions. Yet an honest researcher could still try his best before an objective and fair assessment of any issue is reached.

This paper is a humble attempt in this direction. It brings into focus some of the main issues which relate to the question of Muhammad's prophethood, analyses them, and explores the conclusions to which such analysis may lead. The approach followed, throughout the paper, is hopefully a rational one; one that does not start off with either an unquestioned acceptance of Muhammad's prophethood, or with a prejudicial rejection of the same.

Since the critics of Muhammad, upon whom be peace, raise questions and doubts about his prophethood, a brief word about the changing nature of their critique may be enlightening.

Changing Attitudes of Muhammad's Critics

One simplified way of classifying their critique is to divide it into three slightly overlapping stages:

The Polemic Era. Writers in this group seem to have been motivated by religious prejudices. Their approach did not reflect an honest spirit of enquiry, because their writings were intended, at least partially, to arouse the feeling of hatred and fury against Muslims. This feeling succeeded in generating a poisonous atmosphere which was exploited to satisfy the needs and aspirations of the secular or religious establishments. The crusades against Muslims were perhaps one implication of this attitude. With these mudslinging tendencies, there was hardly any indecent character that was not attributed to Islam and its Prophet. With feverish and fanatical hatred, no room was left for fact-finding, open-mindedness, or even logic. As such, the ends justified the means: distortions, misrepresentations, half-truths, and at times, sheer fabrications were freely used.[1]

Disguised Polemic: As the polemic era lost its momentum, a more careful and disguised polemic was introduced. Writers in this group criticized their predecessors as extremists, refrained from indecent and open attacks on Islam and Muhammad, upon whom be peace. Yet, their motives were not significantly different from their predecessors'. Most of them apparently realized that owing to the forces of history, the masses had become more educated, at least to the extent of ruling out sheer fabrications as effective offensive weapons against Islam. Their approach, however, still reflected an earnest endeavor to develop more effective weapons to destroy Islam or at least to belittle it. It is not a coincidence that such motives were often connected with the writers' colonial or missionary affiliation and orientation.

The Inevitable Inconsistency: A more tolerant yet perplexing attitude then came into being. Some writers even began to give credit to Islam as a powerful and viable ideology and to Muhammad, upon

---

[1]For some examples of this type of polemic, see Ahmad, Khurshid, *Islam and the West,* Islamic Publications Ltd., Lahore, Pakistan, 2nd ed., 1967.

whom be peace, as a man with positive and moral qualities. His sincerity, sacrifices, and the instrumental role he played in bringing about spiritual, moral, and material upliftment to humanity were all admitted. One thing, however, was not admitted as readily. Was Muhammad a true prophet who received divine revelation from God, and was the Qur'an really a divine book or was it of Muhammad's own making?

No matter how courteous, mild, or apparently objective these writers may be, a serious question of consistency would inevitably arise here: how consistent is it to admit the sincerity and high moral character of Muhammad, upon whom be peace, while implying that he was not truthful when he claimed to be a prophet of God, or when he claimed that the Qur'an was not of his own making, or when he claimed that he did not derive his teachings from any human source? It is this latter question that will be explored in some detail in this paper. To do this exploration, however, it would be helpful to clarify the methodology that will be followed.

A Proposed Methodology

In pursuit of an honest answer to the above question, it is logical to begin with Muhammad's claim. Having done this, it would be fair to evaluate and discuss such a claim without accepting it or rejecting it offhand. Such an acceptance or rejection of Muhammad's truthfulness should only follow the analysis and over-all evaluation of the salient arguments, facts, and questions pertaining to the issue.

The Claim

Reference to the Qur'an, to the sayings of Muhammad, upon whom be peace, and to historical material, consistently indicates that Muhammad, upon whom be peace, claimed to be God's Prophet and Messenger to mankind, that the Qur'an was not of his own making, and that what he preached (Islam) was divinely and not humanly inspired.[2]

---

[2]*The Qur'an is God's divine message:*
"So I do call to witness what you see. And what you see not, that this is verily the word of an honored apostle. It is not the word of a poet; little it is you believe. Nor is it the word of a soothsayer: little admonition it is you receive. (This is) a Message sent down from the Lord of the Worlds" (The Qur'an 69: 38-43).

The Qur'an is not produced by anyone save God:
"This Qur'an is not such as can be produced by other than God; on the contrary, it is a confirmation of (revelations) what went before it, and a fuller explanation of the Book— wherein there is no doubt—from the Lord of the worlds. Or do they say (He forged it)? Say: (Bring then a surah like unto it, and Call (to your aid) anyone you can besides God, if it be you speak the truth." (The Qur'an 10:37-38).

It is not up to Muhammad, upon whom be peace, to get it together:
"If you bring them not a revelation, they say: (Why have you not got it together?) Say: 'I but follow what is revealed to me from my Lord: This is (nothing but) Lights from your Lord, and Guidance, and Mercy, for any who have faith!" (The Qur'an 7:203).

The Critique

In evaluating the above claim, there could be two possibilities; first, that this claim was truthful; second, that this claim was not truthful, i.e., a fabrication. If the first possibility is accepted, whether by faith or by reason or by combination thereof, then the question of Muhammad's true prophethood is settled. If, however, the second possibility is still open, how could it be objectively verified or refuted?

Only Two Possibilities: It is important to emphasize at this point that Muhammad's claim of prophethood is subject to only two possibilities: truthfulness or fabrication. It may be contended that many critics of Islam do not use the term fabrication to refer to Muhammad's claim of prophethood. It may be added also that they talk and write about Muhammad with considerable respect and admiration (like many other great men and heroes). Is the mere fact that they say or imply that Muhammad, upon whom be peace, was a great social reformer and a remarkable composer of an influential book, the Qur'an, sufficient to infer that they accuse him of not being a truthful man?

Without beating around the bush, it should be said candidly that it doesn't matter how nicely, diplomatically, or courteously the ideas are stated, the logical implications of such statements cannot be ignored. If an apparently fair writer does not dispute the fact that Muhammad *did claim* that what he taught was neither of his own making nor was it derived from any human source, and if the same writer says or implies later on that Muhammad was the *composer or compiler* of the Qur'an, then what he is really saying is that Muhammad was not truthful (or sane) when he claimed the divine origin of Islam. Muhammad's personal integrity and truthfulness can still be

---

Nor is it up to Muhammad, upon whom be peace, to change any of the contents of the Qur'an:

But when Our Clear Signs are rehearsed unto them, those who rest not their hope on their meeting with Us, say: ('Bring us a Reading other than this, or change this,) Say: ('It is not for me of my own accord, to change it: I follow only what is revealed unto me: if I were to disobey my Lord, I should myself fear the penalty of a great day (to come).' "

(The Qur'an 10:15, see also 10:16)

For nothing is more wicked than inventing a lie against God or making a false claim of receiving revelations from Him:

Who can be more wicked than one who invents a lie against God, or says, '(I have received inspiration,)' when he received none, or (again who says: '(I can reveal the like of what God has revealed?' If you could but see how the wicked (do fare) in the flood of confusion at death! — the angels stretch forth their hands, (saying, 'Yield up your souls: this day shall you receive your reward, — a penalty of shame, for that you used to tell lies against God, and scornfully reject His Signs!' " (The Qur'an 6:93).

It would be highly illogical to say that Muhammad, upon whom be peace, composed the Qur'an whose very verses severely condemn such composition as a shameful act which is not surpassed in its wickedness!

questioned in a nice, courteous, and yet misleading manner. It is this *courteous inconsistency*, and in some cases hypocrisy, that might mislead the reader, Muslim and non-Muslim alike. Diplomatic statements are no substitute for candid, objective and rigorous research in a subject as important as the current one.

But Why Fabricate? To avoid the above courteous inconsistency, a researcher would have to assume either of the two possibilities (truthfulness or dishonesty) and seek all evidence that may verify or refute his assumption. Since these two possibilities are contrary to each other, it makes little difference which one may be assumed to initiate the analysis. Let us see if the assumption of possible fabrication can be substantiated.

If it were true that Muhammad's claim of prophethood was a mere fabrication, then two sub-possibilities may present themselves; 1) that he might have fabricated this claim deliberately and knowingly, or b) that he might have done so unconsciously.

Conscious Fabrication?

Deliberate fabrication, like other patterns of human behavior is likely to have a goal; the satisfaction of certain human needs. Arrogation of prophethood may thus be motivated either by some material benefit or by the aspiration to status, glory, and power. We may as well look into these two possibilities.

Fabrication for Material Gains?

Is it reasonable to assert that Muhammad, upon whom be peace, might have claimed prophethood to attain some material gains? This question may be answered by looking into his financial status before and after prophethood. Before his mission as a prophet, Muhammad, upon whom be peace, had no financial worries. His loving and rich wife, Khadijah, had made available to him all that he needed. As a successful and reputed merchant, Muhammad had a comfortable income. It is ironic that the same man, after his mission as a prophet and because of it, become worse off materially.

Describing their life, his wife, 'Ayshah narrated that a month or two might have elapsed before fire was lit in the Prophet's house (to cook a meal), while the household subsisted on milk and dates.[3] After eighteen years of his mission, when Muslims emerged victorious, we still find a kind of revolt in Muhammad's household in protest to the difficult life characterized by a considerable self-imposed material deprivation. This incident took place at the time when the Muslim treasury was under his disposal.[4] Asked about Muhammad's bedding, Hafash answered, "It

---

[3]Cf. M. Al-Nawawi *Riyadh al-Saliheen Min Kalam Sayyid-il-Mursaleen*, Hadeeth #492 (Several printings of this source were published. The printing cited above is published by Shirkat-al-Shimirley, Cairo, Egypt, no date.)

[4]This incident is referred to in the Qur'an (33:28-29). It is also documented in *Al-Bukhari* and *Muslim*.

comprised of a piece of canvas which I spread double folded under him. Once I did it fourfold in an effort to make it more comfortable. The next morning he asked me: 'What did you spread under me last night'. I replied: 'The same canvas, but I had fourfolded it instead of the customary double fold'. He said: 'Keep it as it was before. The additional softness stands in the way of tahajjud (night prayer)' "⁵ When 'Umar Ibn al-Khattab went to see Muhammad, upon whom be peace, he noticed that the contents of his room were comprised of three pieces of tanned skin and a handful of barley lying in a corner. "I looked about but I failed to find anything else. I began to weep. He said 'Why are you weeping?' I replied: 'O Prophet of Allah, why should I not weep? I can see the mat's imprint on your body, and I am also beholding all that you have in this room. O Prophet of Allah! Pray that Allah may grant ample provisions for us. The Persians and the Romans who have no true faith and who worship not Allah but their kings — the Chosroes and the Caesars — should live in gardens with streams running in their midst, but the chosen prophet and the accepted slave of Allah should live in such a dire poverty!' The Prophet, upon whom be peace, was resting against his pillow, but when he heard me talk like this, he sat against his pillow and said, 'O 'Umar! Are you still in doubt about this matter? Ease and comfort in the hereafter are much better than ease and comfort in this world.' "⁶ In a long narrative by Bilal about what Muhammad, upon whom be peace, did with the gifts and provisions he received, Bilal reported that the Prophet never kept back anything for future use, that he spent what he had on the poor and needy, and that on one occasion, Muhammad received a gift of four loaded camels, yet he took nothing for himself and he further insisted that he would not go home until the *whole* lot was given away to the needy.⁷ At the time of his death, and in spite of all his victories and achievements, Muhammad, upon whom be peace, was in debt, and his shield was in the hands of a Jewish citizen of Madinah as a collateral for that debt!⁸

One may then inquire: Are there any materialistic motives behind Muhammad's claim of prophethood?

---

⁵Idara Isha't-e Diniyat, *The Teachings of Islam*, New Delhi, no date, p. 50.
⁶*Ibid.* pp. 49-50. A similar narrative is also cited in *at-Tirmidhi* and reproduced in *Riyadh al-Saliheen*. op. cit., *Hadith No. 486*.
⁷*The Teachings of Islam*, op. cit., pp. 55-57, see also *Riyadh al-Saliheen*, op. cit., Hadiths No. 465 and 466.
⁸*Riyadh al-Saliheen*, op. cit., Hadith No. 504. The study of the history of Islam shows that Muhammad's example of sacrifice has been followed by many of his companions and their successors until this day.

For further documentation on Muhammad's self-imposed deprivation, one may refer to a large number of narratives reported by his contemporaries. All these narratives show consistently his sacrificial life and the extent of hunger which he chose to undergo from the beginning of his mission until his death. See for example *Riyadh al- Saliheen, Ibid.*, Ahadeeth Nos. 474, 491 and 507 (narrated by his wife 'Ayshah), No. 475 (narrated by his

Fabrication for Worldly Glory and Power?

Is it possible that Muhammad, upon whom be peace, might have claimed prophethood to attain status, worldly greatness, and power? The desire to enjoy status and power is usually associated with good food, fancy clothing, monumental palaces, colorful guards, and indisputable authority.

Do any of these indications apply to Muhammad? Following are a few glimpses of his life that may help answer this question.

Despite his responsibilities as a prophet, a teacher, a statesman, and a judge, Muhammad, upon whom be peace, used to milk his goat, mend his clothes, repair his shoes, and help with the household work. His life was an amazing model of simplicity and humbleness.[9] He sat on the floor, went to the market without any trappings of power; he talked and listened patiently and politely to anyone who stopped him, and he accepted invitations to dine with the poor and ate graciously whatever was served to him. Once he was travelling with some of his companions who began to prepare to cook some food by dividing the work among themselves. Muhammad, upon whom be peace, offered to collect some wood. His companions told him that they could do it for him. Muhammad answered back, "I know you could do it for me, but I hate to have any privilege over you".[10] A stranger once came to him almost trembling out of respect. Muhammad asked the man to come closer to him and with a compassionate pat on the man's shoulder, he told him: "Relax brother, I am born of a woman who used to eat dried bread".[11]

Muhammad's use of authority is quite revealing. His followers loved him, respected him, and trusted him to an amazing extent. Yet, he continued to emphasize that obedience and devotion should be directed to God and not to him personally. As a matter of fact, he made a clear distinction between the specific revelations he received from God and areas left to human discretion. In the latter category, evidence of Muhammad's consultative attitudes is ample. In planning for the defense of Madinah (before the battle of the Trench), Muhammad,

---

brother-in-law, Amr ibn al-Harith), No. 473 (narrated by ʿUmar), Nos. 493, 497 (narrated by Abu Hurairah), Nos. 494 and 421 (narrated by Anas), No. 485 (narrated by Noʿman Ibn Basheer), No. 486 (narrated by Sahl Ibn Saʿd), No. 500 (narrated by Saʿd Ibn Abi Waqqas), No. 520 (narrated by Jaber), and No. 499 (narrated by Abu Musa al-Ashaʿari). Further narratives may be found in standard books of Hadith.

[9]A large number of ahadith (sayings of Muhammad, upon whom be peace), call for simplicity and humbleness and warn against *excessive* indulgence in worldly pleasures. It was Muhammad's practice of what he preached that provided a living example for his followers and commanded their trust. See for example *Ibid.*, Nos. 457, 458, 461, 463, 464, 467, 468, 471, 472, 477, 484, and 516.

[10]Khalid, Khalid M. *Insaniyyat Muhammad*, Maktabat Wahbah, Cairo, Egypt, 2nd Printing, 1963, p. 67.

[11]*Ibid.*, p. 65.

upon whom be peace, asked for the advice of his companions and decided in favor of Salman's proposal to dig a trench around Madinah. Furthermore, he started working with his hands like any other man in his company. A similar behavior was demonstrated in the battle of Badr.[12]

In addition to the simple, humble, and altruistic life of Muhammad, one may also ask: Was there any indication in his early life that demonstated his aspiration for leadership and fame? Critics of Muhammad fail to provide any evidence that he planned or aspired to leadership and fame. Even a writer who goes into a great length to support his guess that Muhammad, upon whom be peace, probably had some "secret desires" to be famous, cannot help but admit that Muhammed was not guilty of planning for his role as a prophet.[13] Not only was Muhammad an ordinary and quiet person, but he even trembled and rushed home in terror when he received the first revelation as a prophet of God. If he were planning or aspiring for fame, he would have come down happy and jubilant that his "secret desires" were finally coming true.[14] Andrae's theory of "secret desires" and similar theories are perhaps modern versions of the pagan Arabs' initial interpretation of Muhammad's motives. Long before there was any prospect of success of the new faith and at the outset of a long and painful era of torture, suffering, and persecution of Muhammad, upon whom be peace, and his followers, he received an interesting offer. An envoy of the pagan leaders, 'Utbah came to him saying, ". . .if you want money, we will collect enough money for you so that you will be the richest among us. If you want leadership we will take you as our leader and will never decide on any matter without your approval. If you want kingship we will crown you as our king. And if you cannot resist the visions that come to you, we will spend all that is needed to seek a cure for you..."[15] Only one concession was required from Muhammad in return for stopping "dividing the people" and to give up this new claim that there is no god but Allah — the Merciful. This was not a high price if Muhammad was pursuing his own benefit. Was Muhammad, upon whom be peace, hesitant when the offer was made? Did he turn it down as a bargaining strategy leaving the door open for a better offer? The following was his answer:

"In the Name of God, Most Gracious, Most Merciful. Ha-

---

[12]Joma'a, Muhammad L., *Thawra'ul-Islam wa Batal al-Anbiya*, Maktabatul-Nahdhah, Cairo, Egypt, 1959, p. 302 and 401. In the battle of Badr, it was the proposal of Al-Habbab Ibn al-Manthir that substituted Muhammad's own proposal, See *Sirat Ibn Hisham*, under Ghazwat Badr al-Kobra (available in several printings, one of which is *Tahtheeb Sirat Ibn Hisham*, compiled by Abdussalam Harun, Dar al-Fikr, 1954, vol. 1, p. 146.

[13]Andrae, Tor, *Mohammed: The Man and His Faith* (Translated by Theophil Menzel, Harper and Row, N.Y., U.S.A., 1955 (Revised ed.), p. 94.

[14]See Joma'a, op. cit., p. 557.

[15]*Tahtheeb Sirat Ibn Hisham*, op. cit., p. 65.

Meem. A revelation from (God), Most Gracious, Most Merciful;
A Book whereof the verses are explained in detail: A Qur'an in
Arabic, for people who understand. Giving good news and
admonition: Yet most of them turn away and so they hear not".[16]

On another occasion and in response to his uncle's plea for
compromise, Muhammad's answer was as decisive and sincere, "I
swear by the name of God, O Uncle!, that if they place the sun in my
right hand and the moon in my left hand in return for giving up this
matter (Islam), I will never desist until either God makes it triumph or I
perish defending it"[17]

History tells us that not only did Muhammad, upon whom be peace,
and his few followers suffer all kinds of torture and sacrifice for thirteen
years, but that on several occasions, he was about to perish physically
because of his steadfastness.

Are these the characteristics of a power-hungry or a self-centered
man? What could justify such a life of suffering and sacrifice, even after
he was fully triumphant over his adversaries? What could explain the
humbleness and nobility which he demonstrated in his most glorious
moments when he insisted that success is due only to God's help and
not to his own genius?

UNCONSCIOUS FABRICATION?

So far, an impartial researcher would fail to find any ground to doubt
Muhammad's truthfulness. Ironically, some orientalists and
missionaries agree with this result. Yet, through diplomacy,
romanticism, and possibly deception, they continue to search for new
ways of denying the divine origin of Islam and of attributing the Qur'an
to Muhammad's own thinking. Some claim that under the influence of
repeated "visions," and with his disenchantment with idol-worship,
Muhammad, because of his pure and upright nature, gradually
convinced himself that he was the reformer or savior of his people!
What is overlooked in this type of theory is that Muhammad's claim of
prophethood was continuously and consistently made throughout the
full twenty-three years of his mission, and that it was not something that
was gradually developed or felt. It was rather a claim that came up
unexpectedly at the age of forty.

What kind of person is he who "convinces himself" for twenty-three
years that his *fabricated* claim of receiving revelation from God is only
an outcome of his *sincere* desire to help his people? A person like this
would have to be notoriously dishonest or mentally sick. As it became
too difficult to show objectively any proof of dishonesty, fishing in the
troubled waters continued by seeking explanation in epilepsy.

---

[16]*Ibid.* p. 65. Muhammad's answer was the recitation of the Qur'an 41:1-38, of which the
translation of the first four verses is cited above.
[17]*Ibid.*, p. 59.

Epilepsy?:

It was contended and still is, perhaps to a lesser extent, that Muhammad, upon whom be peace, was a sincere but epileptic person who, during his epileptic seizures, recited what subsequently became the Qur'an.

What is overlooked in this argument is that during an epileptic seizure, the functioning of the brain is disturbed. As such, sensible speech is not possible since the patient usually mumbles confusing words which he forgets after he has recovered. From all available accounts on Muhammad's life, we consistently find a man with excellent physical and mental health throughout his life, a man who never had epileptic seizures, or the "falling-down" disease that was known to his contemporaries, and a man who faced many critical moments in his life without collapsing, even once, under tension or strain, no matter how great.

Are these the characteristics of an epileptic man? How could his followers, including the most wise and intelligent,[18] believe in him rather than seek a cure for him? Did the believers in this "epilepsy" school of thought bother to open the Qur'an, read it, and see if it looks like a product of epileptic convulsive seizures?

The Logical Conclusion:

If no reasonable argument can be made to support the imputation of dishonesty to Muhammad, upon whom be peace, and if the implicit assumption of fabrication, while seeking psychological explanations for his claim, is only self-contradictory, what other reasons may justify the denial of the divine origin of his message, or to doubt his truthfulness?[19]

JUDEO-CHRISTIAN ORIGINS OF ISLAM?

In orientalist, as well as missionary literature on Islam, there is often some explicit mention or implicit implication that Islam is compiled from Judaism, Christianity or both. This is done by pointing out obvious parallels between Islam and either or both Judaism and Christianity. It is also contended, without sufficient evidence, that it was through Muhammad's contacts with Jews and Christians, especially during his travels, that he learned about religious beliefs and theology. It was this background, they claim, that led Muhammad, upon whom be peace, to formulate his new religion. The clear implication of statements of this kind is to impute dishonesty to him when he claimed that he did not compile Islam from any source except for the revelation he received from God. The soundness of this

---

[18]For example, Abu Bakr, 'Umar, 'Uthman, 'Ali, Talhah, al-Zubair Ibn al-'Awwam, Sa'd Ibn Abi Waqqas, and 'Abd ur-Rahman b. 'Auf.

[19]Unless one rejects all religions based on divine revelations, which is not the typical attitudes of Muhammad's critics, some of whom are missionaries!

assumption was discussed at some length in the preceding pages. It would be interesting, however, to look further into this issue.

None of those who subscribe to the theory of "Judeo-Christian origins" of Islam could present any *conclusive* historical evidence about the alleged teacher(s) of Muhammad. Their claim thus qualified only as an assertion or an assumption but not as a factual statement. By sheer repetition and wide circulation, however, this assertion and the far-reaching judgements based on it were "elevated to the dignity of facts"[20] — a settled issue.

One example of such inaccuracy which disregards the basics of a scientific spirit of inquiry is a statement by Montgomery Watt in his *Islam and Integration of Society:* "Islam would have to admit the *fact* of its *origin*—the historical influence of Judaeo-Christian religious traditions".[21] Commenting on this, a historian says: "Here the question of origins is taken as settled and referred to as a (fact) without any qualification or discussion".[22] If the question of Muhammad's truthfulness was subjected to such a critical investigation, then it is only logical to critically look at the assertion of the Judeo-Christian origins of Islam.

At least three questions may be raised on this issue:

• What was Muhammad's background and education before he started his mission at the age of forty, and to what extent could such a background have resulted in what he brought forth?

• What was the extent of his "contacts" with the Jews and Christians, and to what extent could such contacts have resulted in the faith he proclaimed?

• How far can the Judeo- Christian thought be traced in what Muhammad, upon whom be peace, taught? And if there is any similarity between both teachings, how could that be explained?

• **The Question of Background:** Historically speaking, Muhammad, upon whom be peace, was an illiterate man. There is no evidence that he knew reading or writing. Even the Qur'an, which he stated was the Word of God, was not written down by him, for he dictated it to the "scribes of revelation" who wrote it down and committed it to memory. Another historical document which is still available, is the letter sent by Muhammad, upon whom be peace, to the ruler of Egypt inviting him to accept Islam.[23] This letter written for Muhammad carries his seal rather than his signature. Besides the lack

---

[20]Tibawi, A.L., *English Speaking Orientalist*, The Islamic Centre, Geneva, Switzerland, 1965, p. 17.

[21]Watt, W. Montgomery, *Islam and the Integration of Society*, London, 1961, p. 263, cited in Tibawi, Op. cit., p. 22. Emphasis are mine.

[22]Tibawi, op. cit., p. 22.

[23]This document was reproduced in *Newsletter*, the Muslim Students' Association of the US & Canada, Vol. 5, No. 3, Jan. 1971, p. 10.

of significant education, formal or otherwise, religious or secular, there is no account in his life, until the age of forty, that shows his scholarly tendencies or achievements in any of the spectrum of subjects, which the Qur'an deals with. How could such an illiterate man, suddenly, at the age of forty, bring about an ideological and religious revolution that changed the face of history?

• **The Question of Environment:** As we looked into the man's background, we may as well look into the type of environment in which he was reared to see the extent of his possible exposure to Judeo-Christian thought. Unlike Moses, upon whom be peace, who was reared in a center of learning and civilization, and unlike Jesus, upon whom be peace, and other Israelite prophets who emerged in the center of Judaism, if not the religious hierarchy[24] itself, Muhammad, upon whom be peace, was raised in a predominantly pagan society with no significant Jewish or Christian population. Yathrib (Madinah), where some Jewish tribes lived, was too far to be considered as part of Muhammad's immediate environment, especially when the seventh century means of transportation and communication are considered.

Some may assert, however, that through his travels with the caravans, Muhammad, upon whom be peace, might have learned about Judaism and Christianity. The danger in a statement like this is not in its theoretical possibility: the danger lies instead in the hasty and superficial conclusions that are often based on it. Assuming that Muhammad met some Jews and Christians during his travels, or when the latter visited Makkah, which is a fair assumption, what was the extent of his exposure to their teachings? Was such an exposure sufficient to raise reasonable doubts that he copied or compiled the Qur'an from their scriptures?

Historically speaking, and in spite of the reasonable details about Muhammad's life, there is evidence of two travels that Muhammad made, both to Syria. In one trip, he accompanied his uncle as a twelve-year-old boy. Would it be reasonable to assume that during such a trip, a twelve-year-old boy would learn all the high concepts of theology which were at that time the exclusive knowledge of high priests? In the second trip, Muhammad, upon whom be peace, was twenty-five years old, and he was leading Khadijah's trade caravan.[25] It would be highly imaginary to say that through his occasional chats with Jews and Christians, while busy with his caravan, Muhammad learned enough about either or both religions to formulate a new powerful and viable

---

These facts, however, do not justify the denial of the divine origin of the *original* revelations given to Prophets Moses and Jesus (may peace be upon them). Such denial is much less justified in the case of Muhammad, upon whom be peace. See Joma'a, op. cit., pp. 547-549.

For an account of these two travels, see *Tahtheeb Sirah Ibn Hisham*, op. cit., pp. 42-46.

religion, a task that defied the collective efforts of scholars for centuries. Furthermore, the above assertion does not provide answers to the following six questions:

• Why is it, that in spite of the abundance of historical material on Muhammad's life, and in spite of the extensive research on his life for centuries by his severe critics, it has not been possible to discover that mysterious teacher(s) through whom Muhammad might have learned all that?

• It is known that Muhammad was opposed, ridiculed, and persecuted for nearly thirteen years by his contemporaries. With this magnitude of severe enemies, was it not possible for them to prove to the masses that Muhammad's claim of revelation was sheer fabrication? Was it not possible for them to reveal and name the alleged human source or sources of his teachings?[26] Even some of his adversaries who made this assertion changed their minds later on and accused him instead of magic or of being possessed by evil and so on.

• Muhammad was among his people and every aspect of his life was exposed to them, especially by the openness that characterized tribal life in the desert.[27] How could the multitudes of his contemporaries, including many of his close relatives who knew him so well, believe in his truthfulness if they had any doubt that he was claiming credit for ideas taught to him by some other teachers without bothering to give them credit?

• What kind of teacher might have taught Muhammad a coherent and complete religion that changed the face of history? Why didn't he claim the credit for himself? Why couldn't he or they (if any) speak against the alleged student who continued learning from them, while ignoring them and claiming some other divine source for his teachings?

• How could many Jews and Christians among his contemporaries become Muslims and believe in his truthfulness if they knew that he was copying from their scriptures or learning from their priests or rabbis?

• It is known that some of the Qur'anic revelations came to Muhammad, upon whom be peace, in the presence of people. The Qur'an was revealed over a span of twenty-three years; where then was that mysterious, perhaps invisible human teacher of Muhammad? How could he have hidden himself for so long? Or how could Muhammad, upon whom be peace, who was constantly surrounded by his followers, make frequent secret visits to that mysterious teacher or teachers for twenty-three years without being caught even once?

If Muhammad were an able theologian with a score of Ph.Ds from

---

[26] See Joma'a, op. cit., p. 556.
[27] Addressing the disbelievers of Muhammad's contemporaries, the Qur'an states "Or do they not recognize their messenger, that they deny him."

Oxford, Harvard, and McGill it would be impossible to believe that the Qur'an could be the outcome of this background. The fact that Muhammad was an illiterate man reared in a predominantly pagan and backward society, makes the preceding assertion a ridiculous one.

• **The Question of Parallels:** Many orientalists, especially those with missionary affiliation, have been busy comparing the Qur'an with the Bible, trying to "discover" parallels between both books to show the *influence* of the Bible or the *influence* of "Judaeo-Christian thought"on Islam. Those scholars seem to ignore that methodologically speaking, the similarity between any two compositions is not sufficient to infer that one of them was copied from the other. Both compositions may be based on a third common source.[28] A Muslim may state that all divine revelations came from that same source, the One Universal God. No matter what human changes were introduced into some of these revelations that might have distorted their originality, there are bound to be some areas that remained free from distortion, and thus are common to many religions. It is true that there are some parallels between the Qur'an and the Bible, e.g., some basic moral laws. If these parallels are sufficient to accuse Muhammad, upon whom be peace, of compiling or copying from the Bible, then the same logic should be impartially and consistently applied to all previous Scriptures as well. For example, there are similarities between the teachings of Christianity and Judaism. Is this sufficient to infer that Jesus, upon whom be peace, was not a genuine prophet and that he copied from the Old Testament? Moreover, there are similarities between the Judaic teachings and other older religions such as Hinduism (e.g. in moral laws); is this sufficient to infer that Moses, upon whom be peace, and all other Israelite prophets were false prophets and that they simply compiled their teachings from Hindu and other sources, instead of receiving genuine revelations from God? These would be "heroic inferences" in the cases of Judaism and Christianity, as they are in the case of Islam.

Beyond the Surface

From the above discussion, it does not seem necessary to argue that there are no similarities between Islam and other religions. It is certainly unfair and inaccurate to say so. All divine revelations proceeded from the One Universal God of all. Even with human distortions throughout history, some parallels are bound to exist.

It is important to point out, however, that there are many essential differences that further refute the "Judaeo-Christian origins" thesis. Such differences cover a wide spectrum of topics, including the concept of "original sin," the necessity of blood sacrifice, atonement of

---

[28]Tibawi, op. cit., p. 20.

one's sins by someone else, the question of an intermediary between man and God, the necessity and authority of a religious hierarchy, the concept of Sabbath, the concept of prophethood, essential information about previous prophets, the presence or absence of inherent conflict between material and spirit, body and soul, the conception of man's role on earth, and the meaning of "religion" and whether it is basically a spiritual aspect of man's life or the totality of man's life. Discussion of such differences could extend to almost any length. For brevity, however, a few citations from the Bible and the Qur'an on one essential topic, the Concept of God, may help shed some light on such differences.

The Biblical Concept of God

✓   God is depicted in a human form. In the book of Genesis we read: "And God said, Let us make a man in our image, after our likeness".[29]

✓   He is described as one who gets tired of work and who needs to rest: "And on the seventh day God ended his work which he had made: and he rested on the seventh day from all his work which he had made".[30]

✓   He is described as one who walks in the garden, one from whom man may hide, and one who needs to search for what he is looking for. Narrating what happened after Adam and Eve ate from the forbidden tree, the Bible states: "And they heard the sound of the Lord God walking in the garden in the cool of the day: and the man and his wife hid themselves from the presence of the Lord God among the trees of the garden. But the Lord God called to the man, and said to him, "Where are you?" And he said, 'I heard the sound of You in the garden, and I was afraid because I was naked, and I hid myself'. He said, 'Who told you that you were naked? Have you eaten of the tree which I commanded you not to eat?' "[31]

✓   He is described as One who becomes sorry for making certain decisions which may imply either that he was aware of the future repercussions of his decisions or that he is subject to different moods. In the Bible we read: "And the Lord was sorry that he had made man on the earth and it grieved him to his heart".[32]

✓   He is described frequently as the God of Israel and as one who is jealous. In the Book of Exodus we read: "For you shall worship no other god, for the Lord, whose name is Jealous, is a jealous God".[33]

---

[29]Genesis 1:26, See also Gen. 9:6.
[30]Gen. 2:2, See also Gen. 2:3 and Exodus 20:11. For forgetfulness see Gen. 8:1 and Exodus 2:24.
[31]Gen. 3:8-11.
[32]Gen. 6:6, See also Judges 2:18 and Exodus 32:14.
[33]Exodus 34:14, See also Exodus 20:5.

Although the Bible describes God as the Creator of heavens and earth, there is far less emphasis on Him as the Universal God of all nations and more emphasis on Him as the "God of Israel". Children of Israel are frequently depicted as "His people".

✓ In general, He is depicted as one who is subject to human-like limitations, as one who has nostrils and a mouth[34], that he dwells in thick darkness.[35] He is described as one who needs man's guidance as it is clear in his instructions for the Israelites' flight from Egypt.[36] He is described as one who worries about man's power and unity. The following citation documents this latter point:

"And the Lord came down to see the city and the tower, which the sons of men had built. And the Lord said, 'Behold, they are one people, and they all have one language; and this is only the beginning of what they will do; and nothing that they propose to do will now be impossible for them. Come, let us go down; and there confuse their language, that they may not understand one another's speech.' So the Lord scattered them abroad from there over the face of the earth, and they left off building the city. Therefore its name was called Babel, because there the Lord confused the language of all the earth; and from there the Lord scattered them abroad over the face of all the earth".[37]

The Qur'anic Concept of God

✓ In contrast to the conception of God in a human form, we read in the Qur'an: "Say He is God, The One and the Only God, the Eternal, Absolute. He begets not, nor is He begotton. And there is none like unto Him."[38] Also ". . . there is nothing comparable to Him!"[39]

✓ In contrast to the conception of God as One who gets tired and needs rest, we read in the Qur'an:

"God, there is no god except Him, the Living, the Eternal.
Slumber does not overtake Him, nor does sleep."[40]

✓ In contrast to the conception of God as One who walks, resides in the clouds or in the temple of Solomon, the Qur'an indicates that God is not subject to the limitations of time and space. We read in the Qur'an:

"The East and West are God's. Wherever you may turn, there is God's countenance [Presence.] God is so Ample, Aware."[41]

---

[34]2nd Samuel 22:9-15.
[35]1 Kings 8:12, See also Numbers 11:25.
[36]Exodus 12:13.
[37]Gen. 11:5-9, See also Gen. 3:22-24.
[38]The Qur'an 112:1-4.
[39]*Ibid.*, 42:11.
[40]*Ibid.*, 2:255.
[41]*Ibid.*, 2:115.

"And He is God in the heavens and on earth. He knows what you hide, and what you reveal..."[42]

✓   In contrast to the conception of God as One who discovers the consequences of his decisions as time goes on, the Qur'an emphasizes that God's knowledge is as eternal and as infinite as His Presence. We read in the Qur'an:

"...He knows what is before them and what is behind them and they encompass nothing of His knowledge except what He pleases.."[43]

"He holds the keys to the unseen; only He knows them! He knows everything on land and at sea; no leaf drops down unless He knows it, nor any seed in the darkness of the earth, nor any tender shoot nor any dry [stalk] unless it is in a plain book".[44]

✓   In contrast to the conception of God as the Jealous God of Israel, one fails to find a single verse in the Qur'an in which God is described as the God of Quraishites, the God of Arabs, or the God of Muslims. On the contrary we read in the Qur'an:

"Praise be to God, Lord of the Universe..."[45]

"...We have sent you [O Muhammad] as a messenger to mankind; God suffices as a witness".[46]

✓   In contrast to the conception of God in a human-like form, a conception which is too explicit to think of as only symbolic (See #6 under Biblical Concept), one fails to find similar descriptions of this in the Qur'an. Whenever it was necessary for purposes of communication to describe God in what may seem to be a physical description, we find that the terms used in the Qur'an are clearly figurative. For example, using the term throne of God or His seat to refer to authority and power. Also the use of the word "hand" in an expression like "The Hand of God is above their hands"[47] — refers to power or will. The proper meaning of such terms is clearly understood by referring to the Qur'an itself: "Nothing is comparable to Him [God]".[48]

Such clearly figurative descriptions are hardly analogous to the Biblical anthropomorphism, e.g., saying that God created man in His own image, that He walks in the garden causing noise as He walks, One who rests, One from Whose mouth devouring fire went out, or One who came down with thick darkness under His feet.[49]

---

[42]*Ibid.*, 6:3.
[43]*Ibid.*, 2:255.
[44]*Ibid.*, 6:59.
[45]*Ibid.*, 1:1.
[46]*Ibid.*, 4:79.
[47]*Ibid.*, 48:10.
[48]*Ibid.*, 42:11.
[49]See for example 2 Samuel 22:1-15.

Conclusion

This brief exposition is not intended to over-emphasize the differences between Islam and the "Judaeo-Christian" traditions. Nor does it imply that there is nothing in common between Islam, Judaism, Christianity, or other religions. Such an inference would clearly contradict the Islamic theory of the history of "religions." Such a theory can be summarized as follows: All authentic divine revelations proceeded from the same Universal God. As such, authentic and original teachings of all messengers of God must have been essentially the same. Slight differences might have existed but only in detailed rites and regulations. As time went on, authentic and original teachings of various prophets were lost, changed, or intermingled with philosophical and theological interpretations to the extent that even the concept of God was given various contradictory explanations ranging from attributing divinity to trees, stars, animals, spirits, or even human beings (e.g. Buddha and Jesus). It was by God's grace that His message to humanity was perfected and purified from all alien elements and was presented in its pristine form to humanity at large, no longer subject to any loss or change. Such is the universal, eternal, divine, purified and perfected message that Muhammad brought to humanity.

The fact that God chose an illiterate Arab, who was neither a Jew nor a Christian to carry this noble message does, by no means, justify the tremendous energies spent by Jewish and Christian orientalists and missionaries to belittle his mission by all means. Nor does it justify the distortions, unfairness, and lack of objectivity in what amounts to an attempt to impute dishonesty to the noble character of Muhammad, directly, or indirectly, openly or diplomatically.

Any fair and logical study of Muhammad's history and character would leave no room for doubt about any ulterior motive in claiming prophethood and divine revelation. It does not stand to reason to say that the book (the Qur'an), which caused a far-reaching spiritual, moral, social, political and economic revolution that changed the course of history, was a product of convulsive epileptic seizures! Nor is it reasonable to say that this book was a product of a simple and illiterate desert dweller! The brief discussion of the so-called "Judaeo-Christian Origins" of Islam, even in one single topic is only self-explanatory.

What holds then an honest and open-minded seeker for truth from admitting the divine source of Islam?

Does it seem too much for the "rational" and "scientific" mind to accept the concept of divine revelation?

It would perhaps be plausible if those who denied Muhammad's truthfulness were all athiests, since divine revelation in their view is all superstition. It is hardly plausible to see devout Jewish or Christian orientalists and missionaries, whose own faith is based on divine revelation, trying by all means to dismiss the desert dweller's claim of prophethood, although his life and character leave no reason to doubt his sincerity and truthfulness.

Might it not be better for humanity to turn to its loving Creator, receive His universal message to it, with no prejudice or cynicism, to reflect on it, and implement it in man's life? Could that bring about unity, happiness, and peace to our conflict-torn world?

Chapter V

THE SECRETARIAT
OF THE UNLETTERED
PROPHET

M.M. Azami

Dr. M. M. Azami is a professor of hadith at the University of Imam Muhammad Ibn Sa'ud, Riyadh, Saudi Arabia. Among his renowned works are *Studies in Hadith Methodology and Literature* and *Studies in Early Hadith Literature*, both published by American Trust Publications. The present article was originally published in Arabic under the title *Kuttab an-Nabi* and was rendered into English by Mohi el-Din Saleh. Mohi has taught at Riyadh University and besides his work at the Islamic Teaching Center, Plainfield, is currently teaching at the Indiana-Purdue University, Indianapolis.

The Art of Writing in the Arab Peninsula in Early Islam

The Arabs recognized the importance of the art of writing in the pre-Islamic period. They considered it one of the three basic traits for the perfect man. Said Ibn Sa'd: "The perfect one among them in the pre-Islamic period, as well as in early Islam, was the one who knew how to write in Arabic and was adept in swimming as well as archery."[1]

They disdained certain occupations. Nevertheless, teaching was accorded a higher status, and the most noble among them worked as teachers in the pre-Islamic period as well as in early Islam.[2]

That the pre-Islamic Arabs knew the importance of writing is hardly surprising. Whether they knew its application is rather doubtful. One may say that they were not in need of writing in their every-day life and thus, the number of people who knew the art of reading or writing was very small. It is said "when Islam appeared there were

---

[1]Ibn Sa'd, *at-Tabaqat al-Kubra*, Volume 3, p. 542, edited by Sakhaw, Leiden: 1904-1940 A.D.
[2]Al-Baghadadi, Ibn Habib, *al-Mihbar*, pp. 475, 477, Haydarabad: 1361 A.H./1941 A.D.

seventeen men among the Quraysh who were able to write."[3] Al-Waqidi mentions eleven people in Madinah who were able to write. We cannot take this figure to be accurate, especially if we consider the geographical and commercial location of Makkah and its religious position. The fact, however, remains that ignorance of the written word was predominant in the Arabian peninsula at that time, for the society was described in the Qur'an as composed of unlettered people, to whom an unlettered Prophet, upon whom be peace, was sent for guidance:

"It is He who has sent among the unlettered ones a messenger of their own, to recite unto them His revelations." (62:2) "So believe in Allah and His messenger, the Prophet who can neither read nor write, who believes in Allah and His words and follow him that haply you may be led aright." (7:158).

The Prophet, upon whom be peace, himself described the Islamic society of those early days in these words: "Indeed, we are an unlettered community. We do not write, and we do not employ arithmetic. . ."[4]

It was thus no accident that the first word of the revelation was *iqra'* (read). "Read! In the name of your Lord who created. Created man from a clot. Read! And your Lord is the Most Bounteous, Who taught by the pen. . ." (96:1-4).

As the divine message unfolded itself, the opposition intensified and the Prophet accompanied by his companions migrated to Madinah. His emigration ushered in a new era in Islamic history. Islam eventually established itself though in the small geographical confine of a city, yet it provided a very potent manifestation of itself in its totality. Within a year of his arrival in Madinah, he called for writing down the famous scroll, i.e. "the constitution" of the new state as some researchers have called it. This scroll or constitution was written to organize the relations between the *Muhajireen* (emigrants) and the *Ansar* (the supporters) on one side and between the Muslims and the Jews on the other.[5]

The establishing of a state in Madinah by the Muslims called for an organizational as well as an administrative system.

In the following pages, we shall give a general idea about one aspect of the administrative organization; namely, the establishment of the secretariat at the time of the Prophet and the people who

---

[3]Al-Baladhuri, *Futuh al-Buldan*, pp. 660-661. See *al-'Iqd al-Farid*, Volume 4, p. 175. See also Ibn Qutaybah, Mukhtalaf al-Hadith, p. 287, ed. by 'Umar Anis al-Tabba'a, Beirut, Dar al-Nashr li-al-Jami'iyin, 1377 A.H./1957 A.D.

[4]Al-Bukhari, *al-Sawm* or Fasting, 13; Siyam, 15; *Musnad Ibn Hanbal 2*, p. 122, first edition, Cairo: 1313A.H./1893 A.D.

[5]Hamidullah, Muhammad, *Al-Watha'iq al-Siyasiyyah*, Document number 1, third edition, Beirut: Dar al-Irshad, 1389 A.H.

made it happen.

We have mentioned before that in the incipient phase of Islam, the number of people who knew the art of writing was few; yet, with the initiation of the Prophet's educational policy, literacy spread in such a short time that the number of secretaries who wrote on behalf of the Prophet, upon whom be peace, rose to fifty. Based on the sources available to us, we can draw a general outline for the writing or administrative activity at the time of the Prophet.

Diwans or Administrative Offices
(Permanent Secretariat) at the Time of the Prophet

Diwan is the name of the place where scribes sit. *Diwan* also means a collection of written pages, a copybook in which names of men serving in the army are recorded as well as names of the donors who give donations.[7]

Apparently there were three types of *diwans* in the early period of Islam:

- *Diwan* or the institution of composition.
- *Diwan* of the army.
- *Diwan of Kharaj* or the land tax or the documentation of what enters the treasury, and what was to be allocated to each Muslim.

It is generally known that 'Umar Ibn al-Khattab established these *diwans* or institutions. Abu Hilal al-'Askariy said: "The first man to utilize the *diwan* was 'Umar."[8] As for the institution of composition, al-Qalqashandi said: "It was the first institution to be established in Islam. It was founded in the Prophet's time."[9] And as for the institution of the army he said: "The first to found and organize it was the commander of the believers 'Umar Ibn al-Khattab (Allah be pleased with him) during his caliphate."[10]

Said Abu Yusuf: "The people burnt the *diwan* and as such it has become unknown." He added: "Some old learned men of Madinah are reported to have found in the *diwan* that 'Umar (Allah be pleased with him) confiscated the properties of Kisra (Khusru), his family and of everybody who had fled from the land."[11]

Hasan Ibrahim Hasan said the following about the institution of

---

[6]Al-Qalqashandi, *Subh al-A'sha*, Volume 1, p. 89, Cairo: Ministry of Culture and Public Guidance, 1383 A.H./1963 A.D.

[7]Ibn Manzur, *Lisan al-'Arab*, Al-Ifriqi, the root "doon."

[8]Al-'Askariy, Abu Hilal, *al-Awa'il*, p. 133, ed. by al-Walkil, Muhammad al-Sayyid, Tangier: Dar al-Amal, n.d.

[9]Al-Qalqashandi, *Subh al-A'sha*, Volume 1, p. 91, Cairo: Ministry of Culture and Public Guidance, 1383 A.H./1963 A.D.

[10]Ibid, Volume 1, p. 91.

[11]Hasan, Ibrahim Hasan and Hasan, 'Ali Ibrahim, *al-Nuzum al-Islamiyyah*, p. 170 third edition, Egypt: 1962.

Kharaj: "Umar Ibn al-Khattab started the *diwan* system on the advice of a Persian prince after the extension of Islam." Further he said: " 'Umar adopted the *diwan* system from the Persians. He established the *diwan* for the army to register the soldiers. . . and the *diwan* for *kharaj* (or levying tax) to register what goes to the treasury and what was to be allocated for each Muslim."[12]

But this calls for reconsideration of the issue. It seems that in their simple form the *diwans* were used at the time of the Prophet and when 'Umar received the caliphate and the Islamic state expanded, it became necessary to further develop the administrative system. 'Umar ordered the reorganization of the *diwans* on "a more comprehensive basis." This is corroborated by the fact that the institution of composition, as already stated by al-Qalqashandi, was the first to be established in the history of Islam by the Prophet himself. Concerning the institution of *diwan* in the army, it is stated in the *Sahih al-Bukhari* ". . . Hudhaifah (Allah be pleased with him) narrated that the Prophet, upon whom be peace, said: 'Write down for me every person who has proclaimed the *shahadah*. We wrote down for him the names of one thousand five-hundred men.' "

What makes one feel that the early Muslims used to write down (the names) of those who had to go out for the military expeditions is from a report in *Bukhari's Sahih* "...Ibn 'Abbas narrated that he heard the Prophet, upon whom be peace, saying: 'No man should be alone with a woman. No woman should travel unless with a *mahram*.' A man stood up and said: 'O Messenger of God, I have enrolled myself for the expedition and my wife has set out for hajj'. . ." It is, therefore, understood that they registered every man who was willing to go for *jihad*. This (kind of registration) might be called the *diwan* or the core for such a *diwan*.

As for the institution of *kharaj* or levying tax, there were among the secretaries of the Prophet, as we shall soon see, some who (registered) the Prophet's booties. These booties were actually the state's sources of income at that time, and their record was maintained. If we cannot call this the institution of *kharaj*, at least it can be considered as the beginning of what later became the *diwan* of *kharaj*.

The reported advice of the Persian prince on establishing the *diwans* must be carefully examined since the writing system was already known to the Muslims and was used to record all matters. Books and leafs were also known in the Prophet's time. The *diwan* was nothing but a book in which the names of the soldiers were recorded. In light of this information, the issue of importing the system from the Persians appears doubtful.

---

[12]Abu Yusuf, *al-Kharaj*, p. 57.

The Permanent Secretary and His Functions

If we look at the secretaries from the viewpoint of their competence, we will find that there were certain people who wrote down the Qur'an.[13] In addition to this, there was another group of secretaries who specialized in the secretarial affairs of the state.

Among the secretaries were some who wrote letters to the kings, such as Zayd Ibn Thabit; there were others who wrote the treaties, such as 'Ali Ibn Abi Talib; a few who wrote the needs of the Prophet, such as al-Mughirah Ibn Shu'bah; while some recorded the debts and contracts among the people, such as 'Abdullah Ibn al-Arqam and others. There were also others who registered the booties of the Prophet, upon whom be peace, such as Kamm'uiyqieb Ibn Abi Fatimah ad-Dawsi. And there were still others who wrote down the estimated amount of the dates in Hijaz, such as Hudhaifah Ibn al-Yaman. There was also a man named Handhalah *al-Katib* or Handhalah the secretary, who used to substitute for any of the Prophet's secretaries on leave. The title *katib* became a part of his name.[14]

Translation Department

It is narrated on the authority of Hassan Ibn Thabit: "The Prophet upon whom be peace, said to me: 'I write to people and I fear that they might add or drop something, so learn the Syrian language.' I learned it in 17 days.[15] Thereafter, I wrote to the Jews and I read for him (the Prophet) when they wrote to him."[16]

Some Systems used in Letter Writing or The Correspondence System

Al-Jahshiyari mentioned that the Prophet, upon whom be peace, ordered Handhalah Ibn ar-Rabi' Ibn al-Muraqi al-Katib (the secretary) to stay beside him and to remind him of things after the third day. Does this story mean that the Prophet, upon whom be peace, ordered his secretaries to reply to the letters within three days? This might not be unlikely. The Prophet, upon whom be peace, wanted Handhalah to remind him of the urgent matters so that they might be taken care of in time. This suggests that there were many matters which occupied the Prophet's mind and that he was careful enough not to postpone them for more than three days.

---

[13]Ibn Hajar, *Fath al-Bari Sharh Sahih al-Bukhari*, Volume 9, p. 22; Musnad Ibn Hanbal, Volume 6, p. 250; al-Masahif, Volume 3. Egypt: al-Matba'a al-Salafiyyah, 1380 A.H./1960 A.D.

[14]Al-Jahshyari, *al-Wazara' wa al-Kuttab*, (The Vizirs and the Secretaries), pp. 12, 13, ed. by al-Saqqa, Mustafa and others, first edition, Cairo: 1357 A.H./1937 A.D.

[15]Ibn Hajar, *al-Isaban fi Tamyiz al-Sahabah*, first edition, Volume 1, p. 561, Egypt: Matba'at al-Sa'dah, 1328 A.H./1908 A.D.

[16]Al-Bukhari, *al-Tarikh al-Kabir*, Volume 2/1, p. 381, Haydarabad: 1361 A.H./1941 A.D.

Office of the Secretariat

Was there a special place for the secretaries? It is not easy to answer this question one way or the other. But most probably there was a special place for writing down the Qur'an, and possibly for state correspondence too. Ibn 'Abbas is reported to have said: "The *Masahif* (i.e. the copies of the Qur'an) were not sold. The (man) would come with a scroll to the Prophet, upon whom be peace, and would stand and anticipate God's reward in the hereafter and write. After that another man would stand and write until the copy of the Qur'an was written to the end."[17] Hence, it is very likely that there was a special place in the Prophet's court for copying the Qur'an. This place might well have been used for correspondence as well.

Writing of Drafts

Ibn al-Qasim narrated on the authority of Malik that he (Malik) said: "It came down to me that the Prophet, upon whom be peace, received a letter. He asked (those gathered around him): 'Who would answer this letter for me (or on my behalf)?' 'Abdullah Ibn al-Arqam said: 'I will.' Ibn al-Arqam wrote the answer and brought it back to the Prophet who was pleased with it and dispatched it."[18]

In light of this text we can say: the secretaries used to write first, then they would show the Prophet what they had written to get his approval. It is obvious that he would change, replace or agree with what had been written. The letter would not have its final form until the Prophet, upon whom be peace, agreed with it. This kind of work could be labeled as the writing of the drafts in case the Prophet was not dictating the answer himself.

Recording the Letter and Keeping a Copy

There is no evidence that the secretaries recorded the outgoing mail, or that they retained the copies. But there are some indications that some of the correspondence, if not all, was recorded.

First, the word *naskh* (recording) was known to the Arabs in the pre-Islamic period. Allah said in the Qur'an: "Lo! We have caused (all) that ye did to be recorded." (45:29) In the dictionary of *Lisan Al-'Arab*, the word *naskh* (recording) means to copy a book letter by letter.[19] The peace treaty of al-Hudaybiyah was documented in two copies. The Prophet, upon whom be peace, took one copy and Suhayl Ibn Mada' took

[17]Al-Bayhaqi, *al-Sunan al-Kubra*, Volume 6, p. 16, Haydarabad: 1344 A.H./1924 A.D.
[18]Ibn Hadida al-Ansari, Muhammad Ibn Ahamd Ibn 'Abd ar-Rahman, *al-Misbah al-Mudi' fi Kuttab al-Nabi al-Umiyy wa Rusulihi Ila Muluk al-'Ard min 'Arabi wa 'Ajami*, 31 ab. Manuscript #20, Library of Makkah, Makkah al-Mukarramah.
[19]Al-Ifriqi, Ibn Manzur, *Lisan al-'Arabi*, the root *nasakh*.

the other one. Al-Waqidi says: "When the peace treaty was finalized Suhayl said: 'The peace treaty is to be kept with me.' The Prophet said: 'No, I will keep it,' and they disagreed about that matter. Thereupon, a copy was written for Suhayl. The Prophet, upon whom be peace, took the first and Suhayl took the other."[20]

'Abdullah Ibn 'Amr Ibn al-'Aas said: "The first letter I wrote was the Prophet's letter to the people of Makkah."[21] It is evident that he made a copy of the Prophet's peace treaty of al-Hudaybiyah because 'Abdullah Ibn 'Amr Ibn al-'Aas was not among the secretaries who wrote down the treaty. He must have copied it from the original which was in the possession of the Prophet or he might have copied it from one of the companions. However, this incident bears upon the fact that the official documents were well preserved..

Copies of the Prophet's letters to the different regions were kept by some of the companions, such as Ibn 'Abbas, who kept many copies of the Prophet's letters,[22] Abu Bakr Ibn Hazm[23] and 'Urwah Ibn az-Zubayr.

In the light of this information, we can say that they made copies of the Prophet's letters dispatched to the different regions. The letters, together with their copies, were kept in the general administration department because it was not possible for anybody to collect the dispatched letters of the Prophet, upon whom be peace, unless there was a copy of each letter kept by the companions.

Likewise, Abu Bakr as-Siddiq had the Prophet's register for the charities. [24] 'Umar Ibn al-Khattab used to keep all the treaties and pacts held with notable men.[25]

It was because of such traditions of recordkeeping that within a quarter of a century after the death of the Prophet, upon whom be peace, the *bayt al-qaratis* or the archive was established in the city of Madinah. This archive was apparently next to the house of 'Uthman Ibn 'Affan.[26]

We may call this archive the permanent secretariat of the Islamic state.

---

[20]Al-Waqidi, *al-Maghazi*, p. 612, ed. by Masdin Johns, Oxford University Press, 1966 A.D./1379 A.H.

[21]Al-Kittani, *at-Taratib al-Idariyyah*, Volume 2, p. 244. Rabat: 1346-1349 A.H./1926-1929 A.D.

[22]Az-Zayla'i, *Nasb ar-Rayah*, Volume 4, p. 420 - 2nd edition, Beirut: al-Maktab al-Islami wa al-Majlis al-'Ilmi, 1393 A.H./1973 A.D.

[23]Al-Qudsi, Ibn Tulun, *A'laam al-Sa'ilin 'an Kutub Sayyid al-Mursaliin, Damascus.*

[24]For the details see *al-Watha'iq as-Siyasiyyah*, B104, C104.

[25]Al-Maqrizi, *Khutat al-Maqrizi*, Volume 1, p. 295, Cairo: Matba'at Bulaq, 1270 A.H./1850 A.D.

[26]Al-Baladhuri, *Ansab al-Ashraf*, Volume 1, p. 22 - ed. by Hamidullah, Muhammad, *Tarikh at-Tabari*, Volume 2, p. 790, The European edition.

STYLE OF LETTER WRITING

Introduction

The letters of the Prophet, upon whom be peace, began with *Bism Allah ar-Rahman ar-Rahim.* Ash-Sha'bi reports that writing the words "Bism Allah" at the beginning of the letters underwent several alterations.

Said Ibn Sa'd: "Al-Haytham Ibn 'Ady related to us that Mujahid b. Sa'id and Zakariyya b. Zaida reported to him on the authority of ash-Sha'bi that Allah's Messenger, upon whom be peace, used to write 'Bismika Allahumma' as the Quraysh did until the 'ayah 'embark on the ark, in the name of God, whether it moves or be at rest' (11:41) was revealed to him, upon whom be peace, that he began to write: 'In the name of God.' (He used this form) until this 'ayah: 'Say: Call upon God, or call upon Rahman.' (17:110). Then he wrote 'Bism Allah ar-Rahman' until the 'ayah 'It is from Solomon, and is (as follows): 'In the name of God, Most Gracious, Most Merciful.' (27:30), that he wrote 'Bism Allah ar-Rahman ar-Rahim.' i.e. 'In the name of God, Most Gracious, Most Merciful.' "[27]

This narration is weak. Al-Haytham Ibn 'Adiy used to lie[28] and, therefore, it should not be taken into consideration.

Heading

The secretaries of the Prophet used to give his esteemed name precedence over the name of the addressee.[29] It was an ancient custom, except in rare cases,[30] to start the letter with the name of the greater and nobler person; therefore, when the companions wrote to the Prophet they started first with his name: "To Muhammad, the Messenger of God."

Ibn Hajar said: "Ahmad and Abu Da'ud made the extraction that al-'Ala b. al-Hadrami wrote a letter to the Prophet, upon whom be peace, beginning it with his name."Ibn Hajar also mentioned that the son of 'Umar wrote to Mu'awiyyah and began the letter with his name. "According to al-Bazzaz on the weak authority of Handhala, the secretary, the Prophet, upon whom be peace, sent 'Ali and Khalid Ibn al-Walid on a mission. Khalid wrote to the Prophet beginning with his name, while 'Ali, upon writing to the Prophet, began his letter with the

---

[27]*At-Tabaqat*, Volume 1, pp. 263-64. See also *Sunan Abi Da'ud*, Volume 1, p. 291. See also Abu 'Ubayd, *Fada'il al-Qur'an*, pp. 51-52.

[28]Al-Dhahabi, *Mizan al-'Itidal*, Volume 4, p. 324, *Biography of al-Haytham Ibn 'Adiy*. Ed. by al-Bajawi, Cairo: 1382 A.H./1963 A.D.

[29]See any document from *al-Watha'iq as-Siyasiyyah* (The Political Documents) by Dr. Muhammad Hamidullah. See for instance the Prophet's letter to an-Najashi.

[30]See for instance: *Musnad Ibn Hanbal*, Volume 4, p. 339.

name of the Prophet. The Prophet blamed neither of them."[31]

Separation Between the Contents

Al-Bukhari said: "Rauh Ibn 'Abd al-Mu'min narrated to us and said: Abu Usamah narrated to us on the authority of Hisham Ibn 'Urwah who said. 'I saw some letters of the Prophet, upon whom be peace. Whenever a story (theme) was over, he said *amma ba'd* (i.e. now to our topic).' "[32]

Name of the Secretary

The secretary often used to mention his name at the end of the letter. Sometimes he also mentioned the names of the witnesses.[33]

Seal Imprint of the Letter

Contrary to today's practice of signing the documents in order to make them official, in ancient times, the documents were affixed with a seal.

The usage of seals instead of signatures, however, goes back to Japan and China, several centuries before Christ. In the West, the seal is still used instead of the signatures of kings, governors, and others.[34]

The Prophet, upon whom be peace, began using a seal when he wanted to write to some non-Arabs. He was informed that the Persians do not read an unsealed letter.[35] Thereupon, the Prophet made for himself a silver signet ring with the engraving "Muhammad, the Messenger of Allah."[36] As the signet ring was a seal of the state, the Messenger of God allowed no one to make another signet ring similar to it.[37] Sometimes when he did not have the signet ring with him, he stamped (the letter) with his fingernail.[38]

Dating the Letters

Were the letters dated or not? And more explicitly, did the Messenger of Allah put dates on letters? There is no doubt that his letters generally were not dated, though there were a few documents in

---

[31]Al-Bukhari, *Sahih al-Bukhari ma'a (with) Fath al-Bari*, Volume 8, p. 223, Cairo: al-Maktabah al-Salafiyyah, 1380 A.H./1960 A.D.

[32]Al-Bukhari, *al-Adab al-Mufrad,* Volume 2, p. 559 with the interpretation of Fadl Allah al-Samad. Fadl Allah al-Jilani, Hims: 1388 A.H., Encyclopedia Britannica.

[33]See *al-Wath'iq as-Siyasiyyah* (The Political Documents), Nos. 34, 41, 44 and 124.

[34]See *Encyclopedia Britanica,* article SEAL.

[35]Al-Bukhari, al-libas 25; Ibn Sa'd, *at-Tabaqat,* Volume 1, pg. 471.

[36]Al-Bukhari, (The Political Documents). See the photograph of the document number 58 because it supports this statement.

[37]Al-libas 54; Ibn Sa'd, *at-Tabaqat,* Volume 1, p. 472.

[38]Al-Isabah, Volume 2, p. 431; al-Waqidi, *Al-Maghazi,* 1028, ed. by Masdin Johns, Oxford University Press, 1969 A.D./1379 A.H.

which only the year was mentioned. In the Prophet's treaty with the people of Miqna in document 33 of *The Political Documents* by Muhammad Hamidullah, the words "...and 'Ali the son of Abu Talib wrote in the year 9 A.H."[39] were used.

Ibn Fadl Allah al-'Umari said that he saw the letter of the Prophet, upon whom be peace, to Tamim ad-Dari. This letter was written in the year 9 A.H.[40]

As-Suyuti said: "In one of the al-'Imad's collections, I saw in his handwriting that Ibn as-Salah said: 'I was acquainted with a book of Abu Tahir Muhammad Ibn Mahmash az-Ziyadi in which he mentioned that Allah's Messenger, upon whom be peace, dated his letter a Hijri date to the Christians of Najran and ordered 'Ali to write (the date) in the fifth year after Hijrah. So the one who started dating with the Hijrah was Allah's Messenger, upon whom be peace, and 'Umar followed him in this (matter).' "[41]

Ibn 'Asakir quoted Ibn Shihab: "The Prophet, upon whom be peace, ordered the chronological historiography the day he came to Madinah in the month of Rabi' al-Awwal."[42]

Al-Qalqashandi said: "Abu Ja'far an-Nahhas narrated in (his book) *Sina 'at al-Kuttab* or the Profession of the Secretaries on the authority of Muhammad Ibn Jarir who heard it from Ibn Shihab that when the Prophet came to Madinah—he arrived there in the month of Rabi' al-Awwal—he ordered the chronological style of writing. Thus, the beginning of the Islamic historiography took place in the year of Hijrah[43] and not by an administrative decree of 'Umar during his caliphate, as is commonly held among the scholars.

Ash-Sha'bi said: "Abu Musa wrote to 'Umar consulting him about the undated letters they used to receive. 'Umar gave orders that they should make their chronological historiography with the hijrah of the Prophet, upon whom be peace."[44]

In his book *al-Awa'il,* al-'Askariy mentioned that Abu Musa al-Ash'ari wrote to 'Umar Ibn al-Khattab saying: "We receive letters from the Commander of the Faithful. We do not know how to follow your instructions. Some of them require implementation in Sha'ban. We do

---

[39]Al-Baladhuri, *Futuh al-Buldan*, document no. 33, ed. by 'Umar Anis al-Tabbaa', Beirut, Dar al-Nashr li-al-Jami'iyin, 1377 A.H./1959 A.D.

[40]Al-Munjid, Salah ad-Din, *Tarikh al-Khat al-'Arabi (The History of Arabic Calligraphy)*, pp. 173-75, quoted from *Al-Masalik wa al-Mamalik*.

[41]As-Suyuti, *Ash-Shamarikh fi 'Ilm at-Tarikh*, p. 51; included in the epistles collection of as-Suyuti, Edition of India.

[42]Ibid., pp. 50-51.

[43]Al-Qalqashandi, *Subh al-A'sha*, Volume 6, p. 240, Cairo: Ministry of Culture and Public Guidance, 1383 A.H./1963 A.D.

[44]*Ibn Khayyat, Tarikh Khalifah Ibn Khayyat*, Volume 1, p. 8, ed. by Zakkaar, Suhayl, Damascus: 1968. See also al-Bukhari, at-Tarikh as-Saghir, p. 9.

not know whether they should be implemented in the last or in the coming Sha'ban. 'Umar thereupon originated the chronological historiography."[45]

"Al-Hakim in his book *al-Iklil* transmitted on the authority of Ibn Jurayj, on the authority of Abu Salmah, on the authority of Ibn Shihab az-Zuhriy that when the Prophet, upon whom be peace, came to Madinah he asked Abu Salmah to write the date and he dated it Rabi' al-Awwal. This has caused controversy because the contrary is held, as it will be later explained, that the chronological style of writing was initiated in the time of 'Umar."[46] It is narrated that Sahl the son of Sa'd said: "They did not count from the date of the Prophet's mission nor from the day of his death. They counted only from the day of his arrival in Madinah."[47]

Al-Qalqashandi mentioned another narration that when the companions were faced with the problem of the chronological style of writing they said: "We have to learn this from the Persians; therefore, 'Umar brought al-Hurmuzan. He replied: 'We have a calculation system called *mahruz* which means the calculation of months and days.' Thereupon, 'Umar made the chronological style of writing."[48]

Evidently, al-Hurmuzan's story was dragged in for no reason because days, months and years were known to the Arabs, as indicated by the Qur'an. Moreover, the Arabs used the chronological style of historiography in the pre-Islamic period. They had no stable system for historiography; and therefore, they wrote history according to any serious event.[49]

Some of the Arabs dated from the day of the fall of *Sala'*, which is evident from an inscription found on the door of the Church of Bahran al-Luja in the northern region of the Duruz mountains. This engraved inscription was written in 463 A.D., one year after the collapse of Khaybar.[51]

Before the Prophet's mission, the Arabs dated from the Year of the Elephant,[52] and therefore, there is no good reason to attribute the

---

[45]Al-Qalqashandi, *Subh al A'sha*, Volume 6, pp. 240-41. Cairo: Ministry of Culture and Public Guidance, 1383 A.H./1963 A.D.

[46]*Fath al-Bari*, Volume 7, p. 267.

[47]Al-Bukhari, *Manaqib al-Ansar*, p. 48. See the details and the rest of the sayings in *Fath al-Bari*, Volume 7, pp. 267-69.

[48]*Subh al-A'sha*, Volume 6, p. 241.

[49]Ali Jawad, *Tarikh al-Arab Qabl al-Islam* (Pre-Islamic History of the Arabs), Volume 1, pp. 44-53, Arabic Translation.

[50]Al-Asad, Nasir al-Din, *Masadir al-Shi'r al-Jahili*, p. 29, 2nd edition, Cairo: Dar al-Ma'arif, 1962.

[51]*Op. Cit.*, p. 29. Notice that the Gregorian calendar is not used. For the Gregorian calendar see Barzun, J. and H.F. Graff, *The Modern Researcher*, p. 118.

[52]*Subh al-A'sha*, Volume 6, p. 239.

Islamic Calendar to al-Hurmuzan because the Arabs used to date in the pre-Islamic period. After the advent of Islam the Prophet began to date his letters, especially in the Madani era, but the usage of the chronological style of writing in general was not common. During the Caliphate of 'Umar the need for historiography was felt, and the practice began to take root. The emigration of the Prophet became the starting point.

Enveloping Letters

It appears that the Prophet, upon whom be peace, had sent some letters in envelopes or that he had put his seal on the back of the letter in such a manner that it became covered. The Messenger of God sent 'Amr Ibn al-'Aas to Jaifer and 'Abd the sons of al-Jalandi. 'Amr met 'Abd who referred him to his brother Jaifar. Said 'Amr Ibn al-'Aas: ". . .I dropped in on him and gave him a sealed letter. He opened the seal and read it."[53] From this we can conclude that the letters were put in an envelope.

In conclusion it can be said that the Prophet himself established the secretariat; he also laid down the foundation for the regular army and the receipt of *kharaj* (tax) as well as a special department of translation to render foreign languages into Arabic and vice versa. The work in the secretariat was well organized and was assigned to specialists only.

The following companions served as secretaries for the Prophet at different times:
'Aban b. Sa'id b. al-'Aas
Abu Amamah As'ad b. Zararah b. 'Adas
Abu Ayyub al-Ansari
Abu Bakr as-Siddiq
Abu Hudhayfah b. 'Utbah b. Rabi'
Abu Sufyan
Abu Salamah 'Abdullah b. 'Abd al-Asad
Abu 'Abs b. Jabr b. 'Amr b. Zaid
Ubayy b. Ka'b
Al-Arqam b. Abi al-Arqam 'Abd-Manaf
Usaid b. al-Hudhair b. Sammak
'Aus b. Khoali b. 'Abdullah
Buraidah b. al-Hasib b. 'Abdullah
Bashir b. Sa'd b. Thalbah b. Khalas
Thabit b. Qays b. Shammas
Ja'far b. Abi Talib
Jahm b. Sa'd

---

[53]Ibn Sa'd, *at-Tabaqat al-Kubra*, Volume 1, p. 662, ed. by Sakhaw, Leiden: 1904-1940 A.D.

Juhaim b. al-Sal-t b. Makhramah

Hatib b. 'Amr b. 'Abd-Shams

Hudhayfah b. al-Yaman al-'Absi

Al-Hasain b. Numair

Handhalah b. al-Rabi'e b. Saifiy

Huwaitab b. 'Abd al-Uzza b. Abi Qays

Khalid b. Sa'id al-'Aas b. Umayyah

Al-Zubayr b. al-'Awwam

Zayd b. Arqam b. Zayd b. Qays

Zayd b. Thabit

As-Sijil

Sa'd b. al-Rabbiyyah b. 'Amr al-Ansari

Sa'd b. 'Ubadah b.Dulaim

Sa'id b. Sa'id b. al-'Aas

Sharhabil b. Hasanah

Talhah b. 'Ubaidullah b. 'Uthman

'Amir b. Fuhairah

Al-'Abbas

'Abdullah b. al-Arqam b. 'Abd Yaghuth

'Abdullah b. Abi Bakr as-Siddiq

'Abdullah b. Khatil 'Abd al-'Uzza b. Khatil

'Abdullah b. Rawahah b. Tha'Ibah b. Imri al-Qays

'Abdullah b. Zayd b. 'Abd Rabah al-Ansari

'Abdullah b. Sa'd b. Abi Sarh b. al-Harith

'Abdullah b. 'Abdullah b. Ubayy b. Salul

'Abdullah b. 'Amr b. al-'Aas

'Uthman b. 'Affan b. Abi al-'Aas

'Uqbah

Al-'Ala b. al-Hadrami

Al-'Ala b. 'Uqbah

'Ali b. Abi Talib b. 'Abd al-Muttalib

'Umar b. Al-Khattab b. Nufail

'Amr b. al-'Aas

Muhammad b. Musallamah b. Salamah al- Ansari

Mu'adh b. Jabal al-Khazaraji

Mu'awiyyah b. Abu Sufyan

Ma'n b. 'Adiy b. al-Jadd b. al-'Ajlan

Mu'aiqib b. Abi Fatimah ad-Dusi

Al-Mughairah b. Sh'ubah b. Abi 'Amir

Al-Mundhir b. 'Amr b. Khunais

Muhajir b. Abi. Ummayyah b. al-Mughairah

Nasrani min al-Ansar

Yazid b. Abi Sufyan

Khalid b. al-Walid b. al-Mughairah

Chapter VI

ISLAM
AND
HUMANITY

Hammudah 'Abdalati

Dr. Hammudah 'Abdalati (1928-1976) taught sociology at Utica College of Syracuse University as associate professor. His *Islam in Focus* and *The Family Structure of Islam*, both published by American Trust Publications, are popular works. The present article was first published by *al-ittihad* in its Muharram 1391/March 1971 issue.

The thesis of this discussion is that Islam and humanity have common grounds, and that the essence of both is responsibility and commitment. I shall try to expound this thesis as far as possible.

Islam has been defined in many ways. My chosen definition is that Islam designates submission to the good, benevolent will of God, and obedience to His law. This definition captures the essence of Islam, which is a deep, profound internal commitment of the individual Muslim. This internal commitment is, however, valid only when it is supported by external manifestations, by actual fulfillment of duty, and by dynamic interest in that to which one is committed. Here faith and action join together to integrate the personality of the individual and make his life meaningful. Clearly , there is no viable faith without some purposeful action to reinforce it, nor can there be any meaningful action of perpetual significance without faith. Clearly, too, whenever the word faith is mentioned in any Islamic context, it is always accompanied, either directly or indirectly, by the word action. The two are as inseparable in Islam as they are in reality.

The essence of Islam, then, is an internal commitment reinforced by external manifestations. But how can man commit himself? Can he commit himself? And if he can, should he do so? To what, and why should he make any commitment? It is no exaggeration to say that commitment is the equivalent of life, because to live is to be committed and life would be unthinkable without commitment of some kind.

At face value, the word commitment may imply compulsion and deny the existence of any choice for man. But this is not the case. We are not born with responsibilities and commitments. We learn, as we grow up and run our life cycle, how and when to commit ourselves. Some people commit themselves to professions, others to business still others to the service of humanity, and so on. But within every area, there is a very wide range of choice. And we say, for example, that so and so is committed, or has committed himself, or is going to commit himself to such and such. This sense of commitment is not something we are born with or that we always like; rather, it is something that we learn to make. Commitment, in essence, then implies some choice by man, the existence of alternatives to choose from, choosing one or more of such alternatives to hold dear and binding.

One may ask: does Islam make room for choice and freedom? We cannot go here into the complex problems of freedom and determinism of the scientists, or free will and predestination of the theologians—problems that have puzzled the scientists and the theologians of all ages. But it should be maintained that in Islam man is free to choose his course of faith and action. This freedom cannot be absolute any more than it can be absolutely denied. It is a freedom that is relative and proportionate to man's capacity, to his nature, and to his responsibility. To advocate absolute freedom is irresponsible and unthinkable, but to deny it completely is inhuman and erroneous.

History shows that in every age there are various religions and courses of life and that people choose from among these, each according to his inclinations and circumstances. But not every choice is the best choice, nor is every commitment the right one. People do make mistakes and do not always fulfill their commitment, especially in the area of religion. And this is why God has always come to man's aid. The best choice in religion is, of course, Islam, and the most rewarding work is a true commitment to Islam; for, as God has said in the Holy Qur'an: "Surely, the true religion with God is Islam.[1] And among the last verses of revelations was this: "Now have I perfected your religion for you, completed My favor unto you, and have chosen for you as religion, al-Islam."[2]

But let us not be overtaken by vanity and momentary joy. Let us remember that Islam did not exactly begin with Muhammad, upon him be peace, in sixth century Arabia. Nor was Islam addressed to the Arabs as a racial or national faith. Let us be assured that Islam is the essence of all divine religions and is the mission of all prophets from

---

[1] The Qur'an 3:19.
[2] Ibid. 5:3.

'Adam to Muhammad, upon them be peace. It is the universal call
directed to all men of all times and places without discrimination. The
Arabs were called upon to raise the banner of Islam not because they
were racially or culturally superior to their contemporaries, but in order
that they, too, might do their share of commitment to the religion of
God and make their contributions to humanity. It was precisely for this
reason that Muhammad sometimes felt distressed when he saw some
people turning their backs to the call of God. Righteous, and
concerned as he was, and knowing what Islam meant for humanity,
Muhammad believed and hoped that every man would naturally accept
Islam without reservation. But this did not come through, and
Muhammad like any other committed human being, experienced some
frustration. To overcome this frustration, God revealed to him verses
like these.

> "Had your Lord willed it, everyone on earth would have become a
> believer; do you think that you can force people to believe?"[3]

> "Had your Lord willed, He would have made all people one and
> the same nation! But they will remain differentiated."[4]

> "There is no compulsion in religion."[5]

The significance of this experience and of these revelations may be
briefly outlined as follows: No leader can afford to be indifferent to his
commitment and to those around him. On the other hand, he cannot
afford to be possessed by excessive enthusiasm about things beyond
his control, for this may well shatter his personality and destroy his
entire purpose. True, he is committed and responsible for his commitment. True, too, he must do his utmost to honor his commitment. But
we must remember that responsibility is proportionate to man's
capacity and potential. Between these two poles of indifference and
execessive enthusiasm, there is a very wide range for great actions and
achievements.

The fact that God has not made all people by the force of creation
identical in their faith, nationality, race, or color leaves for man some
work to do, some choice to make, something to desire. If God had
wanted them identical, He could have created them so, but that would
be the work of God only, and man would have no part in it, and would
not be held responsible for anything. Instead, God has created diverse
people and has offered them the chance to participate in the
shaping of history. He has created them differentiated so that they
might know one another, be free to choose their commitments, and be
responsible for their choice. This means that the business of the

---

[3]Ibid. 10:99.
[4]Ibid. 11:118.
[5]Ibid. 2:256.

committed people is unfinished and their responsibility never ceases. This, in turn, gives the committed a sense of continuity, a goal, and a dynamism of motivation.

Man is Neither a Deity
Nor is He Worthless

Turning to the second point of our discussion, we find that one of the most distressing and frustrating areas of human thought is that which deals with human nature and the meaning of life. There is the view advocated by some religions and philosophies that regard man as a worthless creature, doomed from birth to death and condemned from womb to tomb. At the other extreme, there is the humanistic philosophy that almost deifies man and generously confers on humanity every conceivable nobility. This would be highly reassuring and also gratifying if only it were true.

It is obvious that none of these extreme doctrines have been successful in tackling the acute problems of man or human nature. As Muslims, we should endeavor to understand the position of Islam with respect to these crucial problems. Such an understanding is extremely significant because it may help the Muslim to examine himself and explore his spiritual as well as his human resources, to review his philosophy of life and open before him new horizons and frontiers.

It has been contended by many thinkers that the unique quality of man is reason, that human nature is rational and knows how to adapt its means to the desired ends in an economical and pragmatic fashion. But human experience and scientific experimentation cast doubt on this contention and shows that reason is not the exclusive quality of man. Nor is human behavior always or even usually ratinal. In fact, the rationality of animals, birds, and even small insects does seem sometimes to deride the rationality of man.

In a desperate effort, some modern thinkers have tried to rescue man and reassure him of certain unique qualities. They assert that the most unique distinction of man is culture; only man possesses culture and only man is possessed by culture. This means that only man can *think* in abstract categories, *will* and behave *normatively*. In other words, man has great resources at his disposal, a tremendous capacity to conform or deviate from responsibilities to meet or neglect. Speaking Islamically, only man has been singled out by God as a responsible being, commissioned to perform certain tasks, accountable to his Creator, and capable of spiritual and moral excellence. This is something that only man can do. It is man alone who can understand the meaning of the remote past and the significance of the distant future beyond the immediate boundaries of his time and space. It is man alone who is responsible for such understanding and is capable thereof. The essence of human nature, then, is a quality of responsibility and commitment, a sense of meaningfulness and fulfillment. And it is here, at this level of responsibility and fulfillment, that the essence of Islam and the essence of humanity do converge and become indistinc: shable or nearly so.

Man's Potentials
Are Limited

At this point, we should try to see more clearly how Islam treats human nature and approaches human commitment. It is correct to generalize by saying that the Islamic position is, as always, marked with moderation, realistic appraisal, and logical consistency. Such are the underlying principles of the Islamic approach.

The Qur'an does not entertain the religio-philosophical doctrine which hopelessly underrates human nature. Nor would it endorse the humanistic dogma which arbitrarily and unreasonably overestimates the nature of man. The Qur'an states very clearly that man is created by God only for the service and worship of the Creator.[6] This is no oversimplification of the matter. It means that the *ultimate* goal of man is the manifestation of the excellent attributes of God. This applies, without an exception, to every man in every walk of life. Accordingly, there is no racial superiority or caste system and no room for the concept of the Chosen and the Gentile, the privileged and the doomed. With this sense of assured equality, man embarks upon life to play his role.

The role of man is no less and no more than that of God's vicegerent on earth.[7] Again, this is no joke or simple flattery. It is a role which binds man with commitments to fulfill and with responsibilities to meet. It is a demanding yet highly rewarding role, whereby the main objective of man is to implement the Law of God and serve His cause. This role commits man to great tasks, but at the same time, it confers on him yet greater honor and privileges. It takes into consideration the fact that God has honored man[8], and that he is trustworthy and capable of noble achievements.

Is man equipped with the needed assistance to play this role? The answer of Islam is in the affirmative. Man is well-provided with all the aid he needs to achieve the ultimate objective of his being. God has shown him the Right Way of life through the continued, self-reinforcing revelations and the continuing messengership of the prophets. God has extended to man a kind of recognition which gives him confidence and hope, strength and peace, security and guidance. God has also subjected to man everything that is in the heavens and on earth, that he

---

[6]Ibid. 51: 56-58.
[7]Ibid. 2: 28-34; also 6:156.
[8]Ibid. 17:70.

may know and be assured of God's aid.[9]

The spiritual and human resources of man are inexhaustible, and his spiritual growth can reach the highest standards, the standards of prophethood. We must remember that Muhammad was a man. He said time and again that he was only a mortal being, entrusted with the revelations of God.[10] Although Muhammad was the last prophet and the crowning glory of prophethood, the fact remains that he was a man. This is a tremendous credit to every man and an honorable recognition of human nature as capable of spiritual growth and moral excellence.

A major contributor to this spiritual growth is the Islamic principle of natural innocence, which means that every human being is born neutral, that is, on the *fitrah* of Islam or submission to God.

"So set your face for religion being upright, the nature made by Allah in which He created men. There is no altering Allah's creation. This is the straight way — but most people know not."[11]

This further means freedom from inherited or inborn sin. The stand of Islam here clears the human conscience and relieves the human mind of the burdensome worries of Original Sin. This freedom from inborn sin has far-reaching implications. It means that man starts his life on a clean basis and begins his responsible relationship with God in a way more assuring of God's love, justice and mercy. It means, moreover, that man is born free from sin and can remain so, if he so wills. In fact, it is his duty to stay clear and free from sin.

Islam looks to the individual as an essential unit in the community of believers. All believers are brothers to one another;[12] and as such, they form a solid unity in the service of God. It is a unity of purpose and being, a unity which derives from the unity of God, the unity of His religion, and the unity of mankind. Under this unity, all men are equal in the sight of God, and the only valid distinction between them is that of piety and deserved goodness.[13] Here every individual is personally and directly responsible to God for his explicit deeds as well as his most secret intent. Every person is assured of the fruits of his deeds, good or otherwise.[14]

In the view of Islam, man is a total being with a spiritual-material nature. This calls for the fulfillment of the spiritual as well as the material needs in a wholesome, well-balanced manner. Islam is not blind to the realities of human nature. It does not condemn the flesh or the carnal needs. Nor does it condone any neglect of the spiritual aspirations of man.

---

[9]Ibid. 45: 12-13.
[10]Ibid. 18: 110.
[11]Ibid. 30:30.
[12]Ibid. 49:10.
[13]Ibid. 49:13.
[14]Ibid. 99:6-8.

No one can claim that man is perfect and his nature incorruptible. Man has faults and his nature does display deficiencies. One of these is the tendency to plead innocent to any charge, to try to get away from commitments, to avoid responsibility, to blame one's shortcomings on circumstances or on other people. Sometimes a person blames his own nature and calls it wicked or weak to excuse himself and justify his misbehavior. Sometimes he blames his parents, his home environment, his own generation, or his entire society. This was very common in the past just as it is today, particularly in North America. Sometimes a person may even blame God for his own misdeeds. A typical case is recorded in the Qur'an where the unbelievers said:

"Had God willed it otherwise, neither we nor our parents would have worshipped anything beside Him.[15]

But does any of these excuses and rationalizations hold good? Does it exempt man from responsibility? Can it release him from his commitment? In answer to all this, Islam would voice an emphatic no. Man cannot blame his nature, for his nature is innocent, at least at birth, and it becomes what he makes of it. Nor can man categorically blame his environment and society, for every human being is individually responsible to God for himself and is given every opportunity to regain his identity, not to lose it in the crowd. Least of all can he blame God, for God is not a vicious sovereign, but a Loving, Just and Merciful God. Nor can man make excuses on account of his ignorance, for divine knowledge is available to all those who seek it, and God has revealed His will and His Commandments, leaving the implementation thereof up to man.

All this leaves man face-to-face with responsibilities to meet, with commitments to fulfill, with worthy goals to aspire to, and with tasks to perform. This is the essence of being a Muslim. It is also the essence of existence and of humanity. It is the meaning of life if that life is to be a constructive and meaningful one.

---

[15]Ibid. 16:35.

Chapter VII

SOME ECONOMIC ISSUES: REFLECTIONS AND ANSWERS

Shaikh Mahmud Ahmad
and M. Akram Khan

[God willing, the first decade of the 15th-century Hijrah will see a couple of Muslim states making serious attempts to reorder their economies in line with Islam.

In an age of rising expectations and the possibility to realize them, the economy of a nation has assumed an exaggerated importance. Exaggerated in the sense that economic indicators are not the only ones to suggest a nation's health. In a way, sound economic indicators may prognosticate a sick society.

An Islamic state does not promise an affluent society. Any such promise will be antithetical to its raison d'etre. Islam does, however, promise a state based on absolute justice and free from exploitation where man's humanity and his spiritual well being will be far more important than any other aspect of his existence. And if in fulfilling this mission, such a society is blessed materially and beyond, it will be a reward from Allah (The Qur'an 5:66).

The following symposium first appeared in *al-ittihad* of Jumada al-Thani 1401/April 1981 under the title of *Symposium on Islamic Economy*. Our respondents are Shaikh Mahmud Ahmad, Muhammad Akram Khan and Dr. Monzer Kahf. Shaikh Mahmud Ahmad is a retired joint secretary, Government of Pakistan, Muhammad Akram Khan is a deputy director of Foreign Audit Service, Foreign Office, Government of Pakistan.

About the format of the symposium, each question will be addressed first by Shaikh Mahmud Ahmad and then Muhammad Akram Khan. Monzer Kahf will address himself to the issue of a welfare state and an Islamic state following this question-answer format. The questions were formulated by M. Tariq Quraishi, editor *al-ittihad*.]

Q. The strength of the capitalistic economy lies in free enterprise; Islam also stands for free enterprise. In what sense will an Islamic economy be different from a capitalistic economy?

Shaikh Mahmud Ahmad

In the formulations of Adam Smith and of subsequent economists, free enterprise has been presented as the guarantee of fruitful functioning of the capitalist system. This concept has come under thickening clouds during this century, and in particular, after the Second World War. The governments have increasingly taken upon themselves the resolution of diverse contradictions which have manifested themselves on account of the exploitative role of loan-capital. The necessity of containing unemployment has forced governments to pursue expansionary fiscal and monetary policies, which have, in turn, introduced the element of continuous inflation without gaining any significant success in exterminating unemployment. Even a popular textbook, which tends to present midstream economics to the undergraduates, concedes that "no jury of impartial economists could agree on a cure of inflation that was not as bad as the disease itself."[1] The monetary school represented by Friedman, in spite of the legitimacy of linking inflation to money supply, has no answer to the political necessity of providing jobs to the unemployed. The only other significant thinking is associated with the name of Galbraith, who insists on the evolution of an income and employment policy. There are indictions that despite containment of free enterprise as understood until this time, the creep of public policy toward Galbraithian projection is by no means unlikely. Capitalism today is confronted with a crisis whose meaning, significance and sweep are not fully comprehended by it. The only future projection, which appears unavoidable, is that further stumbling forward of capitalism will be increasingly marked by its shedding of free enterprise.

Islam's difference with capitalism is that Islam stands for free enterprise, and appears theoretically capable of working it out without the necessity of having to face the contradictory dilemmas of capitalism. This is on account of Islam's uncompromising hostility to the institution of interest. The exploitative manifestations of loan-capital start with incurable unemployment, which when sought to be overcome by an expansionary monetary policy lands us in inflation. The hike in the interest rate, which is incorrectly regarded as one of the cures for inflation, leads to further unemployment, and this necessitates reversion to further expansionary monetary policy, and therefore, to yet another inflationary wave. In the meantime, the governments are loaded with an increasing public debt, only enhancing the unearned

---

[1]Samuelson, Paul A., *Economics,* 10th Edition. Tokyo, 1976, p. 365.

income of the rentier. The increasing need of debt services and transfer payments on account of relief to the unemployed, call for higher taxes to the deteriment of free enterprise. The fact is that unemployment and inflation will keep on pulverizing man, so long as we do not devise a credit structure which is at once human and productive.

Islam differs from capitalism in its rejection of interest as the basis of credit and in its consequent ability to sustain free enterprise without finding itself confronted with the contradictions which have barred the path of development and restricted the happiness of man. The difference between the two in one sentence can be stated thus: while both claim to support free enterprise, objective reality does not prove the claim of capitalism; and its future projections are likely to whittle down whatever is left of it. Islam's capacity to sustain free enterprise, in spite of its theoretically positivist stance in the face of the challenges of today, is still struggling to externalize itself as an objective reality.

M. Akram Khan

Freedom of enterprise in Islam lends it a deceptive resemblance to capitalism. But the conceptual framework, the contours of its superstructure, and the functioning of an Islamic economy are fundamentally dissimilar to those of capitalism. On the conceptual level, the basic assumptions and value system of capitalism are alien to the basic precepts and societal norms of Islam. For example, capitalism is based on the hedonistic psychology of pleasure and pain, where material acquisitions are held in high esteem and material deprivations are socially undesirable. Therefore, society is geared to produce a larger quantity of material goods, and the index of progress is an increasing rate of consumption by its individuals. It has led to the shift of focus from a moral to a material set of values and traditions. Economic matters have come to possess a central position in the social matrix. Economic criteria are applied to decisions affecting the whole gamut of life.[2]

Second, capitalism presumes that all human beings are selfish and therefore makes selfishly useful decisions to arrive at a socially desirable equilibrium. An invisible hand directs the individualistic forces to combine and converge for the common good.[3]

Third, the material values of capitalism are free from any moral constraints. An individual has freedom to believe, desire, decide and act in any manner he likes so far as he does not dispossess someone else from a similar freedom.

Fourth, the right to own and utilize property are absolute in capitalism. An individual is the sole owner of his property and has an

---

[2]See e.g., B. Ward (1972), p. 25, 99-200, Boulding (9170), p. 131, and Hirsch (1977), p. 60.
[3]Dopfer (1976), pp. 5-6.

uninhibited right to its fruits.

These basic assumptions are in conflict with the Islamic conceptual framework. The Islamic economy is based on a belief system which guides and governs the structure and operation of various relations and institutions. Beliefs such as *tauhid* (The Oneness of God), *risalah* (prophethood) of Muhammad, upon whom be peace, and *akhirah* (hereafter) unravel a lifestyle in which man is a representative of God on this earth. His material endowments are the necessary means at his disposal to carry out his role as God's representative. Like all appointees, he has to account for the utilizaton and application of these resources in the Hereafter.

This belief system assigns a secondary role to economic pursuits. The material possessions of man are only a means to achieve an end. The end is *falah* in the Hereafter. *Falah* is a unique Islamic concept. Success in the life hereafter is *falah*, which is attained by adherence to the *shari'ah* in this world. To the extent that *falah* requires obedience to the divine guidance in every sphere of life, it covers the economic aspect as well. The economic subsystem, however, does not occupy a central position. It is on the periphery, but interacts with other subsystems. Therefore, one fundamental difference between capitalism and Islam is that the latter treats economic relations as a subsystem in the galaxy of other subsystems, and therefore, moves it from the center to the periphery. In Islam, the center is occupied by the moral subsystem. Moral considerations are dicisive in shaping the form and interrelationship of various other subsystems. It further implies that the object of activity in Islam is not to increase the material possessions of individuals, but rather it is *falah* in the Hereafter. Economic resources are only instrumental in achieving *falah*, they are not the be-all and end-all of human activity. The fact that economic resources *(mal)* have a positive and purposive social role is obvious from a number of verses in the Qur'an. The *mal* is a means to attain the necessities of life for oneself and for meeting social obligations. In no case is it to be a source of luxurious life *(itraf)*[4], extravagance *(israf)*[5], exploitation *(zulm)*[6], ostentatious living *(riya)*[7], corruption *(fasad)*[8] and waste *(tabdhir)*.[9] Economic resources, if utilized with a social purpose, have been termed as *khair*,[10] *hasanat*,[11] *tayyebat*,[12] *fadlah*,[13]

---

[4]The Qur'an 21:13, 11:116.
[5]Ibid., 17:27.
[6]Ibid., 4:10.
[7]Ibid., 2:264, 4:38.
[8]Ibid., 2:205, 2:85, 26:183.
[9]Ibid., 17:26.
[10]Ibid., 2:273.
[11]Ibid., 4:78.
[12]Ibid., 2:267, 7:32.
[13]Ibid., 62:10.

rizq,[14] and *ni'am.*[15] The connotation of all these words suggests that economic resources are to be applied in a socially desirable manner.

Second, Islam disagrees with the assumption that man is inherently selfish. The Qur'an informs us that man has been created with the best of frames. Selfishness and lust for material possessions are indices of his degeneration, and he can only overcome them by fulfilling his commitments toward God and society.[16] As compared to this, capitalism has taken selfishness in man as natural.

Third, freedom of enterprise in Islam has been visualized in a framework of socio-economic values. These are positive values such as *iqtisad,* (moderation), *'adl* (justice), *ihsan* (kindness), *amanah* (honesty), *infaq,* (spending to meet social obligations) *sabr* (patience), *shukr* (thanks-giving), *qana* (contentment), *samaha* (generosity) and hospitality. Similarly, a set of negative values such as *bukhl* (miserliness), *zulm* (injustice), *shuhh* (stinginess), *riya* (ostentatious living), cheating, *iktinaz* (hoarding of wealth), *hirs* (greed), and *israf* (extravagance) defines undesirable behavior.

These values have been further integrated into a hierarchy of desirability which defines the dimensions of expected behavior in a given situation. The hierarchy consists of *fard* (obligation), *wajib* (essential), *sunnah* (practice of the Prophet), *mustahab* (desirable), *mubah* (permitted), *makruh* (disliked), *fasid* (void) and *haram* (forbidden). Out of these, the first and the last have the force of law, while the stages in between are left to individual volition. By a process of spiritual training, individuals are required to move up the hierarchy in each case. Therefore, in a society where each action of an individual has a definite moral value in a divine scale, freedom of enterprise cannot mean the same thing as in a society where the most dominant value is one's selfish material interest. It further implies that the profit motive, which is the essence of capitalism, cannot be an unbridled economic force in an Islamic society. While the profit motive has been recognized as a legitimate one, it has to be contained in the preceding value-framework. This tends to keep the inter-sectoral strife for a larger share in the national produce at a lower pitch. The profit motive is thus tamed and subdued to larger moral and social values.

The protection and maintenance of a free market is another distinctive feature of capitalism. Prices are to be determined by the forces of supply and demand, and non-market interference is considered against the rules of the game. In one of his traditions, the Prophet, upon whom be peace, was reported to have declined interference in the market price which had gone up considerably.[17]

---

[14]Ibid., 2:60, 20:131.

[15]Ibid., 39:49.

[16]Ibid., 95:4.

[17]Tirmidhi, *Sunan,* al-Buyu', ch. 73, Abu Da'ud, *Sunan,* al-Buyu', ch. 51.

This has been interpreted by some as an absolute maxim, and any interference in the market mechanism has been termed as un-Islamic.[18] But, perhaps, this is not the precise position. The price level determined by the flows of supply and demand discounts an important factor that may destroy the natural trend. The economic power, which individuals possess at a given time, gives them a relative leverage to interfere in the market price level and to destroy it for their own benefit. This is an every-day phenomenon in a capitalist society and may also occur in an Islamic economy. Therefore, some of the jurists have recommended state interference in the market mechanism to arrive at a just equilibrium.[19] The *just* price level—an Islamic concept—has to be arrived at by taking into consideration the cost and supply and demand flows. But prices may be controlled by the state only as a last resort, since such an act often leads to emergence of a black market. The free operation and market forces have been regulated to forestall unjudicious uses of economic power. The legal framework does not allow *ihtikar*[20] (stockholding to bid prices), *tanajush*[21] (collusion to raise price), speculation,[22] dumping to expel others from market,[23] destruction of output to contain supply[24] and demand by false advertisements.[25] These are only a few examples. The Islamic governments used to have a *muhtasib* who was responsible for looking into the fair operation of market forces. Pricing, especially for essentials, was resorted to quite frequently to save people from hardship.[26]

Capitalism recognizes an absolute right to own property. Islam neither recognizes an absolute right to acquire nor does it grant a free and uninterrupted right to utilize property. The right to acquire has been regulated by restricting it to lawful means. Property may be acquired by *kasb* (earning), *wirathah* (inheritance), *hibah* (gift), *wasiyyah* (bequest), *waqf* (endowment), and *luqata* (stray articles found on the way). In each of these forms, a detailed code of *halal-haram* has been laid down which assigns a definite value (positive or negative) to the property acquired. Property acquired through *haram* means is not recognized as legal and, hence, is not protected. The right to utilize property and receive its income has been subjected to even

[18]Maududi, A.A., *Mu'ashiyat-e Islam,* Islamic Publications Ltd., Lahore, 1969, pp. 413-415.

[19]Ibn Taimiyyah, *al-Hisbah fil Islam,* Dar al-Kutub al-Arabiyah, Beirut, no date, p. 31.

[20]Muslim, *Sahih al-Muslim.* See Kitab al-Buyu'.

[21]Bukhari, *Sahih al-Bukhari,* al-Buyu', ch. 60, 64, 68, 70.

[22]Muslim, op cit. See Kitab al-Buyu'.

[23]Ibn Taimiyyah, op. cit., p. 32.

[24]The Qur'an 2:205.

[25]Muslim, op. cit.

[26]*Encyclopedia of Islam,* (Essay on Hisba.) Leiden E.J. Brill.

greater checks. This takes us to the Islamic theories of consumption, production, and distribution.

Theory of Consumption

Besides laying down a code of *halal-haram* for each article of consumption, the general vision is to keep the level of consumption to a minimum.[27] The holy Prophet himself and his companions led an austere life which has been treated as a virtue throughout Muslim history. Increased production did not mean a higher consumption level. Instead, *self-restraint* had been the principle of consumption in Muslim societies. This is in marked contrast to the concept of *self-gratification* that reigns in any capitalist society. The whole mechanism of production, sale promotion, financing of comforts, and luxuries had been concepts alien to Muslim societies. The samples of income, after keeping the consumption to a minimum, was set aside to meet social obligations. The primary obligations were the maintenance of kith and kin, orphans, widows, invalids and economically infirm members of the society. Such expenditures were covered by the institution of *infaq*. Sharing the surplus with others is emphasized in the Qur'an and the Sunnah of the Prophet. The Prophet, upon whom be peace, would often distribute his provisions among the needy while his own family would go hungry. He would share the mount with his attendant and lend his companions various necessities (ma'un). The institution of *infaq* was sustained by an overriding social concept of *ukkhuwwah* (brotherhood), which the Prophet introduced soon after the establishment of the state of Madinah.

The consumption was kept at a minimum with a number of motives. First, it was in line with the overall philosophy that the life in this world was transitory and the real value was attached to the *akhirah*. So, involvement in increasing the material objects of life would have been a contradiction. Second, the primary concern of the Muslims as a political entity was to preserve their survival. The resources had to be preserved to sustain the group over a long period. All resources were not to be consumed by one generation; instead, a larger part had to be set aside for succeeding generations. It was a very sharp sense of intertemporal allocation of resources that kept the current consumption at a low pitch. It was precisely the reason that the second caliph of Islam did not distribute the conquered lands of Syria, Iraq, Iran, and Egypt among the conquerers. Instead, he set them aside as a perennial source of income for the succeeding generations.[28]

Another source of keeping the cost low in Muslim societies has been the high quality of products prepared by artisans. The items of

---

[27]See e.g., The Qur'an 49.10.
[28]Ala'i, H., *Theory of Income Distribution Under the Islamic Law,* p. 98-119.

household use would last for generations. The clothing and shoes were of such durability that they would remain in use for a number of years. Thus, the rate of turnover for items of personal consumption was very low.[29] The resources thus released were used for investment in long-run projects and public works programs. Besides the state treasuries, public works programs were financed privately. The well-to-do people would often construct inns *(sarays)*, hospitals, wells, mosques, palygrounds, parks, public baths and so on for the common good. These public works were carried out not to earn revenue, but for the convenience of the public. The institution of pious endowments *(awqaf)* was very popular among Muslims.[30] But in case voluntary expenditure on community services was not forthcoming, the office of *hisbah* would force the well-to-do to donate out of their surplus for the welfare of the people.[31]

Keeping personal consumption and turnover for durable articles at a low level, minimized the competition for raw material and maintained the prices of raw materials at a fairly low level. The general objective of Muslim government has been to keep the supply of essential items in abundance and at a cheaper level. This was intended to satisfy the biological needs of the majority. As far as psychological needs were concerned, fewer resources were set aside for them since they were the requirements of the few who could afford to pay a higher price for the satisfaction of their. needs. This is in clear contrast to the consumption pattern of a capitalist society where an increased level of consumption per head is an index of development. The enterpreneurial function in a capitalist society includes the creation of demand for new products, and thus, to change the habits of consumption.

Industrialization also brought in products of a much shorter durability than those of the pre-industrial society. This was partly to keep the turnover of products high so that demand for them would not fall and that heavy investment in plant and machinery would remain productive. A high turnover of products led to a greater strife for resources, and thus introduced friction and waste into the economy.

Another major difference lies in the source of capital. Capital formation in an Islamic society is done at the household level. Since the general principle is to keep consumption to a minimum, enough resources are released by the society for investment. In the past Muslim societies, individuals were their own financiers and the community chieftain afforded credit facilities for agriculture and trade. Everyday consumption loans, while of a much smaller scale than prevalent today, were financed by family members. Professional financiers, bankers,

---

[29]Abu Yusuf, *Kitab al-Kharaj* (Urdu Trans. M.N. Siddiqui), pp. 163-168.
[30]Ala'i, H., op. cit.
[31]Gilani, M. Ahsan, *Islami Mu'ashiyat* (Urdu), pp. 447-451.

underwriters and other financial intermediaries, who would provide finances for a monetary return, were simply not needed. A very rich source of long-term investment finances were the *awqafs* which had usually large tracts of lands, and were managed by the management to the benfit of large-scale production. They also provided medium and long-term finance on the basis of *shirakah* and *mudarabah*. Thus, capital formation in an Islamic society took place at the grass roots. It was made available either as *qard hasan* or on the basis of *shirakah/ mudarabah*.[32]

The application of the Islamic theory of consumption to a modern society would surely release large amounts of funds from current consumption. With a decline in the current rate of consumption, large numbers of industries engaged in the production of consumers' goods would have to be disinvested. These resources would then be re-allocated for building social overhead capital to take basic facilities of life to the remotest corners of towns and villages. At present, most of the Muslim countries are under-developed with islands of high consumption. Resources allocated to the production and import of the requirements of this minority may have to be diffused in the society for the construction of a socio-economic infrastructure. This may take another half a century. It is only after a majority of the population in the economy comes to a comparable level of consumption that the question of raising consumption per capita may come up for consideration. The overall vision is that the whole society has to move up as a single unit keeping the proportionate shares of different groups constant. After an equilibrium of the sort suggested above is achieved, the increase in the production would be shared by the different economic agents proportionate to their equilibrium shares.[33]

The Islamic theory of consumption differs with the capitalist theory in other respects as well. 'Demonstration effect' and 'display effect' are widely known in a capitalist society. People emulate others to keep up with the Joneses. This builds up demand and causes strife. The 'display effect' is the feeling of pride produced by displaying the quantity of material objects one has.[34] Both of these effects conflict with Islamic values. The Qur'an has categorically enjoined Muslims to abstain from such behavior.[35]

---

[32]*Al-Mawardi, Ahkam al-Sultaniyyah*, Maktabat al-Babi al-Halabi, Cairo, 3rd edition. 1973, p. 244.

[33]The whole idea has been squeezed here for the sake of brevity. It has been developed by Ala'i, H. op cit.

[34]Galbraith, J.K., *Economics and the Public Purpose*, Houghton Mifflin Company, Boston, 1973, pp. 241-250.

[35]The Qur'an 4:32, 28:76.

Theory of Production

The Islamic theory of production also delineates the nature of the free enterprise it sustains. First, production is regulated by the *halal-haram* code of the shari'ah. The ownership of the means of production does not grant an absolute right to their investment. Investment is decided upon in the light of moral constraints. Second, the issue of factor of production also needs some discussion. The capitalist theory of the four factors of production, with rewards as rent, wage, interest, and profit, leaves out of focus the persons who own these factors. The reward is treated for the factors and not for the persons who receive it. Not only is it in line with the materialistic stance of capitalism, it reduces human labor (in the case of worker and manager) to an insignificant marketable commodity and hides the exploitative role of the rentier class (in land and capital). Moreover, the question of whether the factor of production may be restricted only to four has also been questioned by some Muslim scholars. It has been suggested that technology,[36] the level of scientific knowledge in a society as a whole, and the spiritual level of a society may also be considered as factors of production.[37] This aspect of Islamic theory needs to be developed further.

Third, in a capitalist society, the returns on the factors of production are determined by market forces. Different theories of rent, wages, interest, and profits take into account economic factors. In contrast to this, the Islamic theory lays down two basic factors in the determination of a proportionate share of each factor of production. These are:

- *Ukhuwwa* (brotherhood)
- *Thaman Mithl* (prevalent rate)

The first one is derived from a number of Qur'anic injunctions and traditions of the Prophet, upon whom be peace. The different factors of production are required to get together in the production process on the basis of *ukhuwwah*. For example, a landlord cannot receive a rent which leaves the tenant with insufficient provisions to feed himself and his family.[38] Similarly if a natural calamity occurs, the principle of *wad al-jawa'ih*, which states that a proportionate discount or concession may be granted to the tenant, is applicable. For labor, not only a prompt fair wage has been enjoined, but the workers are also to be helped if the work is of arduous nature. He may be granted products of his industry at subsidized rates, his unpaid wages may be invested in business, making him more of a partner than a laborer. The laborer is to be treated with dignity as a brother and not as an inferior saleable commodity. Similarly, a laborer is also required to be sincere to his

---

[36] Mufti Shafi, *Circulation of Wealth in Islam*, p. 22.
[37] Uzair, M., *Interest-free Banking*, p. 12.
[38] See e.g., The Qur'an 49:10.

employer and not to steal his things (including his time).[39] Concerning capital, the financier is to take part in business as a partner and not a parasite seeking his share of interest, leaving the loss to others. Thus, all factors of production join together on the basis of *ukhuwwah*. They cooperate in production with the spirit of *ithar* (preferring others to oneself) and do not compete for their share.

The principle of *thaman mithl* (the prevalent price) has been derived from the Qur'an. It has been applied to wages in Muslim history. Where the contract was silent, it was usually applied as a clause of the agreement. For example, if a laborer was employed to perform a duty, and his wages were not settled in advance, it was presumed that his wages would be equal to the prevalent wages in the economy for similar work. The jurists pronounced decrees on the basis of this principle.[40] But the principle can be applied with great benefit in determining the shares of the various factors of production. This would reduce to a large extent, trade union pressure for higher wages. The trade unions demand wages partly to increase the level of consumption per head. The principle of minimum consumption along with principle of *thaman mithl* would dampen the current labor strife to a significant degree. (The question as to how *thamam mithl* would be determined needs separate and detailed treatment).

Theory of Distribution

Capitalism leaves the function of income distribution to market forces. Welfare economics, a relatively young branch, has started off with untested assumptions[41] and has contributed to smoothening the uneven trends in income distribution. Islam does not leave the distribution question to market forces. The institutions of *infaq*, *zakah* and *wirathah* build a mechanism which turns the flow of wealth from the few to the many. Those members of society who happen to possess a larger share of wealth are required to share it with others on a voluntary basis[42] and when they do not respond, the law forces them to do so.

The above discussion shows that free enterprise does not lead to the evolution of capitalism in the Islamic framework. The Islamic system has to be conceived in its entirety, for its partial applications may lead to confusion and contradictions.

Q. Do you think that the allowance for free enterprise in Islam, circumscribed within *haram* and *halal*, will not lead to a capitalistic economy?

---

[39]Muslim, op. cit. al-Buyu', especially al-Muzar'ah.
[40]The Qur'an 2:233.
[41]Dopfer (1976), p. 8.
[42]Ibn Taimiyyah, op. cit., p. 17.

Shaikh Mahmud Ahmad

The obvious answer is no. Capitalism is made up of two main ingredients, namely, capitalistic exploitation through interest and a facade, now crumbling, of free enterprise. Free enterprise is accepted by Islam, the exploitative ramification of interest is not. So it is an entirely different system. If free society and free institutions are to survive, there is no option for man except to turn to the social philosophy of Islam. The basic reality is that both man and money cannot be free. The answer of Islam is to circumscribe money and let man be free. The practice of capitalism is to let money be free to exploit man in any measure it desires, even though it may confine man.

M. Akram Khan

It will be misleading to believe that free enterprise in Islam would lead to a capitalistic economy because the freedom of the market would have to be visualized in the overall Islamic framework. As I said in reply to your earlier question, the values, belief system, and the legal code of Islam shapes an economy distinct from the capitalistic economy both in its foundation and superstructure.

Q. In the recent past, a critique on the welfare state has emerged. Its credentials are being seriously questioned. Such a critique gives a dismal picture of a welfare society where societal interests have suffered and a new parasitic class has been created; laziness and inefficiency have marred the growth; excessive taxation to generate funds for welfare have forced the entrepreneurial class and professional people to leave their country. Such societies, to be precise, have become societies of mediocres. Now it has been said by many of our Islamic writers on economy that Islam stands for a welfare state. What does an Islamic welfare state mean? To what extent will it differ from the contemporary welfare states?

Shaikh Mahmud Ahmad

There is a fundamental difference between the dole-dominated welfare state of the West and the welfare state visualized by Islam. Under capitalism, involuntary unemployment is first forced on the people because of the crippling effect of interest on the efficiency of capital resources and then this situation is remedied by raising taxes and borrowing money to meet unemployment insurance and other social welfare payments. The remedy actually has caused aggravation since rising taxes lower the efficiency of enterprise, and borrowing leads to the perpetual burden of interest payments with obvious baneful consequences.

The welfare concept in an Islamic state really sprouts from its structural compulsion to provide employment to all. If once a credit arrangement is devised in which no payment is demanded for the use of money, there is no theoretical reason why anyone should remain unemployed. Thus, the basic issues of the emergence of a parasitic class, of inefficiency and mismanagement of various transfer payments funds, of rising taxes and indebtedness do not arise in the Islamic welfare state. Even if involuntary unemployment may cease to exist with the extinction of interest, as certain economists visualize,[43] there will still be people who need support from the society, such as orphans, widows, the physically handicapped, the mentally retarded, and the aged. The institution of *zakah* is entirely capable of providing solutions to this part of the problem.

M. Akram Khan

I am not aware of any serious attempt by a Muslim economist to have discussed the concept of an Islamic welfare state. Most of the people who have said any such thing have done so to create an impact of Islam's virtues vis-a-vis Western civilization.

Q. Recently it has been said quite eloquently that the institution of *zakah* will redress wrongs and ensure the satisfaction of people's needs as it did in the early days of Islam. It has also been said that *zakah*, being a tax on capital, retards capital formation and thus insures distribution of wealth on a mass scale in an Islamic society. Such a view is self-defeating because if *zakah* hurts capital formation, it will not sustain its collection in the long run. And, if there is no *zakah*, there is no egalitarian society. How would you reconcile the two? Is not the role of *zakah* in an Islamic economy overplayed?

Shaikh Mahmud Ahmad

The conventional interpretation of *zakah* does not lend itself to the generation of adequate resources for eradication of poverty as it exists in the non-oil producing Islamic states. On this interpretation, the claims about the role of *zakah* are certainly overplayed. But if we revert to original sources, we find that no percentages or items of revenue are prescribed in the Qur'an. We are only asked to give "what is beyond our needs."[44] There is evidence to the effect that the holy Prophet applied different rates of *zakah*, even at the same time. After the conquest of Makkah, the holy Prophet wrote letters to different tribes about the details of *zakah*. The original texts of only two of his letters still exist. The one to Banu Harith b. Kalb is in Bukhari's *Sahih*, "Bab az-Zakah", and the one to the Humair tribes of Yemen is in Ibn Hisham,

---

[43]See e.g., Keynes, *General Theory of Employment, Interest and Money*, MacMillan, London, 1951, pp. 374-377; Harrod, *Dynamic Economics*, MacMillan, London, 1956, pp. 129-159.

[44]The Qur'an 2:219.

Tabari, and several other books.[45] The details about the application of *zakah* in the matter of camels differ in these texts. For the *ghazwah* of Tabuk, 'Umar (Allah be pleased with him) gave half of what he possessed and Abu Bakr (Allah be pleased with him) gave all that he possessed as *sadaqah*.[46] 'Umar added taxes on horses, merchandise, imports, sea produce, and included these in *zakah*, although the holy Prophet had not mentioned them as items of *zakah* revenue. 'Ali (Allah be pleased with him) has indicated the flexibility of items and ratios of *zakah* and also gave the reason for it. According to him, "Owners of wealth have to give enough to meet the needs of the poor."[47] My *Questionnaire on Zakah* elaborated these details along with numerous other authorities, all supporting the contention that only the principle of *zakah* is immutable, and that its details are subject to space-time requirements.

I once put several questions to Maulana Abul Kalam Azad which included the one raised by you, viz the capital retarding consequence of *zakah*, if applied as a capital tax. The last two sentences of his reply given in his letter dated 26th July, 1945, whose plate is printed in *Social Justice in Islam* gives his answer to this question: "This is not unchangeable but is subject to *ijtihad*. It is the duty of those who hold power that they should fix the proper ratio according to the economic conditions and needs of society in every age."[48]

Thus interpreted, the capability of *zakah* to redress all wrongs becomes acceptable and the negative consequence on capital formation can be excluded.

M. Akram Khan

The objection has been visualized in a capitalistic framework. The Islamic economy has its own ever-perpetuating mechanism of capital formation. The principle of minimum consumption leads to a definite surplus of resources. These resources are to be allocated to projects, benefits from which may spill over to succeeding generations. If we imagine an Islamic society today where personal consumption is kept to a minimum by everyone, the savings thus generated would ultimately be deployed for longer-run projects. It would be absurd to believe that these savings would be buried under the ground. The institution of *awqaf* was also an application of the same principle during Muslim history. The well-to-do would save and invest in projects,

---

[45]Ibn Hisham, *Sirah, pp. 258-9; at-Tabari, Tarikh*, Volume 1, pp. 1717-20.
[46]It is to be noted that the difference in meaning given to *sadaqat* and *zakah* is a later development. The Qur'an and ahadith use these two words to convey the same meaning.
[47]Ibn Hazm, *al-Mohalla*, VI:158.
[48]Last Chapter of *Social Justice in Islam*, Institute of Islamic Culture, Lahore, 1979.

income from which would accrue to succeeding generations.

The fear that *zakah* would discourage capital formation is not well-founded. Instead, it may be the other way around. Since capital stock of the economy would be subject to a 2.5 percent tax (*zakah*), the economy would save 27.5 percent of its increment in capital stock each year to maintain itself at the previous level.[49] It indicates a high concern for capital formation in an Islamic society. Moreover, since idle capital would be subject to *zakah*, it may suggest to people that the capital should be invested in productive channels in order to earn enough to pay its own *zakah*. This would also dynamize the resources which is a pre-requisite for capital formation.

Q. Both capitalistic and socialistic economies aim at ameliorating the economic lot of man; it is of special significance to a capitalistic economy in which consumerism is linked to production, production to jobs, and jobs to a better standard of living. Islam is certainly not against creating jobs but at the same time, it does not seem to approve of high consumption and a high standard of living because of its obvious concern for man's moral and spiritual well-being. How would an Islamic economy resolve this paradox of jobs and higher consumption?

Shaikh Mahmud Ahmad

The level of consumption is related to productive capability of a given society. No particular level of consumption is prescribed in Islam. Only adherence to the principle of moderation is called for both in the Qur'an and Hadith: "Half of economics is observing the golden mean in the matter of living."[50]

"High consumption" and "high standard of living" are relative terms. They vary with technological advancement, economic potential, productivity of labor and many similar items. The good things of life are not denied to man by Islam. Only certain *haram* items and excessiveness in anything is prohibited. Within these limits, there is no harm in activating production to the limit of technical capacity and allowing this production to meet the manifold needs of man. In Muslim countries, we are still far from meeting even the basic needs of our people; and therefore, the question of any paradox arising between jobs and consumption is premature.

M. Akram Khan

Again the paradox of capitalism has been transplanted into an Islamic economy. Unemployment is the creation of capitalistic

---

[49]Kahf, M., *The Islamic Economy,* The Muslim Students' Association of U.S. and Canada, Plainfield, Indiana, no date, p. 63.

[50]*Kanz al-'Amal* as quoted in Maulana Mohammad Hafiz ur-Rehman's *Islam ka Iqtisadi Nizam,* 1946, Nadwatul Musannifeen, Delhi, p. 69.

societies. It has been demonstrated in a number of studies that a positive interest rate on capital is the main cause of unemployment in capitalism.[51] Higher consumption itself will not solve unemployment. Minimum consumption, as stressed by Islam, is the ultimate solution. The resources thus generated would be diverted to provide social services such as health, education, social security, construction of roads, bridges, canals and houses. This would create jobs and also distribute wealth more equitably. Even in capitalist economies where the level of general prosperity is very high, the lopsidedness of growth has been demonstrated by writers such as Galbraith.[52] The public sector facilities have not expanded in line with the growth of private sector. Instead of raising the personal consumption of the private sector, if resources are released for building social overhead capital, it would surely create more jobs. The difficulty of the capitalist framework is that individual consumers cannot be persuaded to consume less and then to invest the surplus to meet social obligations without any corresponding material gain.[53] In an Islamic society, the individuals internalize social needs and voluntarily behave to restrain their personal needs. In a way, an Islamic order is not natural in the materialistic sense, since it raises the natural order to a social order composed of individuals who, by their free consent, have agreed to limit their needs. Restraint is a religious obligation.[54]

Q. In Islam, an individual is entitled to the fruit of his toil within, of course, the limitation of *halah* and *haram*. Such a view sounds all right in a pre-industrial society where the means to produce wealth are either limited or not widespread. With the extensive use of technology and an expanded market, wealth has increased a thousand times and so have the rich people. In a sense, today's prosperous world is faced with the problem of wealth — how to create it, how to restrain its use, how to minimize its ill effect on the individual as well as society. These are the major issues of our times. To say that Islam does not mind excessive wealth with the people is anachronistic and not valid. At the same time, any restraint on the individual right to produce wealth and to use it the way he wants, will stifle entrepreneurship. Where does Islam stand in this respect?

---

[51]For example: See Ahmad, S.M., "Interest and Unemployment", Islamic Studies, Islamabad, 8 (I), pp. 9-46.
[52]Galbraith, J.K., *The Affluent Society,* Houghton Mifflin Company, Boston 1976. See his chapters on *The Position of Poverty and Inequality.*
[53]Ibid., see his capter on *The Paramount Position of Production.*
[54]The Qur'an 59:9.

Shaikh Mahmud Ahmad

Islam imposes only two restraints on the individual's possession and utilization of wealth. One is an individual restraint which is concerned with *halal* and *haram*. The other is the social restraint which primarily expresses itself in the obligation to pay *zakah* in such a measure so as to be adequate to root out poverty and privation. But there are other restrictions as well. Islam views with disfavor conspicuous consumption as this generates social friction. Within these limits, Islam is all for the activation of production and, therefore, dislikes any stifling of entrepreneurship. But if wealth tends to polarize, Islam permits the state to take such egalitarian steps which stop short of the extinction of enterprise.

M. Akram Khan

In Islam, there is no absolute right to private property. The concept of limiting private property for the social good (*ijtema*) was developed by early jurists. Some of the methods to limit the right to private property are:

a) Limiting the size of the property so that resources are not disportionately appropriated by one class and thus leaving the majority in distress. This may lead to restricting the size of houses, cars, share holding in joint stock companies, and so on.
b) Nationalization.
c) *Hajar* (Restricting the rights to use property beyond a certain limit).
d) Forced donations to meet social obligations if the public treasury so needs.[55]

These steps may be taken by an Islamic state to rectify any accumulated imbalance or to prevent a misuse of economic power.[56]

Q. The credit system in the capitalistic economy is an important tool to sustain consumption of goods produced. Credit also ties the individual to work ethics and productivity. Since interest is prohibited, is there any substitute for credit in Islam?

Shaikh Mahmud Ahmad

This of course is the question of questions. If we have an answer to the problem of substitution of interest, we have the answer to every question. If we cannot fashion an alternative to interest which may have the same workability, automaticity, and simplicity which interest possesses, but not any of its exploitative, counter productive, and

---

[55]Ibid., 89:18-24
[56]Siddiqui, M.N., *Islam's Theory of Ownership*, 2 vols. (Urdu).

restrictive ramifications, then there is no validity to our claim of a distinctive Islamic social system, capable of giving answers to the conflicts and contradictions so manifest in both the capitalistic and socialistic systems.

The simplistic answer that we have in the concept of *mudarabah* and *shirakah* concerning the creation of a new credit system does not stand close scrutiny. These concepts were relevant to an era of personal credit, and are not easily workable in an age of impersonal institutionalized credit. By their very definition, they are relevant only to productive credit and even, in that area, to situations in which some assurance about business integrity may be available. Assuming the corporate sector as being reliable enough to receive advance, these concepts provide no answer to small productive loans, to consumer loans, to government loans, to the evolution of a basis for hire, purchase and above all, cashing bills of exchange. This last point is important both from historic and practical points of view. The Jews failed to evolve an alternative to interest because they allowed the buying and selling of commercial paper at a discount. If we can evolve a concept wherein commercial paper can be purchased at face value, then we will have discovered the alternative to interest, which can then be applied to every other segment and variety of credit.

Another misconception that we need to outgrow is the generally prevalent idea that the sharing of profit and loss is an exclusively Islamic basis of credit. Actually, this system is as old as ancient Babylonia, and articles 100 to 107 of the Code of Hamurabi spell out the principles of its application. The Jews learned this system from Babylonia during their first exodus,[57] and Christians and Muslims borrowed it from the Jews.

In looking around for an alternative, both in historic times and at present, we appear to have concerned ourselves more with subterfuges than the reality of an alternative to interest. Islam is opposed to interest not because of its specific form, but because of its exploitative content. All conceptual alternatives to interest which concern themselves with the change of form alone, will result only in the intensification of exploitation and therefore, will clash with the spirit of Islam. One of the historical examples of this approach is *bai'al-'ina,* which our *fuqaha'* have very rightly disapproved. But the spirit of manipulation is still active. The suggestions made by the panel of experts in Pakistan, e.g., utilization of the concepts of rent and investment auctioning for credit extension are as far, if not farther from Islam, as the concept of *bai'al-'ina* itself.

Fortunately an idea is gaining ground which has the full potentiality of

---

[57]Singer, *Jewish Encyclopedia,* Funk and Wagnalis Company, New York, 1905, V. 12, p. 391.

meeting all varieties of credit requirements and has stood up against many theological and technical objections. The concept is called "Time Multiple Counter Loan Concept" (hereafter TMCL). It is built on the premise that in a loan, time is as important an element as the amount lent. This means that an advance for a short period can be equal to a fractional advance for a multiple period. For instance, the following advances have an equal loan value:

Rupees ($) 1000 for one year
Rupees ($) 500 for two years
Rupees ($) 250 for four years
Rupees ($) 200 for five years
Rupees ($) 100 for ten years

Recognition of the equal value of these loans opens up the possibility of devising a credit structure in which borrowed sums are counterbalanced by fractional counter loans, given by borrowers to the bank, for a multiple period of time. For instance, an advance of Rupees ($) 1000 for one year can be counterbalanced by a counter loan of Rupees ($) 100 for ten years. Both loans can be returned to the respective lenders at the end of the stipulated period without any addition whatsoever.

On closer examination, the identity between Rupees ($) 1000 for one year and Rupees ($) 100 for ten years appears more theoretical than real. The borrower takes his Rupees ($) 1000 and does with it as he likes and does not pay interest on it or share any part of his profits with the lender. The bank, on the other hand, has to meet all overhead expenses which have to be met prorata from the income of Rupees ($) 100 which it has received as counter loan. But the basic notion of the interconvertibility of time and money is capable of giving an answer to this legitimate objection. If Rupees ($) 100 for ten years does not strike an equilibrium with Rupees ($) 1000 for one year, because of the overhead expenses of the bank, let these overhead expenses be converted into time. This is a problem relating to accountancy, but assuming the overhead costs demand a 50 percent extension in time, the necessary counter loan of Rupees ($) 100 will be extended for 15 years, instead of ten years, and this can solve the issues of overhead costs.

At first, a number of objections were raised about it at the theological level, but after due deliberation, they all subsided and the Islamic Advisory Council in Pakistan expressed its approval of this concept from the Islamic point of view. So a major hurdle to the acceptance of this concept has been removed.[58]

---

[58]Readers who wish to study in some depth the appraisal of this concept from the Islamic and technical points of view, in comparison with various concepts available to us, might look up an Urdu paper of the writer entitled *Sood ki Mutabadil Asas ka Masalah*.

Now we are left with a number of technical considerations. First, what are the banks to do with the counter loan funds that are made available to them against every loan, so that they can meet their overhead costs and make a worthwhile profit as well? Second, since the banks will charge no interest, it is obvious that they will pay no interest to the depositors. What impact will this have on the mobilization of deposits? Third, interest is supposed to be a rationing device. Will not the removal of this sieve result in the misdirection of resources? Fourth, the rate of interest having been brought to zero, might result in an incalculable enhancement of the demand for loans. What assurance is there that a matching supply of credit will be available? Fifth, what is the answer to the inflationary possibilities associated with the lowering of interest in the light of Wicksell's theoretical formulation and accepted monetary policy around the globe?

The first objection relates to the utilization of the counter loan funds made available to the bank and an estimation of their profits compared to their present position. Of course, this will entail a departure from current practice, in so far as banks will assume the role of direct investors in relation to counter loan funds. Precedents of direct investments by banks are by no means non-existent, but in this case, the distinctive trait will be the virtually exclusive nature of the direct investment. The obvious openings are the stock exchange, real estate, and Participation Term Certificates in existing industries.[59] These are, however, likely to be inadequate openings for the vast amounts of funds which this basis is likely to cast in the coffers of banks. They will, therefore, have to institute holding which will invest directly in such industrial and commercial ventures as are likely to give the highest return. Capital intensive ventures are likely to prove more in consonance with the resources available to these banks.

Doubts have been expressed about their adequacy of returns as compared to their present position. Some cirtics have gone to the extent of evaluating the fall in returns to be calculable by the ratio which counter loan funds bear to the total advances, so that if 20 percent is the ratio of counter loans, the fall in income of banks will be of the order of 80 percent. This is a highly superficial way of reckoning the income of these banks. The point that is missed is that the new concept is workable only on the basis of discarding the reserve ratio, which is the instituionalized instrument perpetuating the scarcity of credit. The monetary resources available in every country, including a relatively poor one like Pakistan, are adequate to meet all credit requirements, provided the resreve ratio does not erect a steel barier beyond which credit cannot be extended. TMCL simultaneously compels us to

---

[59]These are substitutes of debentures in which the return is pre-agreed percentage of the profit calculated on the daily product basis.

remove this barrier and also provides a creative alternative to it. With the removal of this brake, the artificial scarcity of capital will cease to exist, but the banking system will not be shorn of its reserves or liquidity, for counter loan funds will keep injecting new resources into it in spite of the 100 percent advancement of loans from deposits.

Probably an example will clarify the working of the new system in contrast with the present one and will also help us to visualize the profitability of the banks under this new system. In Pakistan, the present reserve ratio of banks is 35 percent. This means that the ultimate limit to which credit can be extended is slightly less than three multiples of the total initial advances possible for the banks. Let us assume that the total primary deposits in the country are Rupees ($) 1000, and compare the return available at present and the probable return under the new system. Assuming the reserve ratio to be 35 percent, the lending rate of 14 percent, the depositors return at 7 percent and the loan turnover period as one month, the gross income of the banks during one year comes to Rupees ($) 109.96. Under the TMCL system it works out to Rupees ($) 129.96, assuming the return of 10 percent on counter loan investment, and turnover of advances at one month. The smallest calculator will verify this result. TMCL, instead of starving the banking sector is even more profitable for them, for the prosperity of this sector will emerge on account of the prosperity of the people and not through their exploitation and impoverishment.

About the second objection related to the mistaken notion of interest being an instrument of deposit mobilization, we are in the realm of mythology. This is a myth woven with the sole purpose of perpetuating the exploitation of all productive classes by loan capital. Theoretically, the concept was exploded by Keynes in his *General Theory*, who averred that saving is not a function of interest but of income. He explained that savings result from income, income results from employment, employment results from investment, and investment expands with the lowering of interest.[60] Savings, therefore, are inversely related to interest, instead of having any direct relationship as visualized in the objection. It has not suited economists to adopt this Keynesian thesis, but neither have they been able to advance any reason for its rejection. Perhaps, the empirical experience of the 1970s should be enough to prove the accuracy of Keynesian projection. For the sake of brevity, only two examples will be given. In Pakistan, until 1970-71, the bank rate was 5 percent and savings were of the order of 8.69 percent of G.D.P. Deluded by the myth of savings being a function of interest, the bank rate was raised to 10 percent in 1976-77, with the result that the savings, instead of rising, fell to 7.42 percent. In 1977-78 they declined further to 7.05 percent and in 1978-79 to 5.55 percent.

---

[60]Keynes, *General Theory of Employment, Interest and Money*, op cit., p. 375.

This result is supported by the experience of the US and several European countries. In many of the developed countries, the rate of inflation has been higher than the rate of interest; as a result, the real rate of interest fell below zero. In spite of this, there was no dampening effect on the mobilization of savings. The real rate of interest in Britain during 1971 was -2.68 percent; during 1972, -2.09 percent, during 1973, +1.86 percent; during 1974, -0.87 percent; during 1975, -9.51 percent and during 1976, -10.73 percent.[61] Yet the total deposits (demand and time deposits put together) were in 1971, £ 16.73 billion; in 1972, £ 21.90 billion; in 1973, £ 28.76 billion; in 1974, £ 32.34 billion; in 1975, £ 34.19 billion and in 1976, £ 38.02 billion.[62] There is no indication of any slackening in savings despite the soaring negative rate of interest to a two-digit level. The apprehensions entertained about the drying up of savings after abolishing interest are not only disproved theoretically but also empirically.

The third objection, which derives its strength from a mistaken notion of interest being a rationing device, is equally invalid. Most governments run deficit budgets justified on social and political considerations, and the banking sector is obliged to fill in the gap. From an economic point of view, these loans are not only non-productive ones, they divert valuable resources from significantly valuable productive alternatives to conceivably the most unproductive one. If interest were a rationing device it would not lend any support to this situation. The United States Government has for most years, since the end of World War II, prusued a farm policy which has as its objective the limitation of various farm products at a cost of around 5 billion dollars a year. This obviously counter-productive policy has to be supported by borrowing a massive amount every year. But in no year has the rationing instinct of interest appeared to play a role. In most developing countries and in all socialistic ones, planned economic development has taken the place of involving interest in the determination of its direction. In many countries, including Pakistan, public sector industries of their low and sometimes negative returns, continue gobbling up scarce capital resources and the rate of interest has never prevented anyone from following this policy. Again, in many developing countries, of which Pakistan is a significant example, palatial houses and shopping arcades are swallowing up resources which are badly needed for low-cost houses to replace shacks and slums. Interest is not known to have applied any brake to this or other examples of the misapplication of capital resources.

In fact, interest has no allocative function to perform. It is solely

---

[61]Meade, J.E., *The Structure and Reform of Direct Taxation*, London, 1978, p. 107.
[62]*International Financial Statistics*, Feb. 1979, published by I.M.F., p. 382.

concerned with the security of the advances of which it is a return. If the security is sound, no matter how unsound the project, the loan will be forthcoming; if the security is unsound or inadequate, no matter how sound the economic basis of the project, the advancement of loan will be highly improbable.

To sum up, by abolishing interest, no significant constructive function will be thrown overboard. Only the exploitation of loan capital will cease. The rationing function is inherent in the profit expectation, and no project with a lower profit expectation is undertaken in the presence of a project which promises a possibly higher profit. This is the only rationing device in existence at the moment and this will survive in the new system, completely unimpaired.

The fourth objection relates to the issue of bringing into balance the demand and supply of loanable funds. The abolition of interest is bound to lead to a massive increase in the demand for investible funds, and unless arrangements are devised for a matching massive increase in the supply of loans, a critical situation will be at hand. TMCL is structurally competent to meet this situation. It is the reserve policy which determines the quantum of available capital resources. With a 35 percent reserve we cannot advance more than three multiples of the initial advances, which have to be only 65 percent of initial deposits. At 25 percent, we can advance 4 multiples of deposits, at 20 percent 5 multiples, at 10 percent 10 multiples, and at 5 percent 20 multiples. If by some means, we could do away with this 5 percent also, we could have an interminable supply of capital resources. This is exactly what TMCL achieves. It does not countenance the existence of any reserve restriction of the conventional pattern at all, and can lend out 100 percent of the deposits. In spite of this, neither the solvency of the system nor its liquidity needs to be impaired on account of a 20 percent counter loan that is made available to it with the advancement of every loan. There is, thus, an inherent capability in this concept of matching the supply of loans with the demand.

We now come to the last objection against the possibility of imposing inflationary pressures on account of the expansion of credit. First of all, we have to get over the Wicksellian notion that every fall in the interest rate raises the price level. Though this concept was formulated when classical economics did not allow for the existence of any unemployment, it is unfortunately adhered to even after economics has conceded the existence of unemployment as a virtually ineradicable fact of economic life in the free world. This short reply will not bear a discussion which by its nature has to be extensive to disprove every argument which Wicksell advanced in support of his thesis. If we were to examine his arguments, we would find that these not only do not support his contention but lead to a conclusion which is the exact opposite of the one he wants us to reach.[63] Worse, Wicksell was not willing to accept the empirical evidence available to him which contradicted his formulation. There is internal evidence in Wicksell's writing that he has read Took's monumental History of Prices, which provides limitless evidence that prices and interest rates are related directly and not inversely, as Wicksell would want us to believe. Wicksell proceeded to collect his own figures of prices and interest rates of the Berlin and London markets and found this evidence also to conflict with his theory.[64] Toward his end, he started doubting his concept as attested to by Professor Ohlin in his Introduction to the English translation of Interest and Prices.[65]

Subsequent collection of empirical evidence invariably contradicts the formulation of Wicksell with the result that the direct relationship between interest and prices is called by Keynes "one of the most completely established empirical facts within the whole field of quantitative economics."[66] Its significance for public policy was expressed by him in his greatest work when he pleaded for lowering of interest to fight inflation. "Thus the remedy for the boom," wrote Keynes, "is not a higher rate of interest but a lower rate of interest."[67]

Why has midstream economics failed to accept this fundamental reality? It is very difficult for economics evolving in a capitalistic environment to question such a fundamental notion — the validity of interest. If it agreed with the reality of the matter, it would amount to the demolition of the intellectual citadel of the wealth-owning classes, and the complete removal of the smoke screen which hides the perpetuation of oppression and exploitation. For the greater part, the environment's ethos does not permit even the realization of the reality. For the rest, the exploitative classes have sufficient hold on the universities and research bodies to ensure that the piper does not strike a discordant tune, and there are quite a few instances in which subsidized research has been undertaken with the sole object of providing intellectual support to vested interests.[68] Once in a while, one also comes across a scholar with enough moral courage to confess that the "disgusting morbidity", which love of money has generated, must not be called into question. Writes Samuelson: "For at least another hundred years, we must pretend to ourselves that fair is foul and foul is fair, for foul is useful and fair is not. Avarice and usuary ...

---

[63]Readers interested in locating the theoretical fault in the argument of Wicksell may look up the present writer's Man and Money, pp. 138-155.

[64]Cf, the graphs drawn by him on page 87 of his Selected Paper on Economic Theory, London, 1958.

[65]Wicksell, Interest and Prices, London, 1936, p. XIX.

[66]Keynes, Treatise on Money, p. 198.

[67]Keynes, General Theory of Employment, Interest and Money, op. cit., p. 322.

[68]Some instnces are mentioned in S.E. Harris, The New Economics, London, 1949, p. 60.

must be our gods for a little longer still."[69] He might have added that in calling interest useful, he in indulging in a self-confessed twisting of facts and presenting foul as fair.

But to return to the question of inflation in relation to the abolition of interest, a price level is determined by the quantity of money as compared with the quantity of goods and services that can be purchased with it. If the extension of credit increases the volume of money without creating goods and services, there will be inflation. If on the other hand, expansion of credit is carefully channeled to activate production, the increase in money will be matched by an identical increase in production. It is the supply of money per unit of goods and services that determines the price level. If units of goods increase along with the expansion of credit, there is no risk of inflation. The inflation that has pushed many of us to the very brink of impoverishment is a product of an interest-based economy. It is primarily the result of the hectic pursuit of an expansionary monetary policy by governments around the globe for more than three decades. They are forced to this step because the only alternative is increased unemployment. This unemployment is structurally inescapable in the presence of interest. The reason why capitalistic economics is incapable of devising any remedy for either unemployment or inflation is because it insists on calling "fair is foul and foul is fair." So what is left to it is to indulge in a never ending exercise of "fine tuning." When unemployment becomes politically unacceptable, they increase the money supply, and when inflation creates more hue and cry they, inter alia, raise the rate of interest.

Economy shorn of interest can effectively cure both inflation and unemployment. If capital is made available without interest for every worthwhile productive effort, there is no reason for unemployment to survive. This will not create inflation because the productive employment of resources will lead to an increasing cascade of production which will sop up every accretion in purchasing power. One precaution, of course, will be necessary; fiscal policy will have to become more responsible. Not only will government budgets need to be balanced, but curbs on consumer borrowing will need to be exercised. In an interest free economy, these things will be much easier to attain than they are in the present context. On the one hand, expansion of production will raise the revenue of governments, and on the other, much of the expenditure at present devoted to the activation of production and transfer payments will become unnecessary. To sum

---

[69]Samuelson, Paul A., *Economics*, op. cit., p. 817.

Editor's note: This quote is from J.M. Keynes' "Economic Possibilities for Our Grandchildren," reprinted in his *Essays in Persuasion* (MacMillan, London, 1933).

up, there is no doubt that with the abolition of interest, not only will inflation be curbed, but carefully utilized, this problem can eventually be overcome by TMCL.

Q. How would you solve the problem of transition from the existing economic systems in the Muslim countries to an Islamic economic system?

Shaikh Mahmud Ahmad

Five major steps need to be taken in Muslim countries for a transition from their present economic situation to a system which would be responsive to Islamic behests. They are: 1) abolition of interest and the formulation in its place, not of subterfuge, but of a sensible, workable and creative alternative, 2) *Zakah* should be organized in its original concept as understood in the first century of *Hijrah* when *zakah* and *sadaqat* did not have two different meanings, 3) vestiges of the feudal era like absentee landlords need to be wiped out. The tiller must have the full reward of the fruits of his labor. As a general rule, neither sharing the produce, nor rent is viewed with favor by Islam, although in the context of feudal times, most interpretations have tended toward permissibility, 4) social responsibility has to be imposed. Unless social evils like corruption, smuggling, adulteration, profiteering and other dishonest practices are rooted out, no philosophy can be fruitful. Considering the depth of roots that these evils have grown in our societies in the course of our feudal and colonial past, any punishment short of total confiscation of all property will fail to produce any significant result, and 5) all this needs to be done in a democratic framework. This does not merely mean adoption of the elective principle at the national and provincial levels, but also at all levels below it. Even at the lowest level e.g., a village or a mohallah, we should have a representative institution possessing power to settle disputes, ensure law and order, provide elementary education, attend to public health and sanitation, arrange for creative utilization of unused labor and under-used skill, collect and disburse *zakah* and plan and organize productive ventures which may help augment the resources of our communities. *Amruhum shoora bainahum* is a direction of Islam which is conspicuous by its absence in practically every Muslim land, although we should have been the torch bearers of the elective principle.

M. Akram Khan

The question of transition from the present-day *jahliyy* (un-Islamic) to an Islamic society has not been thoroughly attended to by Muslim scholars. Most of the literature discusses Islamic society in its ideal form and leaves out the question of transition. The reason perhaps has been to convince people about the workability of the Islamic system in the present-day context and to dispel the misleading Western propaganda that Islam was a matter of the past and that its system could be operated only in a medieval setting.

However, the question needs a thorough discussion. The answer would only evolve by discussion and experiment with the Islamic system. The Muslim scholars should critically analyze attempts to Islamize societies now being made in some countries such as Pakistan and Iran. A right answer to this question may emerge out of such a study.

Chapter VIII

THE ISLAMIC STATE AND THE WELFARE STATE: SIMILARITIES AND DIFFERENCES

Monzer Kahf

Dr. **Monzer Kahf** is a prolific writer on the economics in Islam. His latest work, *Islamic Economy,* published by the Muslim Students' Association of the US and Canada, was critically acclaimed. He is the former MSA's director of finance. The present article was written in response to the editor *al-ittihad's* questionnaire on Islamic economy.

Q. In the recent past, a critique on the welfare state has emerged. Its credentials are being seriously questioned. Such a critique gives a dismal picture of a welfare society where societal interests have suffered and a new parasitic class has been created; laziness and inefficiency have marred the growth; excessive taxation to generate funds for welfare have forced the entrepreneurial class and professional people to leave their country. Such societies, to be precise, have become societies of mediocres. Now it has been said by many of our Islamic writers on economy that Islam stands for a welfare state. What does an Islamic welfare state mean? To what extent will it differ from the contemporary welfare states?

Faced with problems of economic decay, poverty and under-development, and stunned by the achievements of the western democracy and eastern socialism, many contemporary Muslim thinkers look to the state to provide the cure for these economic maladies. Thus, several essays have been written on the role of the Islamic state — most of them centering around the notion of "the welfare state."

The term "welfare state" was coined by the British; it filtered into the media during the early post-Second World War years when the labor Government was in power.[1] According to Birch: "The phrase was first used by Archbishop Temple."[2]

The concept of a welfare state is attached to social policies and poor relief. Early poor laws in England go back to 1601, that is, about two centuries before the Industrial Revolution, yet no one tends to claim that seventeenth century Britain was a welfare state. The first steps to a "welfare state" came only after the inadequacy of the capitalist state had become widely accepted, i.e., since the middle of the nineteenth century.[3] By the year 1948, social security was expanded to virtually all people; national health insurance came in full application; unemployment benefits were enacted and extended to cover more workers; widow, orphan and old-age pensions became more comprehensive; the principle of secondary education for all was accepted; and the practice of building houses and letting them at subsidized rent was well established.[4]

The emergence of the notion of a welfare state from the thoughts of British politicians and economists and the practices of the British government contributed a lot to the shaping of this notion and its dimensions. A totalitarian government with an elaborate commitment to social services could not be called a welfare state. A welfare state is the result of economic political compromises that took place within the British form of democracy, and is therefore, an English combination of individualism and collectivism. According to T.H. Marshall, "The welfare state has not rejected the capitalist market economy but gives it only qualified approval since there are some elements in civilized life of greater importance which can be attained only by restricting or supplanting the market."[5]

Aims and Characteristics of a Welfare State

The major aims of a welfare state may be stated as follows:
"Ensuring that all have enough income to keep them out of poverty if they cannot earn, and that no one is prevented by lack of education, medical treatment or adequate housing from realizing his potentialities."[6]

---

[1]Richard M. Titmuss: *Essays on The Welfare State;* George Allen and Unwin Ltd., London, 3rd edition with new introduction by B. Abel-Smith, 1976, Introduction, p. 2.
[2]R.C. Birch: *The Shaping of the Welfare State;* Longman, London, 1974, p. 3. See also William Temple: "The State" in *The Welfare State, Selected Essays*, edited by C.I. Schottland; Happer Torchbooks, NY, 1967, pp. 20-24.
[3]Birch, *ibid.*, pp. 8-19.
[4]J.F. Sleeman: *The Welfare State;* George Allen and Unwin Ltd., London, 1973, pp. 23-38.
[5]William Robson: *Welfare State and Welfare Society;* George Allen and Unwin Ltd., London, 1976, p. 12.
[6]Sleeman: *ibid.*, p. 97.

However, Titmuss has a more comprehensive outlook of the aims of a welfare state, and he extends them to include: (1) increasing the economic efficiency by increasing the productivity, facilitating workers' mobility, and enhancing growth; (2) affecting the birth rate in the desirable direction; (3) integrating minorities into the society; (4) reducing inequality of income and command over resources.[7]

From the aims, policies, and evolution of a welfare state, its characteristics can be derived. Since a welfare state is democratic in nature, the combination of collectivism, individualism and their proportions are a matter of political choice. In the purest democratic practices, the public vote is the determinant of the individual's rights and duties. The extent of his obligations to the state becomes subject to the social contract. This contract of the majority vote defines the degree of political freedom as well as the share of taxes.

Moreover, a welfare state defines welfare and happiness in a utilitarian context. Thus, it tends to measure its achievements in terms of economic gains. A welfare state is not only economically inclined, it is also nationalist, and so must be concerned with the economic well-being of the nation. It was enhanced by military assaults on Britain during the Second World War, and it aims at class and minority integration and solidarity. It has no universal vision to offer the world. And lastly, a welfare state is bureaucratic and creates a huge administrative apparatus.[8]

The Islamic State

The first Islamic state was evolved in Madinah at the time of the Prophet Muhammad, upon whom be peace, and his first four successors. As such, the principles of this state are to be found in the Qur'an and the Sunnah. The essence of an Islamic state is the notion that "all sovereignty belongs to Allah." The state is one of the means that brings human beings closer to Him. Consequently, we find a Muslim scholar like al-Mawardi defining the purpose of an Islamic state as "to continue the function of prophethood in safeguarding the religion and managing worldly affairs" لخلافة النبوة في حراسة الدين وسياسة الدنيا.[9] Ibn Taymiyyah adds that the objective of statehood is "that all religion be to Allah and that Allah's word be supreme."[10] Likewise, Ibn Khaldoon explains the relation between the management of worldly affairs and Allah's word being supreme: "... according to shari'ah, worldly affairs

---

[7]Robson: *ibid.*, p. 24.

[8]D.C. Marsh: *The Welfare State:* Longman, London, 1970, pp. 8-16.

[9]Abu al-Hasan al-Mawardi: *al-Ahkam al-Sultaniyah*, Maktabat al-Babi al-Halabi, Cairo, 3rd edition. 1973, p. 5.

[10]Ahmad Ibn Taimiyyah: *al-Hisbah fi al-Islam*, Dar al-Kutub al-Arabiyah, Beirut, no date. p. 2. حتى يكون الدين لله وتكون كلمة الله هي العليا

are all considered with reference to their benefits in the Hereafter"[11] Ibn Khaldoon, therefore, clarifies the function of an Islamic state as "getting everybody to follow the intent of the shari'ah's position in their worldly and other than worldly affairs."[12]

In this definition of an Islamic state's function, two elements can be pointed out as distinct and unique:

First, a system of rationalization is utilized by the state to determine the relevance, usefulness and efficacy of political decisions and the process of their making. However, it is recognized that every political system has its own rationale, and Ibn Khaldoon himself distinguished among the different kinds of political rationalization: monarchic, democratic, and Islamic. The monarchic rationale is based on a set of values that surrounds and nourishes the desires, zeals and drives of the monarch (مقتضى الغرض والشهوة). The democratic rationale is based on human reasoning without being value committed or guided by divine revelation, while the Islamic rationale is based on human reasoning committed to divine revelation in both values and methodology.

Second, the domain and scope of an Islamic state includes worldly affairs as well as affairs of the Hereafter. As such, the responsibility of the Islamic state toward its citizens is to help them attain the pleasure of Allah. Imam Shatibi says: "The interests of religion are absolutely higher than the interests of the worldly life."[13]

The concept that an Islamic state has a primary role is the cornerstone of the Islamic system of government. It represents the principal characteristic of this system and stands, in contrast to capitalist democracy (rule by the people, for the people, and of the people), and communist democracy (rule for people),[14] because both democracies are limited to worldly affairs.

It is by virtue of this kind of definition and its two fundamental elements that an Islamic state is uniquely and distinctively characterized as the vicegerent of Almighty Allah who is the Source of religion, because an Islamic state "represents" Him by promoting His religion and administering the world according to His commandments.[15]

---

[11]Ibn Khaldoon: al-Muqaddimah, Dar al-Sha'b, Cairo, no date, p. 169.

هي حمل الكافة على مقتضى النظر الشرعي في مصالحهم الآخروية والدنيوية

[12]Ibn Khaldoon, ibid. إذ أحوال الدنيا كلها ترجع عند الشارع الى اعتبارها بمصالح الآخرة

[13]Imam Abu-Ishaq al-Shatibi: Al-Muwafaqat fi 'Usul al-Shari'ah, al-Maktabah al-Tijariyah al-Kubra, Cairo, 2nd edition, 1975, vol. 2, p. 370. المصالح الدينية مقدمة على المصالح الدنيوية على الاطلاق

[14]'Uthman Khalil: al-Dimuqratiyah al-Islamiyah, al-Maktab al-Fanni Li al-Nashr, Cairo, 1958.

[15]Ibn Khaldoon holds the following comparison in distinguishing between three systems: monarchy, democracy, and Islamic. Monarchy wants people to fulfill the desires of the

Economic and Political
Implications of the Concept of an Islamic State

On the basis of the preceding definitions and characteristics of an Islamic state and a welfare state, the remainder of this paper will be devoted to studying the implications of differences between these two types of government. This will be done in the following areas:

Priorities of the political apparatus;

Scope of the function of the state; and

Limitations within which the state operates.

In these three areas, our discussion will concentrate on the political and economic aspects.

Priorities

In an Islamic state, the primary objectives are to safeguard Islam and the supremacy of the Word of Allah; whereas in a welfare state, the main objective is to provide social services to the poor and to bring the society closer to an "economic equality" through the use of social services such as health care, education, pensions for the elderly, and so on.[16]

This difference in priorities has several practical implications. For instance, while a welfare state is service oriented,[17] an Islamic state is geared toward the implementation and expansion of Islam. It was such motivations that pushed the poverty-ridden society of the first Islamic state to devote the majority of its resources to taking people out of the worship of other creatures and into the worship of God, and to moving them from the narrow-mindedness of worldly matters to the vast vision of the whole universe, and from the oppression of religion to the justice of Islam.[18]

In matters of economics, the priorities of an Islamic state represent a clear departure from traditional welfare economics and policies in terms of its objectives as well as its measurements. Economic development, economic equality, and economic equilibrium are relegated to a secondary place, whereas production of goods and services are facilitated, especially in areas that can enhance the defense capability of the state both as a political entity and as a vehicle for worldwide *da'wah* movement.

---

king. Democracy wants people to fulfill the intent of their rational judgement to manage their worldly affairs, and the Islamic state wants people to manage worldly affairs in consideration of their benefit in the Hereafter. *Op. cit.,* pp. 169-170.

[16]Vic George and Paul Wilding: *Ideology and Social Welfare,* Routledge and Kegan Paul, London, 1976, pp. 106-138.

[17]It is noticed that the welfare state originated in the war-tired British society of the forties.

[18]As declared by Rib'i b. 'Amer, the companion of the Prophet, upon whom be peace, to Rustum, the commander of the ancient Persian army before the battle of Qadisiyah.

It should be noted, however, that there are two levels of social services that are usually provided by the state. The first level of services is provided in the form of relief to disaster-stricken areas, where the survival of people and the salvation of their properties are at stake. Included in this category are aids and services provided to people striken by war, famine, production below a certain subsistence level, and so on. The second level of social services aims at improving the economic lot of the poor.

According to shari'ah, the first level of social services can be classi-fied as necessities; as such, it is one of the functions of an Islamic state to seek their fulfillment. Necessities are defined by al-Shatibi as things and services that are "indispensable for the survival of human beings in areas of religion, life, mind, geneological reproduction and property."[19] Consequently, an Islamic state is obliged to provide these services and to procure the necessary resources for them even to the extent of imposing special taxes in addition to zakah.

The second level of social services aims at improving the quality of life rather than maintaining it; thus, an Islamic state is not obliged to guarantee the provision of these services. However, if there is any zakah left over after fulfilling other obligations, it may be used for this level of social services.

As for the welfare measurements, it should be noted that the yardsticks of per capita income, and per capita public spending on social services are inadequate in an Islamic society, since they lack the spiritual and religious content of welfare. This can be explained by quoting an example from the life of the Prophet, upon whom be peace, when a woman came to him and said:

> "I get fits of epilepsy and my body becomes uncovered; please invoke Allah for me." The Prophet, upon whom be peace, said: "If you wish, you can be patient and enter Paradise; and if you wish, I will invoke Allah to cure you." She said: "I will remain patient," and added: "but I become uncovered, so please invoke Allah for me that I may not become uncovered." So he invoked Allah for her.

Moreover, the concept of richness (غنى) was defined by the Prophet, upon whom be peace, as the self-contentment with what one has.[20] Also, the concept of modesty (عفاف) is used in the Qur'an as satisfaction with a little, to the extent that one appears rich.[21]

---

[19]al-Shatibi; op. cit., v. 2, pp. 6-7.

[20]Reported by Bukhari and Muslim; see Kitab al-Mardha, "Riches does not mean having a great amount of property, but riches is self-contentment."

[21]"The ignorant man thinks that they (who don't ask for charity) are rich because of their modesty." The Qur'an 2:273;

Also, in his prayer, the Prophet used to say: "My Lord, give me only the bare sustenance." Reported by Muslim.

With such new elements of *thawab*, *'afaf*, and *ghina al-nafs* entering into the welfare of Muslims, there is a need for creating new criteria to measure welfare for people who would not ask for help, even if it be the state.

Scope of the State's Function

The scope of an Islamic state's function goes beyond the worldly affairs of its people. El-Awa, and al-Mawardi before him, includes as part of the duties of the state:

"...The preservation of faith in its established principles and in the form upon which al-salaf (the predecessors) of the Ummah had unanimously agreed;

...Jihad against those who oppose Islam after calling upon them to embrace it, or to accept protection as non-Muslims, so that the right of Allah is upheld by proclamation of the religion in its entirety."[22]

Consequently, an Islamic state carries a political responsibility for the establishment of Islam (اقامة الدين). This responsibility gives the state a new role by allowing it to adopt policies that help its citizenry to perform their religious obligations to the best of their abilities. In reality, this role may reach as far as the individual's private practice of worship such as prayer and fasting.[23] Besides, an Islamic state is obliged to protect those Muslim minorities outside the Muslim state and to preserve their Islamic identity:

"... But if they seek your aid in religion, it is your duty to help them..." (8:72).

Additionally, an Islamic state is responsible for making the "word of Allah" reach those non-Muslims both inside and outside the state. It is further required to exert its best effort to remove any obstacles that may be in the way of the spread of Islam to non-Muslims.

On the other hand, the economic implications of an Islamic state's function include the reallocation of resources necessary for the establishment of Islam, even through coercion, if need be.[24] The economic implication may also call for imposing some kind of "moral pollution requirements" on the place and environment of work, and the elimination of the immoral goods and services from both production and distribution.

---

[22]M.S. El-Awa: *The Political System of the Islamic State;* American Trust Publications, Indianapolis, 1980, p. 77.

[23]For example, the fuqaha' have decided that the Islamic state is not only required to provide a minimum religious education, but it must also punish those who do not establish their own prayers.

[24]Mohammad al-Mubarak: *al-Dawlah wa Nizam al-Hisbah 'ind Ibn Taimiyyah*, Dar al-Fikr, Beirut, 1967, p. 136.

Limitations on the State's Operation

In a welfare state there are two major constraints on the conduct of its affairs. They are: the state's commitment to equality through social policy, and its commitment to democracy by voting. The first constraint distinguishes a welfare state from a nineteenth century capitalist state, and the second distinguishes it from a totalitarian socialist state.

In the field of economic policy, these limitations imply that a welfare state determines the desired social services and their means of finance by majority voting. And in the political field, these limitations imply an increase in humanitarian concerns and the protection of privacy in shaping the policies and laws of the welfare state. Such restraints expressed themselves in abolishing capital punishment, treating criminals as sick rather than sinful, relaxing the traditional prohibition in marital bonds, and in treating fornication and adultery as private rather than social matters.

On the other hand, an Islamic state has two major limitations that are derived from Islamic ideology: the state's commitment to the shari'ah, and its commitment to shura (mutual consultation).

The shari'ah is, in fact, the *raison d'etre* of the Islamic state; and as such, it can only operate within its bounds. Muslim thinkers distinguish between two areas of state operations that are bounded by the shari'ah. The first area is where the shari'ah provides a complete prescription of Allah's guidance. In this area the state's role is limited to the sincere execution of the shari'ah. This area covers matters like the majority of inheritance rules, penal code for major crimes, prohibition of interest, and imposition of *zakah*. The second area is where the shari'ah provides the principles and the guidelines for the state's operations, leaving to it the task of shaping the rules and regulations. The second area, which is sometimes called "the open area" or "the area of the vacuum,"[25] covers issues such as a penal code for minor crimes (التعزيز), taxation other than *zakah*, capital accumulation, resource allocation, organization of the state and division of authorities.[26]

The commitment to *shura* requires that in all affairs of the state, the believers (i.e., people) should be involved and consulted.[27] Definitely, this applies only to the second area and to the execution of the first area of state operations.

Needless to say, the implications of the different constraints of a welfare state and an Islamic state are tremendous, because while a

---

[25]Mohammad Baqir al-Sadr: *Iqtisaduna*, Dar al-Fikr, Beirut, 1968, p. 362.
[26]*Ibid.*
[27]El-Awa, *op. cit.*, pp. 86-89. For a discussion on whether Shura is binding and its scope, see pp. 90-97.

welfare state can determine what services to provide and how to finance them, and what laws to adopt and how to implement them, the Islamic state is bound by Islam whose Messenger, upon whom be peace, laid the ground for relations among people and between all (or anyone) of them and the state on the basis of what is lawful and what is prohibited (الحلال بين والحرام بين).[28] Consequently, an Islamic state is not free in setting the economic and political priorities, nor is it free in imposing any pattern of governmental spending, taxes or any political, social, or economic limitations on its people that may violate their God-given freedom and rights, knowing certainly that the shari'ah provides the means for dealing with exceptional cases.

The rest of this paper will deal with one case as an example of the difference between a welfare state and an Islamic state — the case of taxation. A welfare state may impose any tax and to any extent that satisfies the quest for social services toward equality, provided the parliament approves of such taxes. An Islamic state cannot do the same.

Many Muslim scholars, past and present, have dealt with the question of whether the state can impose taxes other than *zakah*. Their answers are generally negative in the case of early scholars and affirmative in the case of contemporary one's. However, a survey of the texts, verses and sayings,[29] provided as arguments by the two sides, allows us to deduce the following points:

- ✓ Texts of sayings that directly allow or forbid imposing taxes in addition to *zakah* do not withstand Hadith scrutiny and are not generally acceptable.
- ✓ If *zakah* is defined in a way as it includes duties on agricultural products and cattle, there is no text that can be used as a basis for analogy to allow the state to levy additional taxes.
- ✓ 'Ayah 177 of *al-Baqarah* deals with spending on categories of recipients exactly similar to those included among recipients of *zakah*. Therefore, the most that can be said about this kind of spending is that it becomes obligatory only if *zakah* is not sufficient.
- ✓ Specifically, purposes of welfare, development, and/or economic equilibrium are not referred to in the Qur'an or Sunnah, be they explicit or implicit.
- ✓ Texts of general cooperation and solidarity among Muslims do not serve as evidence for allowing taxes to be imposed on specific people for specific purposes unless it can be proven that there are no means of cooperation and solidarity other than

---

[28]Reported by Bukhari and Muslim
[29]Yusuf al-Qardawi gave a good survey of these texts. See *Fiqh al-Zakah*, Dar al-Irshad, Beirut, 1969, volume 2, pp. 964-984.

such taxes.

✓ There are clear and strong texts that protect private property from any act of aggression whether by the state or by individuals.

✓ There are many texts that allow the violation of a less important rule for the safeguard of a more important rule, and the sacrifice of a minor benefit for a higher benefit in application of: "necessities make forbidden things allowed (الضرورات تبيح المحظورات).

✓ Necessities must not be exaggerated and must be measured with a correct yardstick (الضرورات تقدر بقدرها), because the general rule is that killing or taking property is forbidden unless through the right application of the shari'ah (دماؤهم وأموالهم عليهم حرام الابحقها).

In application, these eight points are carefully utilized in determining the legitimacy of taxes by early Muslim scholars. For example, Imam Malik, who is often quoted as an advocate of taxes,[30] says that "if there were no funds in the treasury or the needs of the army increased above the capacity of the treasury, the state has the right to levy taxes on the rich up to the level that satisfied that need immediately and until the revenues of the treasury appear."

It is worth noticing that Imam Malik mentioned five important conditions: (1) regular revenues are depleted, (2) defense expenses exceed current resources, (3) taxes are levied temporarily, (4) taxes are imposed in total receipts not exceeding the needs, and (5) taxes are levied on the rich only.

Ibn Hazm is also reported to have supported taxation, while he restricts the levying of taxes to the case where the *zakah* proceeds are not sufficient to fulfill the needs of the poor so that the poor people "are given the indispensable food and cloth for winter and summer and a shelter that protects them from rain, sun, and the eyes of passers-by."[32]

'Abd al-Haiy al-Kattani discusses the collective duties that strengthen the interests of the Muslims both in religious and worldly affairs, such as salaries of military personnel, students/researchers in the shari'ah, and teachers of young children. He concludes that such payment should be provided by the treasury of the state. If, however, there is a shortage, Muslims are collectively responsible for raising the necessary funds.[33]

Thus, the imposition of taxes in addition to *zakah* is justified according to Malik, Ibn Hazm, and Kattani in cases of defense needs, assurance of a subsistent living of the poor and the indispensable expenses that cherish the collective interests of Muslims. These three

---

[30]See 'Abd al-Sami' al-Misri: *Nazariyat al-Islam al-Iqtisadiyah*, Maktabat al-Anglo-Misrayah, Cairo, 1971, pp. 151-152.

[31]See Mohammad Abu Zahra: *al-Imam Malik*, Cairo, 1963, pp. 400-401.

[32]See Yusuf al-Qardawi: *op. cit.*, p. 981.

[33]Abd al-Haiy al-Kattani: *al-Tarateeb al-Idariyah*, published by Hasan Ja'va, Beirut, no date, volume 1, pp. 394-396.

thinkers did not mention development, equilibrium, and welfare in justifying the levying of taxes.

From the above discussion, it becomes clear that the levying of taxes, in addition to *zakah* is an exception and not a rule.[34] Taxes can be imposed by an Islamic state under certain circumstances and conditions. To determine these circumstances in a clear way would be ironic.

Two areas deserve our attention in determining these exceptional conditions that provide justification for taxes: First, the kind and urgency of necessities; and second, the alternatives available to respond to these necessities.

Necessities that Justify Taxation

- ✓ Internal and external security, including the cost of regular and emergency forces at times of peace and war, to the extent that these provide security and safeguard for Islam, its land and people, such as freeing Muslim captives in other countries.
- ✓ Current expenses of such activities of the Islamic state as the political apparatus (the cost of running the executive and shura branches of government), judicial and *hisbah* apparatus, and the safeguard and promotion of the ideological and ethical values of Islam.[35]
- ✓ The maintenance of a socially determined subsistence standard of living for all people in an Islamic state. The subsistence level includes what Ibn Hazm described as indispensable food, cloth, and shelter or what 'Ali described as preventing hunger, nakedness, and hardship.[36] Al-Shatibi's definition of necessities provides not only for material and biological needs, but also for needs arising from social and religious living, i.e., the subsistence standard of living must include such services as minimum education, transportation and health care.

A distinction is needed, however, between subsistence and welfare. The difference is basically a matter of degree, and with the help of the definitions of al-Shatibi of necessities (الضروريات), wants (الحاجيات), and luxuries (التحسينات), one can shed some light on this difference. Necessities are indispensable for the survival of humans in areas of religion, life, mind, geneological reproduction, and property. The satisfaction of wants improves the quality of life and removes "bearable hardship and difficulty," while luxuries add beauty, elegance, and fragrance (not reaching prohibited extravagance).[37] The concept of

---

[34]Qardawi, op. cit., pp. 991-992.
[35]See Mohammad al-Mubarak: *Nizam al-Islam: al-Hukm wa al-Dawlah*, Dar al-Fikr, Beirut, 1974, pp. 86-96.
[36]Qardawi, op. cit., p. 983.
[37]Al-Shatibi, op. cite., volume 2, pp. 6-12.

subsistence deals with necessities, whereas the concept of welfare includes wants.

- ✓ To develop production capacity capable of providing the subsistence living mentioned above, if the private sector has failed to perform its role.
- ✓ Relief of economic, social, and psychological pressures resulting from natural disasters, war, or any similar emergency.

Alternative Means of Finance

Theoretically, taxes are the last resort in Islam. Muslim scholars have no disagreement that taxes may be levied when the state has no other resources. Such a taxation must not exceed the deficit of funds. In practice, the early Muslim state did not impose taxes unless warranted by exceptional emergencies.[38] Tax impositions were very few in the history of Islam because the state was rich and rarely needed more resources. This fact, in itself, has two implications: (1) taxes were considered as the last resort by the people in authority, and (2) there were several other resources available to the Islamic state. Consequently, in stating what may be available to a modern Islamic state, one should take the time to see if these "old and traditional" means of finance are to be included. These old and traditional means of finance of an Islamic state include: *al-Kharaj, al-Jiziah,* revenue of public enterprises, public debt, equity finance, fees, and voluntary contributions.

It should be noted that while *zakah* receipts are appropriated for distribution to one or more of the recipient categories mentioned in the Qur'an, the proceeds of most of the above taxes are not, and an Islamic state is free to make the choice of financial resource utilization in light of the Qur'an and the Sunnah.[39] However, other resources may be restricted to specific purposes such as public loans and contributions for special projects and equity sharing. On the other hand, although *zakah* proceeds are designated, their use for the development of a productive capacity adequate to support the defense activities and the subsistence level of living is included under the designation.

As such, state revenues, including *zakah*, may be classified into 'general' and 'designated'. General revenues should be used to supply adequate satisfaction of such necessities as internal and external security, maintaining subsistence living, and government apparatus, and so forth; and then, to support the objectives of the designated revenues. Taxes, other than those mentioned above, may be imposed

---

[38]An example of that is the ruling of Shaikh al-Islam Izzuddin Ibn 'Abd al-Salam to the ruler of Egypt Qutuz that he may impose taxes only after selling the slaves owned by the state. See Qardawi, *op cit.*, pp.1079-1181.

[39]A.A. Na'im, *Nizam al-Dhara'ib fi al-Islam*, 2nd edition, 1975, pp. 203-206.

only if the regular revenues are not sufficient to meet the necessities discussed earlier.

Moreover, forced borrowing is similar to taxes since they both are imposed by the state. Hence, if taxes are the last resort, compulsory borrowing is the one before last. In this sense, forced borrowing represents a close alternative to taxes when the state expects future revenues usable for the same kind of necessity. For example, for defense expenses, the state may not be allowed to levy taxes if it can borrow and pay back from future *zakah* and *kharaj* proceeds. By applying the same rationale, a general equilibrium tax is not allowed as long as the state can substitute it by forced loans from the public payable at times of boom and retiring them at times of recession, since for the purpose of general equilibrium, there is no need for financial revenues. The purpose is rather to withdraw some means of payments from the hands of the public at one time and to return them at another time. Consequently, a tax is not justifiable while a loan may be.

Chapter IX

POLITICAL RIGHTS IN ISLAM

Al-Tayib Zein al-'Abdin

Dr. Al-Tayib Zein al-'Abdin is Director of the Islamic African Center (Khartoum), Sudan. His article was first published in *al-ittihad* of Jumada al-Thani-Sha'ban 1402/April-June 1982.

Man has started to speak about political rights since he discovered that politics is too serious a business to be left to politicians alone. The conduct of public affairs, which is the concern of politics, has become a complicated process that affects all aspects of our lives as citizens in the modern society of today. The national state of today, through its gigantic agents — the professional army and the huge bureaucracy — has been able to control the economy, the health service, the mass media and the institutes of recreation, culture and education. This control over the different segments of society has jeopardized man's freedom. No wonder after a long and painful journey, he is embracing the view upheld by all messengers of God that freedom is the dearest human value worthy of sacrifice. But how close has he come to achieving that goal? The US as a society is supposed by many to be the most advanced and the most open in the world; nevertheless, after two hundred years of constitutional rule in the United States, there has not been a serious candidate for the presidency who is liberal enough to select a black American as his Vice President. Rousseau's statement still holds true, that man is born free and is everywhere in chains. In that respect, the so-called Muslim world is worse than many places! We should not be surprised that the heads and representatives of Muslim states keep postponing the draft on human rights set by the Organization of the Islamic Conference again and again. If this is the situation in the contemporary world, does Islam, as a comprehensive philosophy of life, offer us any alternative of political freedom?

If human freedom is ever divisible, then we may speak of political rights as an essential division in preserving that freedom. There are three major areas of political rights that merit discussion.

First, the formation of government;

Second, the participation in decision-making; and

Third, the freedom of belief and expression of views.

Before going into the details of political rights, some general concepts which illustrate the Islamic concept of human freedom in general have to be explained:

√ The principle of *tauhid* (the Oneness of God) in Islam is the bedrock of human freedom. *Tauhid* is based on the belief that nothing can bring good or evil to man without the will of God, that life on this earth is transitory and the eternal life is yet to come, and that man shall be judged according to his deeds on the Day of Judgment. These beliefs, by their very nature, cause the human soul not to yield to any other being except God and give man an internal freedom whatever his circumstances are.

√ Islam holds that all human beings are equal, as equal as the teeth of a comb. We are all the children of 'Adam, and 'Adam is made of earth. No race, no color, no class, no religion is superior to others. The only criterion of man's nobility is *taqwa* (Allah's consciousness), which does not allow a person any special rights over other human beings. Equality in Islam presupposes that human beings should be equally free.

√ If there is one absolute value in Islam, that value is justice. Everybody is entitled to be treated in a fair manner, irrespective of religion, race, color, or if the person concerned is a friend, a relative or an enemy. Justice in its social dimension, according to Islam, assumes the right of man to live in peace, to work and to be reasonably paid for his work. Further, the state is responsible to secure the basic needs of life for each of its citizens. Without such social guarantees in society, political rights and political freedom may not be anything more than a lip-service to an illusionary high principle.

The Islamic state is not a theocracy in the sense that it should be run by a class of "religious" people. No person or group of persons has any automatic right to be political leaders of the *ummah*. The criteria for selecting a person for a job are his ability to do that job and the strength of his moral character. The Qur'an says: "Surely the best (man) that you can hire is the strong (and) the trustworthy."[1] The Prophet, upon whom be peace, put the same principle in stronger terms: "He who gives a job to a person when he knows that there is another Muslim

---

[1]The Qur'an 28:26

who is better qualified for it, then the covenants of God, of His Messenger, and of Muslims, absolve themselves from such a man." Muslim jurists have set certain moral and intellectual qualifications for senior political offices. The norm is that the Muslims should look around to find the best person for the office, not the person pushing himself forward to seize the office. The office of *khilafah* itself is open for any Muslim who has the right qualifications and has been chosen by the *ummah*.

The procedure to select the *khalifah* is that senior members of the *ummah* who represent the scholars, the social and political forces in society, should deliberate to nominate the person best qualified for the highest political office. That person becomes the *khalifa* only when the *ummah* accepts the nomination and gives him *bay'ah* (pays him homage). That was the classical practice during the period of *al-Khulafa' ar-Rashidun* (the rightly-guided *khalifs*). *Bay'ah* is a political contract, and like all contracts in Islam, it has to be by mutual agreement between the parties concerned. Islam does not allow people to be led by a person whom they do not like, even in a matter as simple as prayers. Government by domination from within or outside society is not permissible. The Qur'an tells us that the foreign and imposed governments can only bring destruction to society: "Lo! Kings when they enter a township, ruin it and make the honor of its people shame. Thus they will do."[2] Muslims are not to stand by when another society is destroyed or its people humiliated. God enjoins us: "How should you not fight for the cause of God and of the feeble — men, women and children."[3] Islam realizes the social norm of life that good needs to be defended by force to overcome evil. The Qur'an says: "For had it not been for God's repelling some men by means of others, cloisters, churches, oratories and mosques, wherein the name of God is often mentioned, would assuredly have been pulled down."[4]

What about the question of removing the *khalifah* from office? In early Islamic history this problem caused bloodshed, as in the cases of murdering the *khalifs* 'Uthman and 'Ali. Muslim jurists sanction the removal of the *khalifah* if he deviates from the shari'ah. In a modern Islamic state, clear regulations would have to be set and institutionalized to allow a peaceful and lawful removal of an erring *khalifah*.

If peaceful removal of *khalifs* was not common in Islamic history, checking their excesses and mistakes was. The *bay'ah* is given to the *khalifah* on the basis that he follows the Qur'an and the Sunnah of the Prophet. Any individual in the *ummah* has the right to check the rulings

---

[2]Ibid. 27:34
[3]Ibid. 4:75
[4]Ibid. 22:40

and policies of the *khalifah*. As a matter of fact, it is not only a right but the duty of all Muslims to correct the ruler's mistakes. In his inauguration speech, the first *khalifah*, Abu Bakr, asked his audience to help him when they found him right and to correct him when he was wrong. 'Umar, the second *khalifah*, made a similar statement and a member in the assembly told him that they would correct him with their swords. Furthermore, rulers in Islam do not have any immunity; anybody may easily bring the *khalifah* before the court, as happened many times in our history. The one who stands up to a tyrant for truth has been addressed by the Prophet, upon whom be peace, as "the master of martyrs." Therefore, checking the excesses of a ruler, in Islam, is a high form of *jihad*.

The second area of political rights is participation in decision-making. This is generally known in Islamic terminology as *shura* (consultation). Two Qur'anic verses speak about *shura*: one is a direct order from God to the Prophet himself that he should consult Muslims in their affairs. The second is more telling — it mentions *shura* as a common quality of the believers: "And those who answer the call of their Lord and establish worship, and whose affairs are a matter of counsel, and who spend of what We have bestowed on them."[5] The verse goes beyond political matters to make *shura* a quality for Muslims in all walks of life in home, at work, as well as in political institutions. Muslim jurists agree that *shura* is a right of the ruled and a duty of the ruler. The Prophet himself, with all his wisdom and divine guidance, practiced *shura* on a wide scale. Abu Hurayrah reported that he never saw anyone who consulted his companions more than the Prophet did.

The issues for *shura* are not limited. Any affair which has not been decided upon by revelation may be a matter of *shura*. The Prophet upon whom be peace, consulted his companions in a variety of problems: economic, political, social and those of a military nature. He even consulted the congregation of the mosque on what to do about the ill-founded rumors concerning the behavior of his wife, Saydah 'Ayshah. He would insist on *shura* when the problem at hand required a degree of sacrifice on behalf of the people. In short, Muslims have the right to *shura*, or participation in decision-making, in any problem that concerns them and for which the Qur'an or Sunnah has not offered a definite solution.

The question may be asked, who should be consulted and on which problems: Muslims of today have to set regulations for that question according to the needs of their time. The practice of our Prophet may be summarized as follows:

- He consulted all people or their known representatives in

---

[5]Ibid. 42:38

matters which concerned them or required some sacrifice on their behalf.

- In technical problems, such as the strategy of wars, the Prophet asked *shura* from those who had a deep knowledge and experience about the problem.

- Lastly, in general, on questions of a complex nature, he sought the *shura* of persons who were known for their wisdom and sound opinion. Abu Bakr as-Siddiq and 'Umar b. al-Khattab were frequently asked by the Prophet to give their opinion on such questions.

No matter whom the ruler consults, the outcome of *shura* is binding on him. As long as the issue is decided on the basis of *ijtihad* and *maslaha* (public good), the Muslim ruler is bound to accept the opinion rendered to him by all or the majority of those he trusted for *shura*. The Prophet himself followed in two clear cases the *shura* given to him, although it differed with his own judgement. Thus, no other human being, especially the feeble rulers of the contemporary Muslim world, should claim a righteous status in decision-making.

The Prophet, upon whom be peace, also recognized the associations of various tribes, of the Jews as well as of the *muhajirun* and *ansar*, and accepted the views of their representatives on a number of issues. The Prophet did not create these groups, they were simply the social and political forces at that time. As such, he recognized them and dealt with their leaders as legitimate spokesmen of their people. Later on, the history of Islam witnessed associations on purely political grounds: the Kharijis, the Shi'is, the Sunnis, the Mu'tazilis, and so on. The Fiqh *madhhabs* were another form of loose association based on religious interpretations. Nevertheless, Muslims, irrespective of their associations, are enjoined to seek the general good of society and should not act in a partisan manner.

The third area of political rights is the freedom of belief and expression of views. Islam recognizes a belief as a matter of conviction and conscience, and no power, as such, is allowed to intervene to compel a change of belief. The Qur'an rejects the arguments of those who adopted certain beliefs simply because of the influence of a despotic ruler or a noble class or traditions of one's forefathers. It says about Fir'un (the Pharoah): "He made fools of his people, and they obeyed him. Truly they were a deviated folk."[6] They were deviators from the Path of God because they allowed themselves to be fooled by a dictator. The other group argued: "Our Lord, we obeyed our nobles and great men, and they misled us from the Way."[7] Lastly, there were those who blindly followed their fathers. "They indeed found their

---

[6]Ibid. 43:54
[7]Ibid. 33:67

fathers astray, but they make haste to follow in their footsteps."[8] Even the belief in God Himself has to be a totally free and voluntary matter. The Qur'an rules: "There is no compulsion in religion. The right direction is henceforth distinct from error."[9] Islam urges people to migrate if they have to in order to live according to their convictions. "When the angels take the souls of those who die doing wrong to themselves, they ask them, in what were you engaged? They answer: we were oppressed in the land. The angels say: was not the earth of God spacious enough that you could have migrated therein? Such men will find their abode in Hell, what an evil refuge."[10]

In a Muslim society, non-believers should be given protection. Thus God instructed His Prophet, "And if anyone of the idolaters seeks your protection, then protect him so that he may hear the word of God, and afterward convey him to his place of safety. That is because they are a folk who know not."[11] Not only that, but their false gods themselves should not be abused. The Qur'an says: "(O Believers), do not revile those whom they invoke besides God lest they should, in ignorance, revile God."[12] Furthermore, we are enjoined to argue with them in a good manner: "Call to the Way of your Lord with wisdom and fair exhortation, reason with them in the better way."[13] A religion which respects the false beliefs of its enemies to this extent can never be intolerant of its own followers' political views. Despite the many deviations that took place, the history of Islam did not witness any persecution on the basis of political views.

The right to express a political view is equally guaranteed and protected. When this view concerns a religious order or a public good, its expression becomes not only a right but a duty which has to be performed whatever the circumstances may be. This, in Islam, is known as enjoining the good and forbidding the evil. In fact, this is the major distinction of the Muslim ummah over other communities. God says: "You are the best community that has been raised up for mankind. You enjoin right conduct and forbid evil, and you believe in God."[14] Enjoining the good and forbidding evil may, in certain conditions, go beyond the mere expression of views to putting things right by force. People should not be harassed, spied upon, or ridiculed because of their views. Man, having a breath of God in his creation, is entitled to a high degree of dignity which has to be preserved in all respects of his life.

---

[8]Ibid. 37:69-70
[9]Ibid. 2:256
[10]Ibid. 4:99
[11]Ibid. 9:6
[12]Ibid. 6:108
[13]Ibid. 14:125
[14]Ibid. 3:110

In conclusion, a few general points:

• Many of the principles mentioned are not actually "political rights" but "political duties" which have to be performed by everybody. This closes the door on certain sections of the population who are more effective in the process of the decision-making than others, simply because they are better organized, or more active, or rich enough... or for any other reason. In other words, Islam is not elitist but populist.

• Those rights or duties are ruled by none else than God Himself. No human being and no government is to suspend, modify or cancel any of them whatever the situation be. The responsibility to guard these rights falls upon the Islamic government, upon the people in general and upon each individual Muslim.

• Lastly, these rights were revealed to a simple Muslim society which was not accustomed to it and did not ask for it. They did not have to make a revolution to gain these rights. Those rights were an integral part of the religion of Islam; they were declared and implemented with the emergence of the Islamic state under the blessed leadership of Prophet Muhammad, upon whom be peace.

Chapter X

ISLAMIC SOCIAL SYSTEM: ITS DIMENSIONS AND CHARACTERISTICS

Hammudah 'Abdalati

Dr. Hammudah 'Abdalati (1928-1976) taught sociology at Utica College of Syracuse University as associate professor. His *Islam in Focus* and *The Family Structure of Islam*, both published by American Trust Publications, are popular works. The present article was first published by *al-ittihad* in its Sha'ban 1391/September 1971 issue.

Ideological Basis of the Islamic Social System

Every social system requires an ideological basis to guide its members and to regulate their behavior. The ideological basis of the Islamic social system is the ideology of unity, *tauhid*. This means the Oneness of God, and the oneness of mankind, and equality as an ultimate human destiny. The ideology of unity is an ideology of active commitment, and the ideology of Islamic social system is, by definition, a system of commitment. For the concept of Islam means submission and obedience to the Will of God and His law in both word and deed.

The Islamic social system is necessarily based on Islam, and maintained by Muslims. They constitute one *ummah* or nation despite any racial, social, geographic, or other differences. This single nation of Muslims earns distinct honor by identifying with God and dedicating to His service. In the words of God: "Verily, this your nation is one nation, and I am your lord, so fear only Me".[1] This single nation of Muslims is designated as the best of all nations, so long as it promotes good, withstands evil, and believes in God: "You are the best of peoples

---

[1]The Qur'an 23:23.

evolved for mankind, enjoining what is right, forbidding what is wrong, and believing in God."[2] Indeed, the *ummah* has a clear mandate from God to do these things, and is only assured of success if it honors this commitment in active and dynamic fashion: "Let there arise out of you a band of people inviting to all that is good, enjoining what is right, and forbidding what is wrong: they are the ones to attain prosperity."[3]

The logical derivative of the underlying ideology of unity is that there must be equality, solidarity, and brotherhood among the members of the *ummah*. This is not merely a logical derivative; it is also a divine commandment emphasized throughout the Qur'an.[4]

But Islamic brotherhood does not exclude human brotherhood. Nor should it be taken for bigotry or ethnocentrism. It is a constructive brotherhood based on righteousness and faith which promotes peace, compassion, and equity among men, combatting at the same time devisive tendencies such as racism, inequity, derision and character assassination. Equality, on the other hand, does not mean absolute sameness. Such absolute equality is neither conceivable nor desirable or attainable. Rather, it is a basic equality of human rights and duties. It is an equality incorporated into a framework of balance and decorum. It welcomes higher levels of excellence, but condemns all injustice and exploitation.

Islamic principles of unity, brotherhood, and equality stem from the fact that we are all created by One Universal God. Each Muslim identifies equally with the Islamic social system. Each is born equally free of sin or stigmas attached to birth. Each has equal opportunities to achieve excellence, and each is equally committed to the system and responsible to God for its success. And, finally, each man will have to leave this world empty-handed just as he came into it empty-handed, and he will have to stand in final judgment before the Supreme Lord of the worlds. Furthermore, the only scale of ranking on that day and in the sight of God, the only criterion of value, is the level of one's faith and piety. This piety is not the product of a closed caste system of hereditary status; it is an acquired excellence; something to be achieved. It lies within every man's reach, and should be every man's goal.

Within the boundaries of unity, equality, and brotherhood, the Islamic social system permits a degree of individual freedom. However, this again is not a matter of absolute freedom, for no society can function on such a principle. It is a degree of individual freedom which remains consistent with the total system while being conducive both to

---

2 Ibid. 3: 110.
3 Ibid 3:104.
4 Ibid 49: 8-13.

stability and progress. The members of an Islamic social system do not labor under the burden of prejudice, whether it be a prejudice that stems from race, caste, birth, or sex. They are all free to achieve spiritual, moral, and material excellence, to pursue legitimate interests and careers so long as they do not militate against the general good of society or its fundamental ideological principles. They are free to inquire into the nature of things, to acquire possessions by lawful means, and to direct their lives as they please, so long as they do not violate the Law of God or the rights of man. Such individual freedom is for the good of the whole system as well as the wholesomeness of the individual member. Such freedom is a logical derivative of Islam, since it conceives of all men as directly responsible to God for themselves and their role in society. The Qur'an continually reminds us of the interplay between individual responsibility and freedom.[5]

Structural Elements of the Social System

All social systems are made up of various human, political, economic, and legal normative elements. The human elements of the social system are its constituents, and are called agents or actors. The Islamic social system, however, possesses certain supra-human elements which must always be kept in mind when assessing the role of the human actor; meaning thereby, that every social relationship involving a Muslim also involves God as an integral part of that situation. This may become clear, as we briefly examine the concept of the actor in the Islamic social framework.

The Muslim as an Actor in Society

Islam views man the human actor as the agent of God on earth, as a created being whose very creation reflects the will, the wisdom, the power, and the infinite mercy of the Creator. To reflect upon man within this context is the key to understanding the eternal problem of human destiny. Being the creation of God places man, the human actor, in a very special position. For in this conception lies the essence of humanity, the purpose of life, and the meaning of existence. I will outline the Islamic conception as follows:

Man is created for a special purpose, an ultimate end, incorporating all ends. This is the axis around which everything that is human revolves, toward which all human actions are directed. This ultimate end is an integral part of the divine scheme of things, as is unequivocally declared in the Holy Qur'an:

"I have only created the jinn and men that they might worship me. I require no sustenance of them, nor do I require that they feed Me. For God alone is the giver of sustenance: Lord of Power, the

---

[5]Ibid. 17: 13-15; 18: 29-31; 18: 41-48.

eternally steadfast."[6]

Man's ultimate end is to worship and glorify God. But that may not be as simple as it sounds, nor should it be given a narrow interpretation. The Islamic concept of worship does not mean simple ritualistic repetitions, withdrawal from life, or passive asceticism. It means the active observance of God and His will in everything, and this is the meaning of *taqwa*. Indeed, man has been created solely for the purpose of worshipping God. God is that master conception which integrates all life and all other ends into a dynamic unity. It permeates every aspect of human life, regulating and directing the entire social experience; it cultivates moral courage, self-discipline, active asceticism, mastery over the world. In sum, it delegates to man constant responsibilities and highest honor.

Man has a unique position in the universe in the midst of all creation as the vicegerent of God on earth. This is his task, and he is given the course of his lifetime to fulfill and discharge this duty:

"And it is He who has made you (His) agents of the earth: He has raised you in ranks, some above others, that He may try you in the gifts He has given unto you: for your Lord is quick in punishment; and yet oft-forgiving, most Merciful."[7]

The implications of this unique position are far-reaching. Man is given a trust and is capable of the most noble achievements; while, of course, also being capable of the most abominable failures. He is a free agent, although his freedom is restricted by spatial and temporal realities. He is above all, a responsible actor; each of his acts, even the most minute, is closely watched, carefully recorded, and judiciously evaluated.

Rarely is the course of life smooth. Rather, it is a test, often trying, sometimes agonizing:

"You will certainly be tried and tested both in your possessions and in your personal selves. And you will certainly hear much that will grieve you, and from those who received the Book before you and from those who worship many gods. But if you will persevere patiently and guard against evil, then that will be a determining factor in all affairs."[8]

Man is a finite being composed of both spiritual and material natures subject to rational, appetitive, and emotional pulls. It is impossible for him to lead a peaceful and balanced life without divine aid. What makes life even more trying for the human actor is the enormous task delegated to him, in addition to his full accountability to his Creator. But this responsibility, fortunately, is matched proportionately to his abilities and limitations. Most important of all, he will be judged by a God

[6]Ibid. 51: 56-58.
[7]Ibid 6: 15.
[8]Ibid. 3:106.

possessed of mercy and forgiveness, whose all-embracing mercy is a permanent element of human experience:

"And if you were to count the favors of God, never would you be able to number them: for God is oft-forgiving, most merciful."[9]

Turning to the nature of the act itself in Islam, we find that every action is of consequence. No action, from a Muslim's point of view, can be appraised simply in terms of being lawful, against the law, or neutral, nor in terms of being merely moral, immoral, or amoral. The consequence and significance of an action does not end on the personal or inter-personal level. It extends far beyond the human realm. Ultimately, the true appraisal of any action lies with God alone. This is true even of the best of actions, since God alone is aware of the motives. So, from the Islamic point of view, each action is delicately weighed on a sensitive scale, a scale designed to evaluate precisely the motivational, cognitive, emotional, and volitional nature of the act. And God's categories of evaluation are comprehensive. For the Muslim, action is of consequence to himself, to the social group, and ultimately to God. Acts are meritorious or worthy of punishment both here and in the life to come. Even if an act is not detected here, it will never escape the scrutiny and judgement of God in the life after death.

Political Dimension of a Muslim Society

From its political standpoint, the Islamic social system cannot be categorized by any standards other than its own. In one sense, it is a democratic system based on the delegation and sharing of authority, as well as the active and watchful participation of its constituents. But it is not the kind of democracy which results in the "Iron Law of Oligarchy," or ends at the human level. It is also a democracy in which the exercise of authority is more a duty than a privilege, and the assumption of power more agonizing than gratifying. It is, moreover, a type of social contract, but the contract is between man and God — not merely between the ruler and the ruled, the elites and the masses. This contract designates God as the ultimate sovereign of any Muslim social system. The ruler and the ruled each have mutual duties over and against each other, but they are both ultimately responsible to God. Exchange of ideas, participation in decision making, and common deliberations, are all part of every Muslim's civic duty and his God-given right.[10] This is a political system in which mutual consultation must be sought by the ruler, and advice given by the ruled.

Economic Dimension of a Muslim Society

The Islamic economic system is neither capitalistic nor communistic. It respects labor, honors work, properly acknowledges excellence, and

---

[9]Ibid. 16: 18.
[10]Ibid. 3:159; 42:38.

richly rewards every effort. It calls upon every Muslim to earn an honorable living, but guarantees the needy and disabled, whether Muslim or non-Muslim, adequate security and support by Muslims in public and private capacities. It defines wealth and all possessions as belonging ultimately to God alone. Man's role is that of a steward or trustee.

The Islamic economic system prescribes equity and compassion, and, as a result, no worker or investor may be denied the fruits of his work or skills. No exploitation is permissible. The wealthy and skilled expert may under no circumstances take advantage of the less skilled, the poor, the unfortuante, or the uninformed. It prescribes a wide circulation and sharing of wealth, expertise, and commodities. Usurpation, usury, monopoly, misrepresentation, and hoarding are forbidden. It prescribes utilization of the natural resources and encourages moderate consumption of all derivative products. Natural resources are rendered subservient to the general welfare and possessions of the community.

Consumption is to be moderate. None should live beyond his means, and none should be deprived. But the indolent, parasitic life styles of a "leisure class" will not be allowed to grow up and undermine the moral and social fabric of society.

Legal Dimension of a Muslim Society

The Islamic social system is governed by the rules and precepts of the shari'ah, the legal principles of the Qur'an and Sunnah. The shari'ah is much more than an ordinary legal system or merely a religious doctrine and law. It is simultaneously religion and law, natural and positive law. It relates man to God. Its origin is divine, its object is human. It deals with the present and the hereafter, encompassing all aspects of human action, whether latent or manifest, open or hidden. It is at once universal and particular, absolute and relative, general and specific, strict and flexible. It tempers formal justice with equity, guarantees liberty, condemns libertinism, encourages excellence, and fights abuse. It welcomes free judicious judgment upon its fundamental principles, but forbids chaos or improvising. It allows dissent and difference of opinion, but is intolerant of dissension. It integrates the human, political, and economic aspects of the Islamic social system into one cohesive and exemplary structure, consistent with itself and intact.

Concluding Remarks

The Islamic social system combines certain unique features. It is not exclusive in any historical, racial, ethnic, social, or even religious sense. Rather, it is an open system capable of incorporating all races, social strata, and the peaceable followers of other religions. It is oriented to constructive interplay with other systems, such as those of other religious groups within the Muslim state, if for no other reason than to propagate Islam and demonstrate to non-Muslims how they may benefit by its blessings. It is a social system based on the multiple and manifold commitment of its members. It is based on moderation and flexibility, proportionate and equitable distribution of rights and duties, and the resourceful use of available alternatives and possibilities. All this is because the Islamic social system grows harmoniously out of the teachings of the Holy Qur'an and Sunnah, oriented to the glory and pleasure of God.

"Surely, this Qur'an guides to that which is best, and brings forth delightful tidings to Believers who do good that theirs is a great reward."[11]

"And for those who fear God, He always prepares a way out; and He provides for him from (sources) he could never have imagined. And if anyone places his trust in God, God is sufficient for him; for God will surely accomplish His purpose: For indeed God has appointed all things with a due proportion."[12]

[11]Ibid. 17:9.
[12]Ibid. 65: 2-3.

Chapter XI

SEX ROLES:
A MUSLIM POINT
OF VIEW
Mahmud Abu Sa'ud

Dr. Mahmud Abu Sa'ud, a former economic advisor to Arab League and the State Bank of Pakistan, is chairman of the Islamic Banking System Luxembourg. He has been a professor at Kabul, Rabat, Muhammad Ibn Sa'ud and Southwest Missouri State Universities. Among his publications, *The Outlines of Islamic Economics,* is well-known. His latest book, *Concept of Islam,* was published by American Trust Publications. The present article first appeared in *al-ittihad* of Sha'ban 1398/July 1978.

The notion of equality between man and woman has often been discussed. In most ot these discussions, however, many Western concepts are alluded to as scientifically irrefutable, many Qur'anic verses are arbitrarily interpreted and many sayings of the Prophet, upon whom be peace, are ignored and described as unauthoritative. One can easily discern the motives behind such arguments and how most of them view the problem from the Western perspective.

To talk about the sex roles in Islam, one has to define "family," its origin and its functioning, the Muslim family as its exists, the Islamic concept of family, and finally, the role of both husband and wife in family life. It is evident that it is the latter part of these elements that will be the core of this study.

ORIGIN OF FAMILY

Biological Factor
The biological coupling of a male and a female is an essential element to constitute a family.

The Cell: All living organisms are made of two kinds of cells: eukaryotes and prokaryotes. The Eukaryotes have nuclei and multiply by mating. The prokaryotes have no distinct nuclei and thus multiply by division. Each cell has its hereditary traits and carries its information in DNA (Deoxyribonucleic acid): ". . .two extremely long strands of it, wrapped around each other in a double helix".[1] It may be of interest to know that only the eukaryotes are "capable of making up the bodies of the marvels of creation - those with hearts, lungs, kidneys and brains."[2] The prokaryotes are parasitic by nature and are deadly enemies of the eukaryotes who eat them up or destroy them with their antiseptics or antibiotics. Human organisms are no more than the sum of their functioning together.

Sex, a word for the exchange of genetic materials, requires two organisms to come together and reproduce. Though there are some organisms that can reproduce without sex, such as some bacteria, their progeny are doomed to be identical to the parent without variation or susceptibility to evolution. The biological evolution needs genetic variety which can only be realized by means of ever new combinations of genes of heterosexual cells - the eukaryotes.

Before exploring the functioning of cells as constituents of human males and females, it is of great interest to know that cells themselves are the product of atoms. Atoms follow an eternal strict code of behavior as if they had some sort of consciousness that brings them together in a highly organized manner. They form molecules in extraordinarily geometric forms; molecules make "tissues that become the organs that inexorably build the organism. . . Every molecule has its own distinct properties by virtue of the atoms that make it up and. . .life has its properties by virtue of the molecule used in constructing living organisms."[3] All living organisms, including bacteria, must use for reproduction nucleic acid organized into genes. The genes are the true carriers of all hereditary traits and properties of the offspring.

Such established elementary knowledge reveals some basic facts of life that concern us in this study. The first fact is that prokaryotes - the unicellular organisms - are parasitic and destructive. They are not capable of evolution and do not constitute any part of our functioning organism.

The second is that eukaryotes cannot continue to exist without mating as they multiply by this process. Their union is the basis of biological evolution through a process of natural selection. They are endowed with a gift to choose the fittest from among themselves and thus genetically improve.

The third is that all molecules belong, in their first origin, to the atom,

---

[1]Cadmure, L.L. Larson, *The Center of Life*, The New York Times Book Co., New York 1977, p. 8.
[2]Ibid., p. 9.
[3]Ibid., p. 28.

which by virtue of its nature does not exist without union. The components of the atom: the protons, the neutrons, and the electrons are likewise bound to unite.

Thus mating or marriage is simply a law of existence, an inherent property ingrained in our cells and constitution without which we cannot continue to live or evolve. In each cellular marriage, there must be the male and the female, or the positive and the negative to match. In the world of the cell, which is our world, everything goes on progressing in meticulous order. Order defines the cell as the cell defines life. "Before there was life, there had to be a system. . . there has to be order. . . it is life. . . Death is disorder."[4]

Human Biology: Much has been discovered about the cell, its composition, its functioning and its reproduction. Yet, nobody has been able to guess how the first cell came into being. The eukaryotes, as mentioned before, are highly organized and specialized cells that build our body and, in fact, bring us into life. Every cell is composed of several layers above layers of molecules separated by membranes, and in its middle there is the nucleus ringed by double membrane. The nucleus holds the genes - the ultimate dictators of the cell - wound into the coils of chromosomes.

Humans reproduce through the union of a male and female cell, exactly as any other offspring is reproduced. When fertilization (union or mating) takes place, a new cell is formed and the sex, together with the physical structure, including the brain, are determined by the genes united in the new cell. Both males and females have the same basis of a chromosome (x). But from the very beginning, if this basis is coupled with one (x) chromosome *or more,* the offspring is a female. If the basis is coupled with one chromosome (y) *or more,* it is a male.

Once the new cell is "born," it starts functioning on its own, activated by its inherent power administered by the new set of genes, and is called, in this early stage, an embryo. Soon after inception, the male secretes a predominant hormone called androgen, while the female secretes estrogen and later on the female hormones: the progesterone and the prolactin. The growth of the embryo, whether male or female, follows the same laws of growth: the reporduction of the specialized cells continues building up our different organs, without any deviation except for hormonal secretions. By the time the child is born, he or she has already been influenced by the most active hormones which affect the functioning of the brain.

The human brain is one of the greatest wonders of creation. In its lower part, there is a small zone called "limbic system," composed of structures which are involved in both human emotion and motivation.

---

[4]Ibid., p. 38.

One of these structures, named Amygdala, is among the major brain parts responsible for our behavior, as it affects some endocrinal secretions, especially those touching upon our sexual dispositions. Moreover, "the cortex also feeds it (the limbic system) with condensed indications of cortical activity, including categorized *representations of the state of the external world. It appraises and evaluates the activities of* (the upper brain - system). . .*and balances current priorities with regard to short-term and long-term needs of the organism and the selection and evaluation of different integrative activities.*"[5]

It is well-established that the structure called "hypothalamus" of the limbic system is *prenatally* formed and becomes indelibly 'sex-typed' through the action of sex-hormones, thereby permanently pre-disposing the animal to male or female *physiological and behavioral responses.* In most animals this critical period of hormone action is thought to occur prenatally and thereafter is immutable. "This irrevocable hormonal 'sex-typing' of the nervous system. . . has the most far-reaching implications for sex differences in human behavior."[6] This means that from the earliest days of conception (the new fertilized cell or embryo), our brain starts its formation, disposition and mode of functioning. When born, an infant carries within himself or herself its own particular way of thinking, imagination, motivation, and manner of evaluation. Even among individuals of the same sex, there are genetic inherent differences owing to the differences in the rates of flow of hormones into the brain. Chromosome (y) is responsible for the male hormones androgen, which are associated with what the psychologists call the "aggression" tendency, meaning that type of behavior which is generally characterized by a direct and overt reaction, competitive acumen, and long-term evaluation and perception. The term also implies some final and actual aggressive action which, unless well disciplined, would cause destructive consequences. As a matter of biological fact, such hormones in a male embryo rely on a hormone called "gonadal," which accounts for the differences between the two sexes and which is thought to influence the behavioral decisions issued by the brain.

In the female, (x) hormones are responsible for the menstrual flow which is directly regulated by the key female hormones: estrogen and progesterone. Less secretion of these hormones causes menstruation usually accompanied by a state of discomfort, inhibition, and often gloomy attitudes. It is believed that the hormonal input in this case affects the functioning of the brain of the female, inhibiting or reviving

---

[5]Symthies, I.R., *Brain Mechanisms and Behavior,* Academic Press, New York 1970, p. 156. (Emphasis added)
[6]Weitz, Shirley, *Sex Roles,* Oxford University Press, New York 1877, p. 7.

her emotional state. Biologists emphasize the fact that the natural disposition in humans is to a female system (x) unless broken by the male chromosome (y) causing production of the male hormone, androgen.[7]

Aggression - as previously defined - is the product of the testestrone hormone, androgen, a hormone that exists in the super-reinal glands of both sexes, but, of course, in widely varied qualities. Aggression in women is mostly owing to an overdose of this hormone, unless the woman is suffering from some societal trauma. A violently aggressive man is likewise greatly motivated by an extra dose of androgen. If such a man is given estrogen, he would calm down in most cases, and develop a calmer behavior. A transsexual individual who choses to become a female undergoes surgical intervention and female hormone therapy without which femininity cannot take its usual course. Hormones, in such circumstances, are necessary to build up the breast, to establish female sexual desires, to eliminate profuse facial and body hair, and so on. Once the new female is given such hormonal treatment, her limbic system functions accordingly: the maternal instinct becomes greatly felt, the desire for talking becomes more persistent, the feminine emotionality supersedes rationality, and the lachrymatory glands secrete more tears during emotional stress.

Nothing perhaps, can be more convincing of the biological dichotomy than MATERNITY. Weitz writes: "Animal evidence does support the concept of the maternal instinct, in that female sex hormones such as estrogen, progesterone and prolactin seem to be implicated in the ontogeny of maternal behavior."[8] The same author relates the experiment of the monkey-mother who killed her newly born babies when given androgen, and the motherly monkey-father who cared for the babies after receiving female hormones. Nowhere in the animal kingdom do fathers assume the basic role of caring for the newly born offspring.[9]

A female child is born with a maternal instinct: she distinctly feels a strong interest in children, and this explains why girls prefer to play with dolls. It has been established that girls with an excess of prenatal androgen "do seem to show less interest in infants than normal girls,"[10] and obviously more than normal boys. The maternity behavior is mainly characterized by tenderness, affective bonds, self-preservation, protectiveness, and self-identification with the child.

---

[7]Moyer, K.E., *Sex Difference in Aggression* - Quoted in R.C. Friedman, R.M. Richart, R.L. Vande Wiele, eds. *Sex Differences in Behavior*, Wile, 1974, p. 156.
[8]Wietz, Shirley, *Sex Roles*, Oxford University Press, New York 1977, p. 42.
[9]Lynn, D.B., *The Father: His Role in Child Development*, Brooks Cole, Monterey, California 1974, pp. 14-21.
[10]Weitz, Shirley, *Sex Roles*, Oxford University Press, New York 1977, p. 42.

To conclude, one can safely say that "sexual behavior of an individual, and thus *gender role*, are not neutral and without initial direction at birth. Nevertheless, sexual predisposition is only a potentiality setting limits to a pattern that is greatly modifiable by ontogenetic experience."[11] In other words, the ontogeny (i.e. the biological development of the individual organism) asserts that a female is born with a maternal instinct carrying genetic predispositions different from those of a male. It is of interest to note that there is differential treatment of children by parents according to their sex. Mothers are more inclined to tolerate boys than girls, while fathers are more tolerant toward girls than boys. This phenomenon prevails among humans and some primates and is quite conspicuous among monkeys.

Socialization Factors

"Conspiracy theories of history which seem to imply that men have kept women down over the centuries through some collective act of will, do not merit serious consideration."[12] There is no doubt that our physiological functioning is affected by our psychological and societal conditions, and that biology, psychology and society have contributed to the present sex roles in their different grades and limits. It is rather impossible to separate the biological factor from the societal. Yet, one has to take into serious consideration that there is a definite predisposition in each sex that takes place in the embryo and the fetus. This prenatal conditioning cannot be owing to a societal agent, but most probably can be a major cause of societal differential treatment of the sexes. When parents give a doll to their daughter, they are aware of her instinctive motherly feelings, and they are responding to her instinctive desires. Instinctive urges can be mollified, re-oriented and mitigated, but never nullified or totally wiped out. To suppress such urges is to cause more harm than good to the individual, and to ignore them is to push the child in a wrong way where he or she tries to fulfill the desires by any means, legitimate or illegitimate, socially acceptable or unacceptable.

Socialization agents, namely: the parents, the school, the peers and the social symbols of the sexes, are supposed to be, and in fact should be, factors of disciplining the instinctive behavior. Our basic sexual desires should be satisfied by marriage and not by adultery and fornication. Our instinctive need for security should be met by honorable and lawful gain and not by theft and violence. Even our innate instinct implanted in the eukaryotes for evolving to the better must be

---

[11]Diamond, M.A., *A Critical Evaluation of the Ontogeny of Human Sexual Behavior,* Quarterly Review of Biology, 40 (1965), pp. 147-175.

[12]Weitz, Shirley, *Sex Roles,* Oxford University Press, New York 1977, p. 5.

encouraged through a proper education leading to a feeling of self-esteem and elation. Failing this, the individual would resort to unhealthy and even anti-social practices to feel the importance of his ego; he or she may develop the bad habits of lying, boasting, or even killing. Any infringement upon instincts is a violation of a natural law of life that conduces to masochism, narcissism, schizophrenia and the rest of the psychotic ailments.

The family has a lasting effect on sex roles as most of the individual's latent behavior is basically formulated in the first seven or eight years of childhood. The major role of parents relates to the child's identification where affective bonds, mechanism of modeling and cognitive categorization should be carefully observed. Here the question generally raised by the *Libs* is whether parents should or should not differentiate in their treatment between males and females. Many of them believe that they should not heed the sex and thus should treat both the boy and the girl as if they were of the same sex. They allege that any differentiation at this early stage leads to some category of inferiority complex in the girl and to a bias in favor of the boy. There is enough evidence in everyday life to support such allegations. However, any fair mind can easily see that it is not the differentiation, per se, that causes such inhibition in the girl, if only because differentiation occurs in families which have girls and no boys. Every individual child is different from others and should accordingly be treated differently. What hurts a child is the way parents associate differentiation with sex. If a doll is given to a girl, it is not because she is inferior to a boy who was presented with a horse or a gun. Girls would only suffer inhibition and inferiority if the parents treat them as inferior, or if when differentiating between both of them, parents explain the act in preferential language.

Another important factor in socialization is the school. Infants in nurseries, children in kindergartens, and boys and girls in higher age-brackets are treated differently in one way or another, in accordance with their sex. In pictures for the very young, in all books and prints, there is always a "he" and a "she." He is tough, daring, exterior-oriented, and somehow aggressive, and she is kind, caring, child-loving, interior-oriented, and somehow self-preservative. Then there are the great differentiations in students' activities: the boys compete in physically rough and hard sports, participate in political and social discussions, and are expected to excel girls in empirical sciences. On the other hand, girls practice light and non-violent sports, domestic arts, and are expected to excel boys in artistic pursuits.

Here again differentiation is undeniably conspicuous, and while it is in essence compatible with human biology, it is condemned by the *Libs*. Their plea is always the same: such treatment leads to the development of a feeling of inferiority in the female. It indoctrinates the subconscious mind of the girl with a view to convincing her of the conspired falsehood, i.e., the superiority of the male. The *Libs* believe that keeping the "traditional roles" of sexes in the school gives an edge to the boy over the girl: he is depicted as the hero, the protector, the leader and even the master! This seems to be an exaggeration.

The staunchest proponent of liberalism cannot deny that the male, in general, is created with more muscular strength, that biologically speaking, he is more "aggressive," that his mind is more outwardly inclined, and that he is more free from physiological cyclical effects. The female is created with other excellences and distinctions by virtue of her constitution. Her motherhood instincts, her feminine tenderness and her physiologically receptive aptitude for procreation. These clear facts should induce us to accept - at least - such differentiations that confirm and correspond with the distinct natural characteristics of each sex. It follows that there must be differentiations in all schools to respond to these basic biological divergent requirements.

The so-called peer group effects and the symbolic agents of sex roles are very akin to each other, especially among adults. Clubs of men and women, the distinction in public behavior, and the discriminatory treatment of the sexes in many public and social functions do exist in all present societies. One has to admit that some of this differentiation is owing to societal factors and/or obsolete inherited tradition. But one cannot also deny that there are genuine irrefutable reasons for differentiation in this field. Despite the equal opportunities open to both sexes in education and public life, women have been active in fields that do not require much "aggressiveness," and where there is a concurrence of biological effect and societal functioning. In such activities, there is no reason, whatsoever, for a woman not to succeed and even excel man.

Socialization Versus Biology

There is evidence that socialization factors, when carried out extensively at an early age affect the biological functioning of the child. That is how we notice the "sissy" boy and the "tomboyish" girl. Also, over-secretion of female hormones in a male would produce the same effect, despite any socialization effort to the contrary. In both cases, the situation becomes unhealthy and the individual suffers from some perversion and could develop transsexualism. The correct attitude is obvious: we have to adapt our socialization processes in such a manner that they correspond to our biological functioning. The indelible male and female characteristics installed in our limbic systems as a result of the prenatal hormonal secretions must be the basis of our socialization process. There must be harmony between the act of creation (natural state) and the willful human action. Failing this, a grave imbalance takes place, shaking the personality of the individual to its very roots. Thus, the *Libs* claim, for identical treatment of males and females in every domain, denies the biological constitution of the human mind and body and nullifies masculinity and femininity. Homosexuality, at present assuming some prominence in industrialized Western societies, is the product of lopsided thinking and is bound to fail.

A female must be brought up in a manner that makes her feel proud of her femininity and not ashamed of it. She must be treated with equity, must not be equated with the male. They are different and can never be equals, as each of them has a domain predestined from his or her conception.

Structure and Function of the Family

We have seen that there is no continuity of life without marriage - a union between male and female - and that life is order. Death is entropy or disorder. In Cadmure's words: "Life is mainly to reproduce and to feel."[13] The marriage of cells which constitute our body, brain, and nerves is a highly organized "institution" administered by sophisticated laws and geared by strict discipline. Humans are no more than their cells, and the rule of order and discipline is the essence of their existence. Any violation of this rule is a step toward entropy or self-destruction.

As we live, we reproduce - we marry. Humans learn to live in heterogeneous couples and reproduce within a certain orderly social framework called the "family institution." The word "social" here is not a mere fabrication by man, it is necessarily biological in the sense that one human cell cannot alienate itself from other similar cells. Whenever a group of cells (families) comes together, the necessity for order and discipline becomes incumbent. Hence, those who believe that there should be - or even could be - a society of human cells (families) without rules administering the relationships between its individuals, are asking for the impossible, the anti-natural. Such a chaotic grouping does not exist in nature.

Oparin, a Russian biologist, demonstrated that if a collection of molecules (he calls them coacervates) is given a chance to act, they have order. He set a chemical reaction in the solution where the coacervates were floating and found that they formed an inexplicable and unpredicted order: Heads outward and tails inward. There was a mystifying difference between the rate of reaction outside and inside the coacervates. According to Oparin, this difference accounts for the formation of the cell.[14]

Sociologically speaking, a family is operationally defined as ". . . a

---

[13]Cadmure, L.L. Larson, *The Center of Life,* The New York Times Book Co., New York 1977, p. 8.
[14]Ibid., p. 39.

special kind of structure whose principals are related to one another through blood ties and/or material relationships, and whose relatedness is of such a nature as to entail 'mutual expectations' that are prescribed by religion, reinforced by law, and internalized by the individual. "[15] This definition takes into account the general aspect of any family and the Islamic point of view.

'Abdalati, a present-day Muslim writer, accordingly, specifies the purposes of marriage as:

✓ a means of emotional and sexual gratification,
✓ a mechanism of tension reduction,
✓ a means of legitimate procreation,
✓ social placement,
✓ an approach to inter-family alliance and group solidarity, and
✓ above all, an act of piety.[16]

The preceding definitions and purposes are quite elaborate and spell out views about the functions of the family. Nevertheless, there is an intricate cause and effect relationship between the family and society.

The culture of any society comprises many traditions installed in its individuals' minds and are passed on from one generation to another. As man is conservative by instinct, he does not try to change such traditions except under the great pressure of evolutionary requirements. This perpetual struggle between the two instincts, conservatism and evolution, plays an important role in delimiting the family institution in every society. Both instincts are dynamic and must be kept in good balance for any sane society to develop. Traditions constitute a part of the established ideology of a people, while evolution is the active element that steers the present status toward a future one, and as such, it formulates another part of the ideology. Amid this continuous process the family exists, caught between the two parts. The family is there to conserve what is best and most appropriate in tradition, and to adopt and practice what is best and most appropriate in the new evolution.

To apply the above philosophy, functions, and definitions to the Muslim family in the States, we come immediately to a host of variegated and intertwined problems. Islam is integral, and Muslims are supposed to adopt it in its entirety:

"You believe in part of the Scripture and disbelieve in part thereof? And what is the reward of those who do so save ignominy in the life of this world, and in the Day of Resurrection they will be consigned to the most grievous doom. . ."[17]

---

[15]'Abdalati, Hammudah, *The Family Structure in Islam,* American Trust Publications, Indianapolis 1977, p. 19.
[16]Ibid., pp. 54-55.
[17]The Qur'an 2:85.

Accordingly, they are required to apply the Islamic laws concerning all matrimonial matters. Yet, being residents in a non-Muslim country, they are bound to meet with a complex of contradictory situations. Such complication is exacerbated by the lack of consolidated Muslim communities and the absence of any Islamic order that could help solve the problems.

To begin with, there is the problem of the marriage contract. Muslims, who intend to live here for a protracted length of time or forever, are obliged to register their marriage in accordance with the laws of the state in which they wed. Once this is done, the rights and obligations of both spouses are defined by what these laws stipulate and not by Islamic injunctions. This applies, in fact, to all subsequent familial issues. The husband's financial obligation toward his wife and household, the wife's duties toward her husband and household, and the social code which should be observed by both - all these important issues become subject to local American jurisprudence. In case of divorce, it is again the state laws that adjudge the final separation act, irrespective of the Islamic injunctions.

Another important issue that affects the Muslim family in the States is the economic status. In many cases, both spouses are obliged to work and gain more income to make ends meet and to save something as a security for the future. This economic aspect is very common to most American families and is taken for granted by them, with its good and bad effects. It does not constitute a major problem to them as it is consistent with their material civilization and ideology. Westerners have developed a certain philosophy of life in regard to the status of women as a result of their past heritage and present industrialized societies. It is common knowledge that Athenians treated women as a commodity which could be bought and sold. The Romans considered women to be the property of the father and/or the husband until the days of Justinian (5th century) when some separate identity of women was legally acknowledged. Judaism looks down upon women as a curse worse than death and considers them essentially evil. The Christian views on women varied from considering them to be living beings without souls to humans without identity. The British law until 1801 allowed the husband to sell his wife. The list of historical abuses of women in the West is too long to be enumerated here.

It is only very recently that non-Muslim societies agreed to give women some independent status. Even today, the renowned liberal American wife cannot buy property without the consent of her husband, nor is she allowed to stick to her maiden name without adding that of her husband.[18] In Switzerland she cannot enter into any contractual transaction without her husband's written consent, and if

---

[18]Lately, a few States have allowed married women to use their maiden names.

she earns any money from her work, he is legally entitled to half her income. All over the West, the husband can deprive his wife of his legacy after death.

No wonder, then, we hear women claiming "equality" with man and justice in treatment. The present culture, predominantly influenced by the economic or materialistic agent, gave "justice", "equality", and "liberation" a material implication - pecuniary value. In their industrial age where money is power, where rich is good and poor is bad, where "dog eat dog" are accepted premises of individuals' interrelations, and where moral values have been dumped into the garbage bin, women are contending for economic independence as a basis for their claim for equal human rights. To achieve this end, they did not mind the commercialization of their femininity, the loss of their chastity, the destruction of their family, and the perturbation of their emotions. This yearning for "liberation" pushed the Western woman into deep waters. Her desire for independence dragged her into competition and "aggression," and her pride alienated her from the affectionate society. In her solitude, she accepted permissiveness, and along with her struggle for survival she nurtured bitterness and rancour. In the midst of her secular preoccupation, she suppressed her spiritual values and trod on her motherly instincts.

The American concept of family and marriage has undergone a radical change in the last few decades. Originally, as Edward Westermack puts it, "Marriage is rooted in the family, and not the family in marriage." The family in turn was the foundation of society. Hence, the regulation of all family relations was considered a necessity called for by two fundamental exigencies: wholesome human procreation and preservation of society. The modern industrial culture upset the past norm of family life and greatly changed the purposes of marriage. New opportunities of material gain were opened to married and unmarried women making them economically independent from their husbands and male providers. The women's emancipation movement accordingly declared that there was no more reason for tolerating subjugation to the male and cultivated the eccentric tendencies against the traditional functioning and sex roles in the family. "The woman's new freedom has greatly increased sexual opportunity outside marriage, supported by the contraception and abortion."[19]

The main purpose of marriage has become to satiate the desires of the couple, or what the *Libs* call "to achieve individual fulfillment and to ascertain the spouse's identity." The new concept has become tantamount to fulfilling the "desire of each other's need for individual

---

[19]Williams, R.H., *To Live and To Die;* Mace, David R., *Marriage: Whence and Whither,* Springer-Verland, New York 1973, p. 298.

happiness" and "the development of man-woman relationship." This, according to them, would lead to giving the wife the same status as the husband without differentiation or discrimination. Thus, a new concept of marriage rooted in the family had to be developed, and four substitutes are being practiced in modern societies:

✓ Serial monogamy, where a series of marriages take place one after the other. This is what prevails in the United States at present where divorce occurs in 40 percent of marriages and where 75 percent of the divorced remarry. There are some modernists who suggest the "bypass of divorce by requiring renewal or cancellation of all marriage contracts at three year intervals."[20]

✓ Open marriage, where the exclusivity of husband-wife (sexually and otherwise) is eliminated. Those who advocate this category of marriage practice wife "swapping" or "swinging." They claim that extramarital experiences would reduce jealousy, relieve tensions and ease the pressures of personal conflict.

✓ Polygamy and group marriage, where an association of husbands and wives and their children mix together without restriction or constraint. The claim is that the multiplicity of parenthood for adults and children would offer a wider variety of interactive experiences in meeting individual needs.

✓ Homosexuality, where women "marry" women and men "marry" men. Such a relationship, it is asserted, is without the usual conflict, which is inevitable in every new normal marriage.

All such approaches can never succeed in creating a happy family because they ignore the biological and the spiritual elements. Humans cannot survive without a society, and no society can survive without the family.

Serial monogamy, open marriage, group marriage and homosexuality lack the premordial basics of the family. Humans are the only species where the offspring needs parental catering for a relatively long period after birth, not only physically but emotionally as well. The new frustrated efforts, as reflected in the modern abnormal family life, do not unite man and woman in a bond where both enjoy material and emotional security, stability, and contentment. They do not cure the ailments created by the prevailing technological culture: alienation, loneliness, envy, lack of love, and anxiety. "Search any average human being, and you soon find evidence of heart-hunger for closeness and intimacy and the shared life as the only dependable sources of a sustained sense of self-esteem and of personal worth."[21]

The women's emancipation movement in this country is revolting

---

[20]Ibid., p. 299.
[21]Ibid., p. 304.

against long-standing inequitable treatment, against a biased, unjust legal system and a domineering economic exploitation. In their revolt, and in the absence of any effective religious or moral guidance, women have gone to the extreme which has brought down on them the misery of "civilized prostitution and adultery."

THE ISLAMIC SOLUTION

Biology and Socialization

There is nothing more compatible with human nature than Islamic teachings and injunctions, if only because they take the individual as a fallible being, subject to trial and error and subject to correction and evolution.

"On no soul does God place a burden greater than it can bear. It gets every good that it earns, and it suffers every ill that it earns."[22]

As we are concerned here with the Muslim family, it is natural that whatever solution we may suggest, it must be in acordance with Islam. Luckily enough, Islam decides upon every issue, taking human nature in consideration and exhorting us to abide by the eternal laws of creation. Empirical sciences have discovered many facts concerning our biological structure and physiological functioning but there are still many more of life's secrets to be uncovered. There is not a single scientific *fact* that runs contrary to any Islamic injunction; but there are many postulates, ideas and theories that may be incompatible with Islamic teachings. Under such uncertain conditions, a Muslim is supposed to follow the Islamic rules irrespective of the "scientific" points of view and his personal desires.

Of traditions and cultures that affect the Muslims' socialization factors, one must bear in mind that these are the product of certain ideas prevailing at a given time in a certain society. This is an extremely important element in the Islamic solutions to societal problems. Islam, as a system, delineates the purpose of human life, the relation between man, nature, and the Creator. It draws the broad outlines of the social, political, economic and esthetic aspects of human existence. Such philosophical definitions and doctrinal delineations are confined to the basic facts which do not evolve or change with the continuous human evolution. Facts are absolute and are not subject to change, otherwise they are neither facts nor absolute.

Whatever solutions we find in Islam, they are based on such absolute facts whether known to our contemporary scientists or unknown to them. The entire concept of the family and roles of its members is a part

---

[22]Ibid., 2:286.

of the general concept of the Islamic society. Marriage is dictated by our biological need and not just a matter of individual option."And of everything we have created pairs."[23]

The word *zawj* is used in the Qur'an as a pair or a mate; in usage both connote marriage. "Do they not look at the earth, how many pairs of noble things we have produced therein."[24] Even in the Paradise, the Qur'an informs us that we shall have mates.[25] God created humans from one soul, which could be the first cell. From this soul He created the male and the female. The story of creating Eve (the first female) from a rib of 'Adam (the first male) is not mentioned in the Qur'an.

"And among His signs is this, that He created for you mates from yourself that you may find rest (and peace) in them."[26]

"O mankind, heed (in reverence) your Lord Who created you from a single soul and from it created its mate and from them twain both spread multitude of men and women."[27]

Our Prophet orders us to get married as soon as we can. The family is the nucleus of the Islamic society, and marriage is the only way to bring about such an institution. Extra-marital relations are categorically condemned and prohibited.

"Nor come nigh to adultery (or fornication), for it is a shameful deed and an evil, opening the road to other evils."[28]

It is only logical that Islam sets up the rules to regulate the functioning of the family whereby both spouses can find peace, love, security, and relatedness. These elements are necessary for accomplishing the greatest purpose of marriage: the worship of God. By worship it is not only meant the performance of rituals, but it essentially implies righteousness in all transactional behavior. Every good deed, every service to humanity, every useful productive effort, and even every good word are a part of a true Muslim worship of his God. If both husband and wife observe this main purpose, this cardinal purpose of their union, they would easily learn how to help each other achieve this goal - a goal greater than themselves. They would learn how to tolerate each other, how to love God in themselves and in other beings, and how to overcome their difficulties and their shortcomings.

The second purpose of marriage is to respond to the basic biological instinct of procreation. Children are the realization of motherhood and

---

[23]Ibid., 50:49.
[24]Ibid., 31:19; 50:7; 26:7.
[25]Ibid., 2:25; 4:57.
[26]Ibid., 30:21.
[27]Ibid., 4:1.
[28]Ibid., 17:32.

fatherhood. Islam is particular in providing the most possible wholesome atmosphere for bringing up the offspring. To give birth to children and neglect them is a crime toward society, the children, and of the parents themselves. The child who is deprived of the ample love of his or her parents, who is not properly tutored at an early age, and who is left to babysitters and nurseries will develop many anti-social behavioral patterns and may end up with crime, perversion and corruption. Such a child may never find his or her identity as he or she could have felt it in a systematic manner during his or her childhood. Without a family life, governed by Islamic order and discipline, how can we expect a child to have the Muslim conscience and the Islamic value of righteousness.

Islam prescribes clear rights and obligations on parents and their descendents. Parents are legally responsible for the education and maintenance of their children. These, by turn, are legally responsible for accommodating and maintaining their parents, if they so require, in their old age. Both parents and children inherit from each other according to a prescribed and accurate law of inheritance specified in the Qur'an. Neither of them can deprive the other of their respective shares in the legacy.

This is only part of the long family code in Islam. What is of import here is the husband-wife relationship - their sex roles - within the context of Islamic comprehension:

> "and among His Signs is this, that He created for you mates from among yourselves, that you may find rest (and peace) in them. And He has put love and mercy between your (hearts). Verily in this are signs for those who reflect."[29]

Despite the importance of these moral values: rest, peace, love and mercy, Islam did not stop there. It bolstered its original concept of the family by defining the roles of man and woman in such a manner that each should act in accordance with his or her biological merits. The man, with his aggression, is charged with what is called the "instrumental" functions: maintenance, protection, dealings with the outworldly matters and leadership within the family. The woman is entrusted with caring for and rearing the children, organizing the home, and creating the loving atmosphere inside. It must be clear from the beginning that in an Islamic society the wife is not expected to be pushed to work to gain money. Even the unmarried woman, the divorcee, and the widow are guaranteed by law an income that helps them lead a reasonably comfortable life. Work or trade is not prohibited to woman. Yet, she is not recommended to undertake

---

[29]Ibid., 30:21.

such activities unless there is a justification for them and without prejudice to their husband's rights. Once the woman gets married, she accepts the Islamic ruling on the functioning of the family. Her role becomes mainly to achieve the welfare of her household and to look after the internal family affairs. If she wants to work, she is bound to ask the explicit approval of her husband. However, if she has her own property or fortune, and if she opts to run or to invest such wealth, she is entitled to do so without her husband's permission, provided this does not infringe upon her marital obligations.

The Islamic Family

In Islam, as in biology, there is no family without union or marriage, and there is no marriage without rules and discipline. The family in Islam is a unit in which two independent persons unite and share life together. The husband's dignity is an integral part of his wife's dignity. Accordingly, neither of them is better than the other. To unite and share, there must be mutual love and compassion - a genuine feeling which unless translated into action and behavior would be mere illusion and futile emotion. One can hardly accept the claim of love of the spouse who does not care for his or her sick partner or who does not share the family responsibilities. This fundamental basis, if well understood and observed, makes the first loyalty of both spouses to their family which is supposed to serve God in piety as the main purpose of marriage. It implies that they act as if they were one person with many organs. The head of the human is not better than the heart, and the hand is not better than the foot. If the man is charged with the duty of leadership and maintenance, he is not better than the woman who is assigned the duty of keeping the household. Imam Mohammad 'Abduh emphasizes this point as vital for the right understanding of the sex roles of spouses. He adds that the Qur-anic verse: "And covet not those things in which God has bestowed His gifts more freely on some of you than on others: to men is allotted what they earn, and to women what they earn. . ."[30] does not imply that every man is better than every woman or vice versa. According to him, each sex, in general, has some preferential advantage over the other, though men have a degree over women.[31]

There has been much controversy about this "degree." Some interpret it as the delegation of leadership, surveillance, and maintenance bestowed on men. Others say that this degree is the tolerance with which men must treat their wives. A third view is that it is men's natural gift for judging matters and managing external problems. However, the consensus is that this "degree" comprises the principle of

---

[30]Ibid., 4:32.
[31]*Tasfeer al-Manar*, V. 5, p. 68 and seq.

"guardianship" or *qiyamah*.

Imam 'Abduh in the course of interpreting the preceding Qur'anic verse, stated that *qiyamah* or guardianship has four elements: protection, surveillance, custody, and maintenance. 'Abdalati considered the element of obedience over and above the preceding four elements - the most important indication of *qiyamah*. Obedience, in his view and in accordance with the Qur'an and Hadith, comprises the following:

First, she must not receive male strangers or accept gifts from them without his approval.

Second, the husband has the legal right to restrict her freedom of movement and prevent her from leaving her home without his permission. She must comply with this right unless there is a necessity or legitimate advantage for her to do otherwise. However, it is his religious obligation to be compassionate so as to relax his right to restrict her freedom of movement. If there arises a conflict between this right of his and wife's parents' right to visit and be visited by their daughter, his right prevails. Yet it is religiously recommended that he be considerate enough to waive his right and avoid estrangement within his conjugal family or between any member of this family and close relatives - the wife's parents.

Third, a refractory wife has no legal right to object to the husband's exercise of his disciplining authority. Islamic Law, in common with most other systems of law, recognizes the husband's right to discipline his wife for disobedience.

Fourth, the wife may not legally object to the husband's right to take another wife or to exercise his right of divorce. The marital contract establishes her implicit consent to these rights. However, if she wishes to restrict his freedom in this regard or to have similar rights, she is legally allowed to do so. She may stipulate in the marital agreement that she too, will have the right to divorce, or that she will keep the marriage bond only so long as she remains the only wife; should he take a second wife, the first will have the right to seek a divorce in accordance with the marriage agreement.

Finally, if the husband insists on patrilocality or neolocality, the wife must comply"[32]

Conclusion

The problems facing Muslim families living in non-Islamic societies can be dealt with in compliance with Islamic teachings and principles if we accept them as binding. If the spouses are really devout, they will have no difficulty in encountering the evils of the Western culture and in

---

[32]'Abdalati, Hammudah, *The Family Structure in Islam,* American Trust Publications, Indianapolis 1977, p. 172-173.

escaping the anti-Islamic societal factors that may run contrary to Islam. The guidelines as we see them would be:

First, the main purpose of marriage is to live in piety and to serve the Islamic cause.

Second, the roles of the spouses are biologically determined. Islam affirms this differentiation and inscribes basic rules for socialization:

✓ The family is a vital mechanism for the sane structure of the society. It must be based on legitimate marriage.

✓ It is the law of creation that in every grouping there must be order. In animals in general, and in humans in particular, there must be a leader for every herd of animals, flock of birds and any human grouping.

✓ Males are biologically endowed with specific characteristics that qualify them to shoulder the responsibility of leadership. In Islam, the male is the head of the family and the head of any political formation (the State).

✓ There are moral and legal rights and obligations that become consequential on marriage. Unless both are accepted with conviction and contentment, no happy family relationship can be continued. The main moral values of an Islamic marriage are unity and sharing, always keeping the main purpose of marriage in view. By adopting the moral values, the question of "equality" becomes invalid because it does not arise. Man and woman are treated equally by their Creator and are subject to the same transactional and behavioral laws of the Qur'an.

✓ Because of their different physiological structures and biological functions, each sex is assigned a role to play in the family. This role is only compatible with and emanates from their respective biological formation.

Coming back to practical problems that a Muslim family faces in this Western society, the Islamic solution could be as follows:

Maintenance

It is the husband who is supposed to provide for the family. If he cannot gain enough to support the family, or if his income is too low to provide for a relatively acceptable standard of living, and provided the wife is willing, both of them may work for gain.

However:

✓ The husband has the right to terminate the wife's working whenever he deems it necessary.

✓ He has the right to object to any job if he feels that it would expose his wife to any harm, seduction or humiliation.

✓ The wife has the right to discontinue working whenever she pleases.

Household

When the wife is not employed, the household becomes her first occupation. By household it is meant the rearing of the children and all domestic services required for maintaining a clean and comfortable habitation. (The Prophet, upon whom be peace, says: "Cleanliness is a part of faith.") Motherhood is highly praised in Islam and is the most elated value second to the worship of God.

Marriage, Disputes and Divorce

Marriage

Muslims should marry according to Islamic traditions and rules. The marriage will have to be registered with the state in which they wed to give it a legal force. This legal procedure subjects the marriage contract to the jurisdiction of secular laws which, in most cases, contradict many Islamic rulings. However, such contradiction does not happen unless there is a dispute that both spouses fail to solve in accordance with the shari'ah.

Disputes

Disputes are expected to arise in all matrimonial relations. Islam-abiding spouses must learn how to compromise and tolerate each other. Their guide is the teaching of their Religion and the good example for them is their Prophet.

However, in case they fail to solve their own problems, they have to resort to arbitration. The spouse who refuses this Qur'anic injunction or who defies the other partner taking shelter under the umbrella of American laws is failing in his or her religious commitment. The Qur'anic arbitration is meant to be binding on both spouses and would, indeed, relieve the Muslim family of most of its problems.

Divorce

If one of the spouses refuses arbitration, non-Islamic divorce is bound to take place, leaving a deep painful scar on both of them. Arbitration may end in divorce, but in this case it would be least harmful as both would feel more content when *shari'ah is justly applied*. It is a pity that sometime the litigants in divorce think that non-Islamic law would serve their interest more than the Islamic's. This is not only wrong, but the consequences of litigation generally leaves more ill feeling than should be.

Environment and Children

Nobody can deny the impact of environment upon adults and children. Until now, one can safely say that Muslims of America could not constitute any physical or moral community comparable to that of the Jews or the Chinese. Granted that there are some groupings in scattered localities, yet there is no community that could respond to many basic needs. The family must live in a "society," and unless an Islamic community is established, the Muslim family will have no alternative but to merge in a non-Muslim one.

The danger is so imminent that it forms the major part of the family problems in the United States. Both adults and children are influenced by American values and traditions, and by American behavior and manners. There is no escape from this "assimilation" except by strengthening the family bonds and by steadfast observation of Islamic teachings. The husband must lead her by strict adherence to Islamic ways of life and by requiring the same from his wife.

Such are the sex roles in Islam and the main problems facing Muslim families in the United States and, indeed, in all non-Muslim countries. The preceding solutions entirely depend upon the faith of the spouses and their earnest desire to live up to their Religion. God, according to the Qur'an, has made men in charge of their wives, has ordered them to maintain and protect them, and has ordered women to obey their husbands and guard their property and secrets.[33]

> "Say: This is my Way: I call toward Allah with sure knowledge and whoever follows me - Glory be to Allah! - and never will I join gods with Allah."[34]

---

[33]The Qur'an 4:34-35.
[34]Ibid., 12:108.

Chapter XII

THE TREATMENT
OF WIVES
IN ISLAM

Jamal al-Din M. Zarabozo

Jamal al-Din M. Zarabozo is a doctoral candidate in economics at the University of California, Davis. His article was first published in tne Ramadan 1403/July 1982 issue of *al-ittihad.*

For centuries, women have been exploited and mistreated. Reasons could be many, but two are very obvious: one, the physiological difference between man and woman, which puts the former in a physically advantageous position; and second, the absence of respect for woman in a value system. That is why societies divested of Islam, pseudo-Muslim as well as non-Muslim, are more prone to mistreatment of women than the Islamic one.

For Muslims, just the fact that women are dressed in *hijab* does not mean Islam is being applied to this aspect of the relationship between the husband and the wife. Furthermore, the role of family in the overall social structure of Islam is great, and if we fail to grasp its importance, the whole edifice will collapse. In other words, if we do not return to Islam in its entirety, then we have not really achieved the goal of *jihad*, but merely modified the existing situation to our own liking.

The Qur'an and the Sunnah of the Prophet are the primary sources of guidance for an Islamic way of life. True believers who have tasted the sweetness of faith should, according to a hadith of the Prophet, be in a state where they are pleased with Allah, their Lord, Islam as their religion and Prophet Muhammad as God's Messenger (Muslim). Furthermore, the Prophet has told the Muslims that none of them believe until their desires are subservient to what he has brought (Nawawi). The Qur'an strongly warns against following one's desires or the actions of one's fathers, especially where they were misguided.

When Allah mentions marriage or the relationship between the husband and the wife in the Qur'an, He describes it as one of love, mercy, and harmony between two human beings who have entered into a mutual contract. For example, "And among His wonders is this: He creates for you mates out of your own kind, so that you may incline toward them, and he engenders love and tenderness between you: in this, behold, there are messages indeed for people who think."[1] And, "It is He who has created you out of one living entity, so that man might incline (with love) toward women."[2] Thus according to the Qur'an, the relationship between a man and his wife should be one of love, mercy and mutual understanding. Allah also commands men to treat their wives kindly in the verse, "And consort with your wives in a goodly manner, for if you dislike them, it may be well that you dislike something which God might yet make a source of abundant good."[3]

The ahadith are filled with words enjoining kind treatment to wives. The Messenger of Allah said, "The best among you is he who is best to his family, and I am the best of you to my family." (Tirmidhi, Ibn Majah) A hadith in Sunan Abu Da'ud states that a virtuous wife is the best treasure a man should hoard. A version in Muslim reports that the best commodity of this world is a virtuous wife. In a hadith narrated by both Bukhari and Muslim, the Prophet gives a strong warning to the Muslims with respect to the treatment of their wives. The Prophet said, "Act kindly towards women, for they have certainly been created from the upper part of the rib, and the most crooked part of a rib is the upper part. If you then try to make it straight, you will break it off; if you leave it, it will remain crooked. So give exhort to women accordingly."

If this is so, then why is it that maltreatment of wives is not a rare occurrence among Muslim people? Most likely, I suspect, it comes from a misinterpretation of a Qur'anic verse and some ahadith. The verse and the ahadith in question are the following: And as for those women whose ill-will you have reason to fear, admonish them (first); then leave them alone in bed; than beat them; and if thereupon they pay no heed, do not seek harm to them.[4]

'Umar reported from the Holy Prophet who said, "No man shall be questioned for beating his wife." (Abu Da'ud, Ibn Majah) "Had I ordered anyone to prostrate before anyone, I would have ordered women to prostrate before their husbands on account of their duties towards them ordained by Allah." (Abu Da'ud, Ahmad and something similar by Tirmidhi)

Iyas b. 'Abd Allah reported that the Messenger of Allah said: "Don't beat the maids of Allah." Then 'Umar came to the Messenger of Allah

---

[1]The Qur'an 20:21.
[2]Ibid. 7:189.
[3]Ibid. 4:19.
[4]Ibid. 4:34.

and said, "Women have become daring against their husbands." So he allowed them to beat them. Many women were loitering around the house of the Messenger of Allah complaining against their husbands. The Messenger of Allah said, "Many women are loitering around the household of Muhammad complaining against their husbands. Their husbands are not the best among you." (Abu Da'ud, Ibn Majah)

Let us discuss the ahadith first. The interpretation given for the first hadith quoted is not that Allah will not call anyone to account for beating his wife. Such an interpretation is absurd as obviously the free beating of a wife in which there is no justification and causing bodily harm is definitely *haram* (prohibited); and , therefore, one cannot expect that Allah will not call one to account for it as He says in His Book, "In his favor shall be whatever good he does, and against him whatever evil he does"[5] ..."And he who shall have done an atom's weight of evil shall behold it."[6] The correct interpretation is the following as offered by Fazlul Karim: "So for mild beatings no man from outside should interfere, as it is wise that others should not meddle in the affairs between a husband and a wife."[7] Thus, this hadith is not justification for the beating of wives. Two points should be noticed. First, this hadith should be read within the context of many other ahadith and, second, if the beating is illegal the wife can have recourse to a judge to dissolve the marriage.

The second hadith only states that the husband has certain rights over the wife to such an extent that the wife at all times, during the day and night, will be subject to his command and calling, e.g., the call to sex, staying at home, and so on. This hadith is, however, not sound because its narrators lack credibility.

The last hadith simply shows that the Prophet was against the beating of wives and that he allowed it only due to expediency. But this privilege was abused and the Prophet had come out against those who beat their wives. Such people, he said, were not from among the good men.

In opposition to these ahadith, there exists many ahadith that disapprove of beating. For example, "None of you shall whip his wife the way a slave is whipped and afterwards cohabit with her at the end of the day." And in another narration, "Some of you may be inclined to beat his wife the way a slave is beaten, but perchance he may cohabit with her at the end of his day." (Bukhari and Muslim) These ahadith certainly discourage beating. In the following hadith, the Prophet disapproved of beating as a way of solving any domestic problem. Laqit

[5]Ibid. 2:286.

[6]Ibid. 99:8.

[7]Karim, Fazlul, Translator and Commentator, *al-Hadith,* The Book House, Pakistan, p. 215.

asked the Prophet, "O Messenger of Allah, I have a wife in whose tongue there is something, meaning foul speech. " The Prophet said, "Divorce her." Laqit replied, "I have got a son by her and have had intercourse with her." The Prophet answered, "Enjoin on her, and if there be any good in her, she will receive it; and never beat your consort the way a slave girl is beaten." (Abu Da'ud).

How about the verses cited above. Abu al-A'la Maududi in his work *Tafhim al-Qur'an* translates the 'ayah under discussion in the following way: "As for those women whose defiance you have cause to fear, admonish them and keep them apart from your beds and beat them." He does, however, explain it further and says:

> If the wife is defiant and does not obey her husband or does not guard his rights, three measures have been mentioned, but it does not mean that all three are to be taken at one and the same time. Though these have been permitted, they are to be administered with a sense of proportion according to the nature and extent of the offence. If a mere light admonition proves effective, there is no need to resort to a severer step. As to the beating, the Holy Prophet allowed it very reluctantly and even then did not like it. But the fact is that there are certain women who do not mend their ways without a beating. In such a case, the Holy Prophet has instructed that she would not be beaten on the face or cruelly, or with anything that might leave a mark on the body.[8]

Unfortunately, in his comment, Maududi does not elaborate the nature of the command to be obeyed by the wife and in what case of disobedience may she be reprimanded. I will discuss these matters later.

Yusuf Ali's translation and interpretation are the following:

> As to those women on whose part you fear disloyalty and ill-conduct, admonish them (first), (next) refuse to share their beds, (and last) beat them (lightly). In case of family disputes, four steps are mentioned to be taken in that order: (1) perhaps verbal advice or admonition may be sufficient; (2) if not, sexual relations may be suspended; (3) if this is not sufficient, some slight physical correction may be administered; but Imam Shafi'i considers this inadvisable, though permissible, and all authorities are unanimous in deprecating any sort of cruelty, even of the nagging kind as mentioned in the next clause [of verse 34]; (4) if all this fails, a family council is recommended in iv. 35. . .[9]

---

[8]Maududi, A.A., *The Meaning of the Qur'an*, Islamic Publications Ltd., Lahore, Pakistan, 1971, Volume II, p. 325.

[9]Ali, Yusuf, translator and commentator, *The Glorious Qur'an*, American Trust Publications, Indianapolis, IN, 1977, p. 190.

'Abdul Hameed Siddiqui defines *nushuz*, the term used in the above verse, as a wife rising against her husband. About beating he says: ...it is the last resort. The first is exhortation and persuasion, then suspending the conjugal relations for a short time, exceeding not more than four months. (2:226) And if those measures miserably fail, then chastisement is allowed, but it should be a mild chastisement and not a severe one causing harm to any part of the body. There is a consensus of opinion amongst the jurists that though punishment is allowed in extreme cases, it is not desirable and should be avoided as far as possible. The Prophet is reported to have said, (Beat your wives if you find it absolutely necessary) but the good amongst you would never beat them.[10]

Muhammad Asad in his *tafsir* of the Qur'an gives a comment that includes the opinion of many authorities. First, he defines the word *nushuz:*

The term *nushuz* "rebellion"—here rendered as "ill-will" comprises every kind of deliberate bad behavior of a wife towards her husband or of a husband towards his wife, including what is nowadays described as "mental cruelty"; with reference to the husband, it denotes "ill-treatment," physical sense, of his wife (cf. verse 128 of this surah). In this context, a wife's "ill-will" implies a *deliberate, persistent breach of her marital obligations.*[11] (emphasis added)

On beating he states:

It is evident from many authentic traditions that the Prophet himself intensively detested the idea of beating one's wife, and said on more than one occasion, "Could anyone of you beat his wife as he would beat a slave, and then lie with her in the evening?" (Bukhari and Muslim) According to another tradition, he forbade the beating of *any* woman with the words, "Never beat God's handmaidens (Abu Da'ud, Ibn Majah, Ahmad Ibn Hanbal, Ibn Hibban and Hakim, on the authority of Iyas ibn 'Abd Allah; Ibn Hibban, on the authority of 'Abd Allah Ibn 'Abbas; and Bayhaqi on the authority of Umm Kulthem). When the above Qur'anic verse authorizing the beating of a refractory wife was revealed, the Prophet is reported to have ṣaid: "I wanted one thing, but God has willed another thing—and what God has willed must be the best" (see *Manar* V, 74). With all this, he stipulated in his sermon on the occasion of the Farewell Pilgrimage, shortly before his death, that beating should be resorted to only if the wife "has

---

[10]Siddiqui, Abdul Hameed, translator and commentator, *The Holy Qur'an*, Islamic Book Centre, Lahore, Pakistan, no date, Part III, p. 323. (Ahkam al-Qur'an, Ibn Arabi)

[11]Asad, Muhammad, translator and commentator, *The Message of the Qur'an*, Dar al-Audulus, Gibraltar, 1980, p. 109.

become guilty, in an obvious manner, of immoral conduct", and that it should be done "in such a way as not to cause pain *(ghayr mubarrih)*;" authentic traditions to this effect are found in Muslim, Tirmidhi, Abu Da'ud, Nasa'i and Ibn Majah. On the basis of these traditions, all the authorities stress that this "beating", if resorted to at all, should be more or less symbolic—"with a toothbrush, or some such thing" (Tabari, quoting the views of scholars of the earliest times), or even "with a folded handkerchief" (Razi); and some of the greatest Muslim scholars (e.g., Ash-Shafi'i) are of the opinion that it is just barely permissible, and should preferably be avoided; and they justify this opinion by the Prophet's personal feelings with regard to this problem.[12]

Thus, it can be seen that this verse in no way sanctions the free willed beating of one's wife. It should be resorted to only in the case of *nushuz* and only after admonition and separation from bed do not help in bringing about a change in attitude. Most of the women beaten nowadays are not beaten because these two conditions have been met with, but are in fact, beaten because of the husband's anger over some petty issue. Such behavior is not that of a sincere Muslim and the words of the Prophet should be recalled when he said that the strongest one among us is not the best wrestler, but the one who can withhold his anger. As long as the above conditions are not met there is no Qur'anic justification for the beating of any woman. There exists many ahadith that support Shafi'i's view that it is most reprehensible to beat one's wife, and certainly this is true if one wishes to be good to Allah and His Messenger and wishes for the success in the Hereafter. It should be noted that even if the conditions are met, the beating should be of a symbolic type and it is not allowed, even in the case of *nushuz*, to beat a woman in such a way that marks are left on her body from the beating.

The Prophet in a hadith throws more light on when a wife can be beaten. The Messenger of Allah said, "Fear Allah regarding women. Verily you have married them on a trust from Allah and made their private parts lawful with the word of Allah. You have rights over them that they should entertain no one to your beds which you dislike. If they do this, give them a beating without causing injury to them. They have rights over you with respect to their food and clothing according to your means." (Bukhari and Muslim)

From a fiqh point of view Imam Nawawi writes in his *Minhaj at-Talibeen :*

At the first indication of disobedience to marital authority, a wife should be exhorted by her husband without his immediately breaking off relations with her. When she manifests her disobedience by an act which, although isolated, leaves no doubt to her intentions, he should repeat his exhortations, and confine her to her chamber, but without striking her. . .Only where there are repeated acts of disobedience may a husband inflict corporal chastisement.[13]

Summarizing this lengthy discussion about beating in Islam, I shall simply quote from Fazlul Karim:

Beating shall not be resorted to in the case of general disobedience because that will cause estrangement of feelings suicidal to domestic peace and conjugal happiness. In some extreme cases. . .mild beating is allowed; but it is also a condition that it should never be inflicted on the face. The Holy Qur'an also prescribes some preliminaries before this mild beating; namely, admonition and separation from bed (4:16Q). In spite of this reservation of beating in case of emergency, the Holy Prophet discouraged it in practice for the best of husbands. Beating may be done with small things such as a tooth-stick, but never with a whip or stick.

The admonition and the beating are, however, only allowed in the case of *nushuz* according to the Qur'anic verse. The term *nushuz* is not disobedience but is somewhat equivalent to a breach of the agreements implied in the marriage contract.

This brings us to the duties of the wife in Islam which, as wife alone and not as mother, are basically four:

(1) She must allow her husband to have sexual intercourse with her at any time he desires, provided, obviously, that she is not on her period. This is clear from many ahadith of the Prophet. The Messenger of Allah said, "When a man calls his wife to satisfy his desire, let her come to him although she is occupied at the oven." (Tirmidhi) A hadith in *Sahih Muslim* gives an example of the Prophet calling his wife Zainab to him while she was tanning leather. Other ahadith point to the fact that the angels curse the woman who refuses to allow her husband to be satisfied by her. (Bukhari)

The right of the husband in this case is so great that even the wife's extra-religious practices *(nafl)* may have to be shortened if the husband desires, as the following hadith clearly shows:

Abu Sa'ed al-Khudri reported that a woman came to the Prophet and said, "My husband, Safwan ibn Muattal, beats me while I pray, breaks my fast while I keep fast and does not recite the morning prayer until the sun has risen." Safwan was nearby so the Prophet asked him about his wife's statement. Safwan said,

---

[13]An-Nawawi, Mahiuddin, Translation of *Minhaj at-Talibin*, Law Publishing Co., Lahore, Pakistan, 1977, p. 418.

[14]Karim, Fazlul, *al-Hadith*, p. 198.

"O Messenger of Allah, as for her saying 'He beats me while I pray;' it is because she prays with two chapters so I prevented her." Safwan continued, "And as for her saying 'He breaks my fast while I keep fast,' it is because she goes on fasting while I am a young man and cannot therefore keep patient." Then the Prophet said, "No woman shall keep fast without the permission of her husband." Safwan then said, "And as for her saying 'I don't pray until the sun has risen,' it is because I am a member of a family which is well known for that. We cannot get up from sleep until the sun rises. The Prophet told him, "O Safwan, when you get up from sleep, pray." (Abu Da'ud, Ibn Majah)

On this point it should be noted that the woman has rights also. These are related to the nature of sexual intercourse, which are not too widely discussed today. The Prophet said, "You must not throw yourselves on your wives as do beasts, but first there must be a messenger between you." "What messenger?" asked his companions. "Sweet words and kisses" was his reply. Many of the earlier scholars discussed the nature of sexual relations in great detail. 'Abdul Rauf discusses some of their conclusions. For example:

Muslim writers also emphasize that the husband should endeavor to achieve mutual orgasm. If he should fail to hold out sufficiently for his partner, they say he should continue his efforts to have her reach a climax. To rush away from her too soon may be injurious.[15]

Indeed most of the well-known scholars of Islam have discussed this point at one time or another. Minai states:

Imam Ghazali agreed that sexual fulfillment was essential for a woman's health as well as for her virtue, and instructed husbands on the proper techniques to satisfy their wives. Men were not to be preoccupied exclusively with their own pleasure; for example: they were to wait for their wives to reach orgasm. "A woman's ejaculation is often delayed, which excites her sexual desires even further," the imam explained.[16]

Obviously, according to the preceding ahadith, the woman must succumb to the man on command. Some authors also add that the man should be willing to succumb to the woman on command according to the Qur'anic verse that a woman has rights similar to those over her. For the believer who wants to please Allah, and will therefore be concerned with how he treats his spouse, care should be taken to cater to the sexual needs and feelings of the wife.

---

[15]Abdul-Rauf, Muhammad, *Marriage in Islam: A Manual*, Exposition Press, New York, 1972, p. 51.
[16]Minai, Laila, *Women in Islam: Tradition and Transition in the Middle East*, Seaview Books, New York, 1981, p. 157.

(2)   It is well-known from many ahadith that the woman is not to allow anyone inside the house of her husband if the husband is known to dislike such a person. This is the second duty of the wife.

(3)   There is also a hadith that a woman should not leave her house without the permission of her husband. "When a woman steps out of her house against the will of her husband, she is cursed by every angel in the Heavens and by everything other than man and jinn by which she passes, until she returns," is the meaning of a hadith.[17] But she is allowed to leave the house to meet her needs (Bukhari) and cannot be stopped from going to the *masjid* (Muslim). As for the relationship between this duty, the first duty above and the rights the wife may demand, the *Hedaya* has the following to say:

> If a wife be disobedient or refractory, and go abroad without her
> husband's consent, she is not entitled to any support from him,
> until she returns and makes submission, because the rejection of
> the matrimonial restraint in this instance originated with her; but
> when she returns home, she is then subject to it, for which reason
> she again becomes entitled to her support as before. It is
> otherwise where a woman, residing in the house of her husband,
> refuses to admit him to the conjugal embrace, as she is entitled to
> maintenance, notwithstanding her opposition, because being
> then in his power, he may, if he pleases, enjoy her by force.[18]

(4)   She must guard her husband's property in his absence, as the following hadith states. "Next to fear of Allah, the believer finds nothing better for him than a virtuous wife. If he bids her, she obeys him. If he looks at her, she gives him pleasure. If she gives him a promise, she fulfills it. And if he is absent from her, she guards herself and his property." (Ibn Majah)

This hadith states that the wife should obey her husband, but to what extent? Obviously, she cannot obey her husband in anything that is *haram*. Not only that but the obedience of the wife is only in those four duties listed above, viz., with regard to sex, staying home, guarding his property, and not allowing others into his house.

We now come to those things that are not a breach of the marriage obligations and in fact are not part of the wife's duties, and therefore, she cannot rightfully be punished for any shortcomings on her part with regard to them.

If we look at the example of the Prophet, upon whom be peace, even the striking of the husband by the wife does not justify cruel treatment by the husband toward his wife. A hadith states that once the Prophet

---

[17]Maududi, A. A., *Purdah and the Status of Women in Islam*, Islamic Publications Ltd., Lahore, Pakistan, 1976, pp. 144-145.
[18]Hamilton, Charles, translator, *Hedaya*, Premier Book House, Lahore, Pakistan, 1975, p. 141.

was struck in the chest by his wife 'Ayshah, and her mother got upset and was about to reprimand her. The Prophet at that instant said, "Leave her alone; they do worse than that."[19] There also exists the well-known hadith that tells about the Prophet's wives nagging him for more material possessions.

Some husbands get upset when their wives refuse to do this or that around the house. This has subjected many wives to physical mistreatment. But the following incident from a book on *fiqh* clearly shows that it is not the duty of the wife to tend after the house; and therefore, it can in no way justify any sort of retort on the part of the husband. In fact, the following quote would make it seem that many women nowadays should be the ones complaining as they are forced to do work that they are not responsible for:

It is reported that a man once came to 'Umar, the second Caliph, with the intention of bringing to his notice certain complaints he had against his wife. When he reached the door of 'Umar's house, he heard the Caliph's wife railing against him. Hearing this, he went back as he thought that the Caliph himself was in the same predicament and could, therefore, be hardly expected to set matters right for him. 'Umar, coming out of his house, saw the person going back. So he called him out and inquired as to the purpose which had brought him to his house. He said that he had come to him with some complaints against his wife, but turned back on finding that the Caliph himself was subject to the same treatment from his wife. 'Umar said to him that he patiently bore the excesses of his wife because she had certain rights over him. "Is it not true that she cooks my food, washes my clothes and suckles my children, thus relieving me of the necessity of employing a cook, a washerman and a nurse, although she is not in the slightest degree responsible for this? Not only that, I enjoy peace of mind on account of her and I am protected from committing the sin of adultery. In view of these advantages, I put up with her excesses. You should also do the same."[20]

According to *Hedaya*, a well-known work on fiqh:

The maintenance of the wife's servants is incumbent upon her husband, as well as that of the wife herself, provided he be in opulent circumstances, because he is obliged to provide his wife's maintenance, "so far as may suffice" (as aforesaid), and it is not sufficient, unless her servants also be supported, they being essential to her ease and comfort; but it is not absolutely incumbent upon him to provide a maintenance for more than one

---

[19]Abdul-Rauf, Muhammad, *Marriage in Islam: A Manual,* p. 48.
[20]Siddiqi, M. Mazheruddin, *Women in Islam,* Institute of Islamic Culture, Lahore, Pakistan, 1975, pp. 83-84.

servant, according to Haneefa and Muhammad. Aboo Yoosaf says he must provide maintenance for two servants, as one is required for service within the house, and the other out-of-doors. The arguments of Haneefa and Muhammed on this point are twofold: First, one servant may answer both purposes whence two are unnecessary. Secondly, if the husband were himself to undertake all the services required by the wife, it would suffice, and a servant would be unnecessary; and, in the same manner, it suffices if he constitutes any single servant his substitute therein; wherefore a second servant is not requisite. The learned in the law say that the rate of maintenance due from an opulent husband to his wife's servants is the same as that due from a poor husband to his wife—namely, the lowest that can be admitted as sufficient. Haneefa says that a husband who is poor is not required to find maintenance for his wife's servants; and this is an approved doctrine, as it is to be supposed that the wife of a poor man will serve herself. Muhammad holds that it is due from a poor husband in the same manner as from one more opulent.[21]

Thus, we see that the husband is not only responsible for the maintenance of the wife, but is also responsible for the cooking, cleaning, and general maintenance of the house by either hiring a servant, doing the work himself or by being lucky enough to have a wife who is willing to do it out of her own free will. If the wife refuses to help out in these areas, she is not to be held responsible and cannot be reprimanded.

In summary, there is the following hadith from the Prophet on the rights of a wife. A person asked the Messenger of Allah, "What rights does the wife of one among us have over him?" His answer was, "It is that you shall give her food when you take your food, you shall clothe her when you clothe yourself, you shall not slap her on the face, nor revile her, nor leave her alone except within the house." (Ahmad, Abu Da'ud, Ibn Majah).

Another point that should be taken into consideration is education. As we know, the Prophet said that education is incumbent upon all Muslims, men and women. In these days, especially for Muslims in a non-Islamic society, it is a responsibility of the husband to make sure that the wife gets a proper Islamic education. The Prophet said that we are each responsible for a ward and part of the ward of the husband is his wife; therefore, if the husband fails in his responsibility of making sure that his wife gets a proper education, he may be accountable to Allah for this shortcoming. Furthermore, the husband can in no way prohibit his wife from going to the mosque. A trip to the mosque is educational for the woman just as it is for the man, especially if there

---

[21]Hamilton, Charles, *Hedaya*, p. 112.

is a talk or some other useful activity.

I will just add one small note on the position of a wife in a polygamous situation. Basically, when it comes to material considerations, each wife must be treated equally, although in case of feelings, there may be some things that the husband cannot control, as the ahadith show. The Holy Prophet said, "When a man has two wives and he does not deal equitably between them, he will come on the Resurrection Day with a side hanging down." (Tirmidhi, Abu Da'ud, Nasa'i) 'Ayesha reported that the Messenger of Allah used to divide turns among his wives and that was just. He used to say, "Allahumma, this is my division in what I control, so don't rebuke me regarding that over which Thou has control while I have not, i.e., what he feels in his heart." (Tirmidhi, Ahmad, Nasa'i).

In conclusion, we feel that the wife has certain duties and responsibilities and in these duties she must completely obey her husband. These are in the matter of sex, staying within the house, and not allowing people into her home her husband does not like. We have seen that she can only be beaten in the case of *nushuz*, which refers to the aspects discussed earlier in which she must be completely obedient to her husband, and that too only after she has been admonished and has been separated from the husband's bed. A great scholar, such as Imam Shafi'i, has practically prohibited beating. Furthermore, we have seen that she is not responsible for taking care of the house or even of her own self and needs. In fact, Imam Shaibani has said that even a poor man is responsible for getting a servant for his wife or taking care of her affairs himself. Also, education is incumbent upon Muslim women and it seems to fall within the responsibilities of the husband to make sure that she is educated properly. Thus, we see that the position of the Muslim wife, when given her full Islamic rights and responsibilities, is a far cry from the existing situation among many of the Muslim people of today. This should be of no surprise as the Muslims have strayed very far from Islam in almost every aspect of their lives!

Chapter XIII
_____

THE
PERIMETER OF
AN ISLAMIC DRESS

Jamal A. Badawi

Dr. Jamal Badwi is a well-known speaker and writer on Islam. He teaches industrial management at Saint Mary's University, Halifax, N.S., Canada. His article first appeared in *al-ittihad* of Spring 1973 issue.

To some, the Muslim code of dress may sound like a trivial subject. The shari'ah, however, assigns it moral, social, and legal dimensions. According to the Qur'an, one basic requirement to be a true believer is to make one's opinions, feelings, and inclinations subservient to the commandments of Allah and his Messenger:

> "It is not befitting for a believer, man or woman, when a matter has been decided by Allah and His Apostle, to have any option about their decision: if any one disobeys Allah and His Apostle, he is indeed on a clearly wrong path."[1]

Placing, therefore, one's personal opinions, feelings, or inclination above or at the same level as the commandments of Allah is the ultimate in human pride and vanity. This means, in effect, that a mortal is responding to Allah's guidance by saying: "O my Creator! Your law is Your Own opinion. I have my own opinion, and I know best what is good for me." This attitude is befitting for unbelievers and hypocrites, but not for a believer, no matter how imperfect one may be in implementing Islam in one's life.[2]

_____

[1] The Qur'an 33:36.

[2] A distinction should be made between a) the acceptance of Allah's word as true and supreme in itself, while not succeeding to implement it fully in one's life, hoping and trying to reach that goal, and b) regarding one's own opinions or other social values and pressures as more valid than Allah's injunctions and trying to find various excuses to

The exposition of truth in an honest and straightforward way may thus cause some unease even to good and sincere Muslims. It may seem safer and "diplomatic" to avoid the issue altogether, or to present it in a diluted and vague way. It is even safer and more "diplomatic" to explicitly or implicitly condone each others' infractions, to help each other find excuses and to rationalize our disobedience to Almighty Allah. This attitude is neither new, nor is it without consequences. As the Qur'an says:

"Curses were pronounced on those among the children of Israel who rejected faith, by the tongue of Da'ud (David) and of 'Esa (Jesus) the son of Mary; because they disobeyed and persisted in excesses.

Nor did they (ususally) forbid one another the iniquities which they committed. Evil indeed were the deeds which they did."[3]

Requirements of Muslim Women's Clothing

The First Requirement: Extent of Covering

The dress must cover the whole body except for the areas specifically exempted.

"Say to the believing men that they should lower their gaze and guard their modesty: that will make far greater purity for them: And Allah is well acquainted with all they do.

And say to the believing women that they should lower their gaze and guard their modesty; that they should not display their beauty and ornaments except what (must ordinarily) appear thereof: that they should draw their veils over their bosoms and not display their beauty except to their husbands, their fathers, their husbands' fathers, their sons, their husbands' sons, their brothers or their brothers' sons, or their sisters' sons, or their women, or the slaves whom their right hands possess, or male servants free of physical needs, or small children who have no sense of the shame of sex: and that they should not strike their feet in order to draw attention to their hidden ornaments. And O you believers! Turn all toward Allah that you may attain bliss."[4]

These 'ayahs contain, among other things, two main injunctions:

✓ A Muslim woman should not display her beauty and adornment (zeenah) except for "that which must ordinarily appear of it"[5] (ma

---

justify one's breaking of the law of Allah. It is the latter attitude which is not only blameworthy but akin to unbelief.
[3]The Qur'an 78-79.
[4]Ibid., 24:30-31.
[5]Ali, Yusuf, op. cit. p. 904.

dhahara minha), or "that which is apparent."[6]

The word *zeenah*[7], exempted from the above injunction, was interpreted in two ways:

a.   The face and the hands. This is the interpretation of the majority of the jurists, past and present.[9] This interpretation is confirmed by *ijma'* (consensus) that a Muslim woman is allowed by Islam to uncover her face and hands during pilgrimage and even during the prayers, while the rest of her body is regarded as *'awrah* (that which should be covered).[10] This interpretation is based on the authority of Prophet Muhammad, upon whom be peace, especially in the *hadith* in which he says:

> "... If the woman reaches the age of puberty, no (part of her body — should be seen but this — and he pointed to his face and hands."

b.   Whatever appears of the woman's body owing to uncontrollable factors such as the blowing of the wind, or out of necessity such as the bracelets or even the outer clothes themselves."

✓   The headcovers (*khumur*) should be drawn over the neck slits (*juyoob*). *Khumur* is the plural of the Arabic word *khimar* which means a headcover.[12] *Juyoob* is the plural of the Arabic word *jaiyb* (a derivative of *jawb* or cutting) and refers to the neck slit (of the dress). This means that the headcover should be drawn so as to cover not only the hair, but it should also be drawn over the neck and be extended over the bosom.

---

[6]M.M. Pickthall, *The Meaning of the Glorious Koran*, p. 25.

[7]According to *Lisan al-Arab* (Dictionary of Arabic language), the term *zeenah* includes "all that which beautifies," quoted in (Mrs. Ne'mat Sidqy, *At-Tabarruj*, 17th Printing, Dar ul-I'tisam, Egypt, 1975, pp. 20-21.

[8]The term *zeenah* is used in the Qur'an with reference to children, wealth, and natural beauty in Allah's creation. See example Qur'an 3:14, 16:8, 17:47, and 37:6.

[9]This is the interpretation of Malik, ash-Shafi'i, Abu Hanifah and a version of Ahmad b. Hanbal. See Muhammad N. Hijab Albani's *al-Mar'at al-Muslimah fi al-Kitab wa as-sunnah,* al-Maktab al-Islam, Beirut, Lebanon, 1969, pp. 41-42.

[10]Albani provides ample evidence that the covering of the face and hands is not required. Suffice it to say that the woman is allowed to uncover her face and hands during such spiritual acts as the prayers and pilgrimage. See pp. 25-46.

[11]One weakness with this more stringent interpretation is that "uncontrollable" factors are automatically forgiven without any need for specification. The fact that the Qur'an 24:31 exempts from all "*zeenah*" that which is regarded as "ma dhahara minha" is itself an indication of a concession. This concession is confirmed by the hadith (related to 'Asma as will be seen in the discussion of the third requirement. See al-Albani, Ibid. pp. 25-46.

[12]According to Albani, this meaning of "khimar" was explained in such authorities as Ibn al-Atheer's *an-Hihayah* and *Tafseer al-Hafiz Ibn Kathir* and others. Albani reports that he knows of no difference on this point. See Albani, Ibid., pp. 33-34.

The Second Requirement: Looseness

The dress must be loose enough so as not to describe the shape of a woman's body. This is consistent with the intent of the preceding 'ayahs and is surely a crucial aspect of hiding zeenah. Even moderately-tight clothes, which may cover the whole body, could describe the shape of such attractive parts of the woman's body as the bustline, the waist, the buttocks, the back and the thighs. If these are not part of the natural beauty of zeenah, what else is?

Prophet Muhammad once received a thick garment as a gift. He gave it to Usamah b. Zayd, who in turn gave it to his wife. When asked by the Prophet why he did not wear it, Usamah indicated that he gave it to his wife. The Prophet then said to him, Usamah, "Ask her to use a gholalah under it (the garment), for I fear that it (the garment) may describe the size of her bones."[13] The word gholalah in Arabic means a thick fabric worn under the dress to prevent it from describing the shape of the body.

A highly desirable way of concealing the shape of the body is to wear a cloak over the garment. The Prophet, however, indicated that if the woman's dress meets the Islamic standards, it suffices (without a cloak) even for the validity of prayers.[14]

The Third Requirement: Thickness

The dress should be thick enough so as not to show the color of the skin it covers, or the shape of the body which it is supposed to hide.

The purpose of 'ayah (24:31) is to hide the Muslim women's body except ma dhahara minha (the face and hands). It is obvious that this purpose cannot be served if the dress is thin enough to reveal the color of the skin or the beauty of the body. This is eloquently explained by Prophet Muhammad, upon whom be peace: "In later (generations) of my ummah there will be women who will be dressed but naked. On top of their heads they will have (what looks) like camel humps. Curse them for they are truly cursed." In another version he added that they "will not enter into paradise or (even) get a smell of it "[15]

On one occasion, 'Asma, the daughter of Abu Bakr, was visiting her sister 'Ayshah, wife of the Prophet. When he noted that 'Asma's dress was not thick enough, he turned his face away in anger and said, "If the woman reaches the age of puberty, no part of her body should be seen but this,[15] and he pointed to his face and his hands.[16]

---

[13]This hadith appears in Musnad Ahmad, also in al-Bayhaqi, and is confirmed in other sources of hadith such as Sunan Abi Da'ud. See Albani, Ibid., pp. 59-63.

[14]See Sayyid Sabiq's Fiqh as-Sunnah, Dar al-Kitab al-Arabi, Beirut, Lebanon, 1969, vol. 1, p. 127.

[15]At-Tabarani and Sahih Muslim. See Albani, op. cit., p. 56.

[16]On another occasion when the Prophet, upon whom be peace, saw a bride in a thin dress he said, "She is not a woman who believes in Surat an-Noor who wears this." Surat an-

The Fourth Requirement: Overall Appearance

The dress should not be such that it attracts men's attention to the woman's beauty. The Qur'an clearly prescribes the requirements of the woman's dress for the purpose of concealing *zeenah* (adornment). How could such *zeenah* be concealed if the dress is designed in a way that it attracts men's eyes to the woman?

That is why, addressing the Prophet's wives as the examples for Muslim women, the Qur'an says:

"Dress not yourselves with the dress of the Time of Ignorance..."[17]

Additional Requirements

In addition to the above four main and clearly spelled out requirements, there are other requirements[18] whose specific applications may vary with time and location. These include:

The dress should not be similar to what is known as a male costume. Ibn 'Abbas narrated that "the Prophet cursed the men who act like women and the women who act like men."[19]

It should not be similar to what is known as the costume of unbelievers. This requirement is derived from the general rule of shari'ah that Muslims should have their distinct personality and should differentiate their practices and appearances from the unbelievers.[20]

At the same time, it should not be a dress of fame, pride, and vanity. Such fame may be sought by wearing an excessively fancy dress as a status symbol or an excessively ragged dress to gain others' admiration or one's selflessness. Both motives are improper by Islamic standards. The Prophet says:

Noor is the surah where the main requirements of the Muslim woman's dress are outlined. On yet another occasion some women from the tribe of Bani Tameem came to visit 'Ayshah in thin clothes. Upon seeing them, the Prophet, upon whom be peace, said, "If you are believers, these are not believers' clothing." See Yusuf al-Qaradwi, *al-Halal wa al-Haram fi al-Islam*, Maktabat Wahbah, Cairo (1976), p. 160.

[17]The term used in the Qur'an is *tabarruj* which means displaying of beauty. Another derivative of *tabarruj* is *burooj* which is used in the Qur'an (e.g. 4:77, 15:16, 25:61, 85:1) Burooj means towers because of their clear visibility. Clear "visibility" of the woman may result from the type of dress, the way she walks, or the way she behaves.

[18]According to Albani, a further requirement is that the dress should not be perfumed. In fact, this requirement extends beyond dress. There are several ahadith which make it clearly forbidden for a Muslim woman to wear perfumes when she goes out of her home, even if she is going to the mosque. See Albani, op. cit., pp. 64-66.

[19]*Al-Bukhari, Abu Da'ud, Ahmad, ad-Darimi.* For this and other ahadith on the same subject see Albani. Ibid, pp. 66-69.

[20]For an excellent discussion of this principle on the basis of the Qur'an and Sunnah, see Albani, Ibid, pp. 89-109.

"Whoever wears a dress of fame in this world, Allah will clothe him with a dress of humiliation on the day of resurrection, then set it afire."[21]

Requirements of Muslim Men's Clothing, Extent, Looseness, Thickness and Appearance

The basic requirements of the Muslim woman's dress apply as well to the Muslim man's clothing, with the difference being mainly in degree. This can best be understood by looking into what Islam defines as 'awrah which refers to the part of the body that should be covered at all times unless there is an expressed exception. The covering of 'awrah is also a condition for prayer of both men and women.

The jurists agree on the basis of the Qur'an and Sunnah that 'awrah for the woman is defined as the whole body except for the face and hands. For the man, the 'awrah is defined as the area between the navel and the knees.[22]

Within the definition of 'awrah for men and women, all the four basic requirements discussed in this paper are essentially the same:

A man should fully cover his 'awrah.

Men's clothes should be loose enough to cover his 'awrah.

They should be thick enough to conceal the color of the skin or the parts required to be covered.

They should not be designed in a way to attract attention. The basic rule of modesty and simple clothes applies to men as well as women.

Additional Requirements

The other three additional requirements discussed under the Muslim woman's code of dress apply to men's clothes as well:

They should not be similar to what is known as the female dress.

They should not be similar to what could be identified as the dress of unbelievers.

They should not be clothes of fame, pride, and vanity.

Besides, men are not allowed to wear silk and gold. This does not apply to women.

---

[21]For this and other versions of the hadith see al-Albani, Ibid, pp. 110-111.

[22]Differences exist, however, among jurists whether the knees and the thighs should be included in the definition of the man's 'awrah. For a good discussion of the evidence related to both views, see Sayyid Sabiq's Fiqh as-Sunnah, Dar al-Kitab al-Arabi, Beirut, Lebanon (1973), volume 1, pp. 125-127.

Conclusion

There are surely many other issues pertaining to the subjects that are not covered in this paper. Its main focus is on the documented injunctions of Allah (subhanahu wa ta'la) as derived from His word (the Qur'an) and as explained by the chosen Messenger, Muhammad, upon whom be peace. These injunctions are to be complied with by all Muslim men and women, and in case of transgression, they will be held accountable in the hereafter. Truly, husbands, wives, fathers and mothers do have an obligation to remind, exhort and help each other to achieve the pleasure of Allah and to avoid His wrath. In the final analysis, however, it is not coercion or force which is likely to bring about obedience to Allah. It is but the love of Allah, the acceptance of His guidance as the supreme Truth, even if contrary to one's personal opinions, that will bring about the change.

Chapter XIV

ISLAMIC ART: ITS DOCTRINE AND FORMATION

Muhammad 'Abdel Wahab

Dr. Muhammad 'Abdul Wahab was an associate professor of Islamics, University of Michigan, Ann Arbor at the time of his contribution to *al-ittihad* of Rabi' al-Awwal 1400/April 1980.

About the genesis of Islamic art, there are two facts that call for consideration. First, Islamic art was born with the *hijrah* (emigration)— a fact ignored or understated by the orientalists. Islamic architecture, in their estimation, assumed form subsequent to the conquests. Thus, they try to conclude that Islamic architecture was not born in Arabia and not by the Arabs. Second, the term 'Islamic Art' does not mean sensuality as seen in dancing, acting, singing, painting, sculpture, and so forth which is a characteristic of the arts other than Islamic. Art is considered here as 'architecture,' the first or principal art form to which all other art media are subservient, such as minor arts, applied arts, fine arts and decorative arts. In the study of Islamic art we term all of them as 'pure arts.'

Islamic Architecture in the Time of the Prophet

After the Prophet, upon whom be peace, left Makkah and before he reached Yathrib (Madinah), he stopped in Quba' where he built the first mosque.

"There is a mosque whose foundation was laid from the first day on piety."[1]

---

[1] The Qur'an 1:108.

For this reason, the mosque at Quba' has been known as the "Mosque of Piety" and "Mosque of the Power of Islam." On reaching Yathrib, the Prophet, upon whom be peace, build the second mosque of Islam.

When these two mosques were planned (figure 1) the *qiblah* was fixed and a *mihrab* was built in the middle of the *qiblah* wall. It is obvious that the *qiblah* is the focal point in the planning. This is a new theme which is not known in any other religious architecture. They posted columns of palm stems in rows parallel to the *qiblah* wall. The building was covered with wood and reeds. This building proper is known as *Bait al-Salah*, "the House of Prayer."

The Prophet's home was then connected with the mosque by two side *diwans*. The space between the house of prayer and the Prophet's home was left open to the sky and was known as *sahn* or open court (figure 1)

Elements of Islamic religious function were added, such as the *minbar*. The Prophet, upon whom be peace, used to climb its steps so that he could be seen by the Muslims while giving his Friday *khutbah* (speech). The minbar was a necessity in the mosque to enable the Prophet to preach Almighty Allah's most perfect religion. When Muslims stood up for prayer behind the Prophet, upon whom be peace, they made straight lines as if they were a stretched wall.

From this illustration it is proved that the Prophet, by building the mosque, paved the way to Islamic architecture. Thus, the first Muslims did not go out of their land to look for architectural elements. The orientalists have dropped these two mosques from their consideration while using the mosques of al-Basrah, al-Kufah, Damascus, and al-Fustat to find supportive evidence for relating their elements to the pre-Islamic civilization in Iraq, Syria, and Egypt.

The question is from where did the Prophet, upon whom be peace, extract the architectural elements of the mosque? Before we answer this question, we must explain the Prophet's role.

The Prophet was not just a deliverer of the message; he had to exemplify the message in his own life and build a new Muslim ummah. His every action was guided by Allah.

The Qur'an contains these architectural elements:

And We (Allah) appointed the qiblah
to which you were used.
Only to test those who followed
the Prophet from those
who would turn on their heels.[2]

So from wherever
you start forth, turn

---

[2]The Qur'an 2:143.

your face in the direction
of the Sacred Mosque;
and wherever you are
turn your face to it.[3]

The *qiblah* is the direction Muslims face in prayer; and, as is evident from the above *'ayahs* of the Qur'an, its concept was drawn from the revelation. Before *hijrah* to Madinah, the Muslims prayed facing Jerusalem, a city sacred to the People of the Book. But after sixteen months in Madinah, Muslims were divinely ordained to change their *qiblah* to the Ka'bah in Makkah. This change restored to the Ka'bah, the oldest center of Ibrahim, its rightful place; Jerusalem assumed a second place.

The *mihrab*, the second important element of Islamic architecture, has also been referred to in the Qur'an:

Every time that Zakariya entered
her Mihrab he found
her supplied with sustenance.
He said: O Mary! Whence
(comes) this to you.
She said: From Allah
for Allah provides sustenance
to whom He pleases
without measures.

The angels called unto him (Zakariya)
while he was standing
in prayer in the Mihrab.[4]

Thus, the post-*hijrah* mosques at Quba' and Madinah enshrined the concepts of *qiblah* and *mihrab* under divine guidance.

As the center of faith and community life, the subsequent mosques in Arabia and other parts of the world followed the same basic pattern.

The mosques of Allah
shall be visited and maintained
by such as believe in Allah
and the last day.[5]

The Motivation of Religion

In the orientalists' view, Islam does not motivate art; instead, it opposes art. Unfortunately, some Muslim scholars have followed their track. We oppose this view by a new theory which proves that Islamic art evolved from its main source, the Qur'an. Those who assert that the

---

[3] Ibid. 2:150.
[4] Ibid. 3:37, 39.
[5] Ibid. 9:18.

so-called Islamic art, as manifested in Muslim architecture, has little or nothing to do with the faith of Islam, are guilty of misstatement. In fact, all arts are inspiration, but Islamic art is religious. Its universality renders it adaptable to other religions, too. It is distinctive even to the layman.

Motivated by Islam, the Muslim artist, as opposed to the Greek, the Roman, and the Christian, expressed his artistic inclinations with humility because he did not desire to be in competition with his Creator.

> Such is Allah, your God
> the Creator of all things.[6]

He further says:

> And has given you shape
> and made your shapes
> beautiful.[7]

The artistic excellence of Allah reaches its high mark in the creation of man:

> He is it who shapes you
> in the wombs as He wills.[8]

Separating each role from the other, Allah emphasized that He is the Creator, the Inspirator, and the Painter:

> He is Allah, the Creator,
> the Evolver,
> the Bestower of shapes (and colors).[9]

This *'ayah* tells us very vividly about His creativity. God does not merely create, but also gives inner spiritual and outer physical forms. He is also the *Musawwir* who fashions and colors to complete the visible shapes of creation. The artistic concepts such as form and shape, which confuse many an art scholar, are clearly delineated in the Qur'an:

> He who has made everything which He has created
> most good: He began
> the creation of man
> with clay
> He created man
> from sound clay
> like unto pottery.[10]

---

[6] Ibid. 40:62.
[7] Ibid. 40:64.
[8] Ibid. 3:6.
[9] Ibid. 59:23.
[10] Ibid. 55:14.

Only by Almighty Allah's Will, will man have some of his abilities.

> Then will Allah say:
> O, Jesus, son of Mary!...
> And Behold! you make
> out of clay, as it were,
> the figure of a bird,
> by My leave,
> and you breathe into it,
> and it becomes a bird
> by My leave.[11]

The Muslim artist did not use sculpture as an art form nor did he use the human body as an art object because he feared to imitate Allah's creativity. The Christian artist, who considered a mortal man as God, and God as having a human form, penetrated into the human form, studied its anatomy and portrayed it into the most realistic sculpture known to mankind. Michelangelo painted "The Creation of Adam" on the Sistine Chapel of the Vatican. He represented both Allah and 'Adam as human beings. 'Adam's hand stretches for the Almighty's hand, but they do not touch, even though the distance is so close. Both God and 'Adam are nude and God has his arm around a woman! According to Michelangelo's philosophy, if the fingers had touched, life would have generated in his painting of 'Adam.

The Christian artists presented God as human and portrayed Him as a powerful elderly man, knowledgeable and wise. They represented Jesus as a strong young man when alive, and as a tragic, helpless man during the crucifixion.

Contrary to Judeo-Christian tradition, the Muslim artists never represented God whose shape will be revealed to them in the Day of Resurrection or Hereafter. Artists never dared to represent the Prophet's features, upon whom be peace, even though the Muslims have vivid details of his person preserved in ahadith.

Dignified Representation of Women

Islamic teachings have influenced the artist in the representation of women. In the first place, he avoided her as an object; but even when he portrayed her, he abided by the Qur'anic teachings and did not violate the sanctity of her body.

> ...There is no blame on them
> if they lay aside
> their (outer) garments, provided
> they make not a wanton display
> of their beauty and ornament.[12]

---

[11]Ibid. 5:113.
[12]Ibid. 24:60.

And say to the believing women
that they should lower
their gaze and guard
their modesty; that they
should not display their
beauty and ornaments except
what (must ordinarily) appear
thereof; that they should
draw their veils over
their bosoms and not display
their beauty...[13]

For this reason, women are not seen in Islamic art naked or semi-naked. In other religious arts women are nude or partially nude. Their bodies are revealed in very realistic proportions. The Christian artist was the first to use women as live models.

Natural Representation

The Qur'an delivers ideas, subjects, and themes for art representation. There are several 'ayahs which indicate that animals, birds, plants, trees, palms and other elements of nature are available for artistic themes. They have their own beauty and decorative value. These natural elements passed through stages of conventionality (figure 2) and abstraction.

And (Allah has created) horses,
mules and donkeys, for you
to ride and use for ornamentation[14]

That which is on earth
we have made but as
a glittering ornamentation for the earth.[15]

And We ornamented
the lower heaven
with lamps (stars) light.[16]

Do they not look
at the sky above them?
How We have made it
and ornamented it.[17]

---

[13]Ibid. 24:31.
[14]Ibid. 16:8.
[15]Ibid. 18:7.
[16]Ibid. 41:12.
[17]Ibid. 50:6.

Arabesque

To avoid realism, the Muslim artist went for abstraction. He invented a style of decoration which has been named in the West as "Arab Decoration" or "Arabesque." It is a mixture of mingled, interlaced abstracted floral (figure 3) and geometric (figure 4) elements. Also, animals and birds are mingled within the same style of the whole decoration. One of its main characteristics is the infinite of the linear and themes, even beyond the frame. As a main feature of the Islamic art, it is admired by all tastes. It has been copied, but in vain; never approaching close to one made by a motivated and inspired Muslim hand.

Islamic Calligraphy

As a decorative theme, calligraphy among Muslims was also motivated by the Qur'an. It became the second *pure art* after Islamic architecture. In Christianity, Pope Gregory, called upon the artists to paint Christian subjects for the education of the illiterate masses. Scenes such as: the Announcement, the birth of Christ, the Flight into Egypt, Christ Walking on the Water, the Crucifixion, the Descent from the Cross, the Wailing of Christ... and so forth were the main subjects for the artists up to the eighteenth century.

Instead of painting and sculpture, the Muslim artist took a relatively unknown art form and used it for educating people about Islam. This reflects an intellectual approach on behalf of the artist and his viewers. The name Allah (figure 5) and the Qur'an were written in glorified letters. The Qur'anic *'ayahs* were written as decorative themes in mosques, mausoleums, *madrasahs*(schools) and parts of buildings, such as mihrabs, domes, entrances and so forth. Some of these are mentioned in this paper.

al-Mishkawat

There are some words and verses in the Qur'an which are rich in symbolism and contain parables of exceptional imaginative value. The artist applied them successfully. One such example is the *mishkawat* (glass lamps), which Allah has invoked to explain the mysterious nature of His being:

Allah is the light
of the heavens and the earth;
the similitude of His light
is as a niche
and within it a lamp,
the lamp enclosed in a glass,
the glass as it were
a brilliant star:
lit from a blessed tree —

an olive, neither of the East
nor of the West,
whose oil is well-nigh
luminous,
though fire scarce touched it
light upon light
Allah does guide
whom He wills
to His light,
Allah does set forth parables
for men, and Allah
does know all things.[18]

The Qur'an sets for the Muslims the origins and rules of their Islamic civilization. Stimulated by the divine words, the Muslim artist turned *mishkah* into a most graceful form of art to light the most honorable building on earth, the mosque.

The Muslim Artist was Motivated but not Obligated

Say: who has forbidden
the beautiful ornamentation of Allah,
which He has produced
for His worshippers...[19]

Contrary to the Muslim tradition, which did not tamper with the artist's freedom, the Christian church controlled the arts. The artists were used to serve religion, even though most of them hated such controls. The Pope obliged Michaelangelo to paint the Vatican, even though his medium was not painting, but sculpture. His work was even thankless and without pay. Writing in May 1557 to his friend Vasari, he complains: "God is my witness how much against my will it was that Pope Paul forced me into this work...."[20] The Muslim clergy never imposed their will on the artist.

---

[18]Ibid. 23:35.
[19]Ibid. 7:32.
[20]Clements, Robert J., *Michelangelo: A Self-Portrait*, Prentice-Hall, Englewood Cliff, N.J., 1964, p.57.

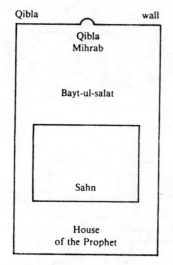

The main plan of the Mosque built by the Prophet in Madinah - figure 1

Abstracted birds
figure 2.

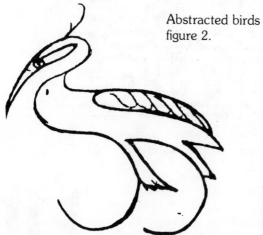

From Syria, Six century Hijrah.

From Iraq,
Fourth Century Hijrah.

First step of Arabesque Egypt,
Third Century Hijrah - figure 3.

Floral Arabesque, Iraq, Early seventh century Hijrah.
This is the second drawing of figure 3 Arabesque.

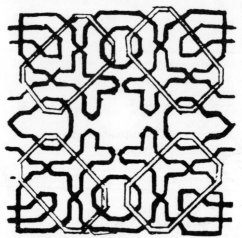

Geometric Arabesque, al-Hamhra,
al-Andalus, Seventh Century Hijrah.
figure 4.

Naskh, Six Century Hijrah.
figure 5.

Foliated Kufi
Fourth Century Hijrah.

Early Kufi, Qur'an,
Third Century Hijrah.

"Revolution has never been a happening only in the domain of civilization, economy, society, or politics. Every true revolution is a member of faith, exaltation, justice, longing, sacrifice, and death—the feelings which are beyond interest and existence. Everybody who took part in a revolution or followed its development from close by could affirm the presence of those ethical features. They saw it as an epic poem and not just a mechanical overthrow or a simple change of the ruling machinery. This might explain the inability of the workers in today's capitalist countries to revolt and, on the other hand, the enthusiasm of poets, artists, and other religious people for a revolution which can be atheistic in its declarations. Considered from the inside, not as a process but as a part of life, revolution appears as a drama which affects men as only religions do. From the outside, political, "real" point of view, it can have a quite different character and aim.

A community affected by the feelings of solidarity, sacrifice, and a common destiny is in a "state of religion." This is the atmosphere of "increased temperature," which appears in emergencies and at feasts, when people feel like brothers and friends.

A society incapable of religion is also incapable of revolution. The countries in revolutionary fervor are the countries of living religious feelings as well. The feeling of brotherhood, solidarity, and justice—religious in their very essence—are in revolution turned to this world's justice, to this world's paradise.

Both religion and revolution are born in pain and suffering and die in well-being and comfort. Their true life is as long as their struggle to be realized. Their "realization" is their death. Both religion and revolution, becoming real, produce institutions and structures which eventually suffocate them. The official institutions are neither revolutionary nor religious.

If a revolution had its adversaries in religion, it had them in the official religion only, in the church and hierarchy—in the institutional, false religion. And conversely, the pseudo-revolution—revolution converted to structure, to bureaucracy—always had its ally in the religion converted to structure, to bureaucracy. Having begun to lie and betray itself, the revolution could go along with the false religion."

'Alija 'Ali Izetbegovic
from *Islam Between East and West*

INDEX